WOMEN IN BRITISH TRADE UNIONS
1874-1976

Norbert C. Soldon

Women in British Trade Unions 1874-1976

GILL AND MACMILLAN
ROWMAN AND LITTLEFIELD

First published 1978 by
Gill and Macmillan Ltd
15/17 Eden Quay
Dublin 1
with associated companies in
London, New York, Delhi, Hong Kong,
Melbourne, Johannesburg, Lagos,
Singapore, Tokyo

7171 0824 4

First published in the United States by
Rowman and Littlefield,
81 Adams Drive, Totowa, N.J.

ISBN 0–8476–6056–7

Printed and bound in Great Britain by
Bristol Typesetting Co. Ltd, Barton Manor, St Philips, Bristol

Contents

List of Illustrations

Between pp. 82 and 83

List of illustrations continued

ABBREVIATIONS

ACUCWW	Annual Conference of representatives of trade Unions Catering for Women Workers.
AEF	Amalgamated Union of Engineering and Foundry Workers.
AEU	Amalgamated Engineering Union.
ASE	Amalgamated Society of Engineers (later, Amalgamated Engineering Union).
AUEW	Amalgamated Union of Electrical Workers.
CBI	Confederation of British Industries.
CWO	Chief Woman Officer.
ETU	Electrical Trades Union.
FBI	Federation of British Industries.
FLDA	Freedom of Labour Defence Association (formerly Women's Employment Defence League).
ILO	International Labour Organisation.
ILP	Independent Labour Party.
ITWU	Irish Textile Workers' Union.
IWWU	Irish Women Workers' Union.
LCCSA	London County Council Staff Association.
MWTLC	Manchester Women's Trades and Labour Council.
NATSOPA	National Association of Operative Printers and Assistants.
NFWW	National Federation of Women Workers.
NUBSO	National Union of Boot and Shoe Operatives.
NUDAW	National Union of Distributive and Allied Workers.
NUGMW	National Union of General and Municipal Workers (formerly NUGW).
NUGW	National Union of General Workers.
NUR	National Union of Railwaymen.
NUTGW	National Union of Tailor and Garment Workers.
NUWW	National Union of Women Workers.
ODC	Open Door Council.
SCWT	Scottish Council for Women's Trades.
SDF	Social Democratic Federation.
STUC	Scottish Trades Union Congress.
T&GWU	Transport and General Workers Union.
TOS	Textiles Operatives Society.
TUC	Trade Union Congress.
UCWW	Unions Catering for Women Workers.
USDAW	Union of Shop Distributive and Allied Workers.
WPPL	Women's Advisory Committee.
WAC	Woman's Employment Defence League.
WEDL	Working Men's Club and Institute Union.
WMCIU	Women's Protective and Provident League.
WSPU	Women's Social and Political Union.
WTUA	Women's Trade Union Association.
WTUL	Women's Trade Union League (formerly WTUPL).
WTUPL	Women's Trade Union and Provident League.
WU	Workers' Union.
WWG	Women Workers' Group.

Preface

WHILE concern in Britain regarding women's political and economic status began in the 1850s, it was not until the 1960s that there was a renewal of feminine activism culminating in the passage of the Equal Pay Act of 1970 which on the economic front matched the progress made by women politically during the early decades of the twentieth century. This movement stimulated new interest in the role of women in history; although it was not as militant, it is equally important and interesting. While much attention has been focused on accounts of the exciting struggle of the suffragettes to achieve their political objectives, the economic side of the endeavour has received little study. Some exceptions are Sheila Rowbotham's *Hidden From History*, which is a lively account of women in socialist thought, and Lee Holcombe's excellent *Victorian Ladies at Work: Middle Class Working Women in England and Wales, 1850–1914* which, true to its title, deals only with middle-class 'ladies' and fails to discuss 'blue blouse' trade union women who are the main subject of this book. Until the above publications anyone seeking information on the latter subject had to use Mrs Barbara Drake's *Women in Trade Unions*; however it is out of print and only covers the period up to 1921. It is hoped that by utilising the largely untapped information in the *Women's Union Journal, The Woman Worker* and the *Annual Reports of the Women's Trade Union League* and employing some of the recent research on the subject, the period before 1921 can be re-examined and the story brought up-to-date by tracing the story from 1921 to the present. Unfortunately no valuably relevant collections of correspondence exist. The book is also intended to acquaint students with a number of personalities and problems worthy of further research and to provide members of today's trade union movement with a view of its feminine side.

The growth of women's trade unionism really was a story of 'women in labour'. The long and painful struggle to improve working conditions, hours of work and subsistence-level wages encountered obstacles from employers, male trade unionists and even the apathetic or intimidated women workers themselves. In many ways it mirrored the rise of male trade unionism but with a time-lag caused by four social or economic factors : (1) the quality and intellectual background of women's trade union leadership, (2) the volume of trade and general rate of the labour market, (3) the attitude of men and their trade unions and (4) the attitude of women trade unionists towards government regulation. The movement which started so feebly in the 1850s has grown as the result of the heroic efforts of a number of women who have failed to receive the recognition given their male counterparts. Emma Paterson, Lady Dilke, Clementina Black, Mary MacArthur, Julia Varley, Anne Loughlin and Florence Hancock and others deserve to be remembered by present-day women workers for their efforts—some were successful, while others were thwarted by the economic climate or attitude of male trade unionists. Brief biographies of these leaders are included to enable the reader to see how each leader's background shaped her response to the challenges that she faced.

According to the TUC Women's Advisory Committee's Report to the Women's Conference in March 1975, there are 2,613,139 women members within the TUC representing twenty-six per cent of the total membership. This means that more than a quarter of women workers compared to approximately one-half of all male workers are in trade unions. Between 1965 and 1975 over one million women became affiliated with the TUC; yet there are only seventy-one women full-time union officials as compared with 2,259 male full-time officials. The careers of leaders and an increase in numbers are important parts of the tale, but the real story is the courage of the rank and file who in spite of numerous difficulties organised to better their lot. The reader should bear in mind that statistics provided, listing the number of women employed, are only those covered by the national unemployment plans until 1948, and thereafter those covered by the new comprehensive National Insurance scheme.

I owe thanks to a number of people who have assisted me in accomplishing my task : first to Mrs Helena Murray whose interest in Emma Paterson initially introduced me to the need for further research in the field, then also to Ms Thelma Eberle who typed the entire manuscript more than once, to the staff of the Francis Harvey Green Library of West Chester State College, Mrs Hampson, Mrs Revoir and especially Ms Jesse Bostelle who cheerfully obtained and maintained numerous inter-library loans, to Ms Stephie Grier who made the resources of the University of Delaware Library available to me and to Ms Christine Bryan and Ms Christine Coates of the TUC Library.

In addition I wish to thank all the directors and librarians of the following institutions: British Museum; Scottish Records Office; George Howell Collection, Bishopsgate Institute, London; New York Public Library; Labour Party Library and Amalgamated Engineering Union; Clapham, Institute for Historical Studies, University of London and London School of Economics; and General and Municipal Workers' Union Research Department.

This book is dedicated to my grandfather Paul Witkowski, a school custodian who taught me to love books, my grandmother Helen Witkowski and my parents Stephen and Leona Soldon, whose early careers spent in stocking-mill, coal mine and silk mill awakened in me an interest in labour history.

Finally I wish to thank my wife Alice and daughters Shawn, Sherry and Sarah for allowing me the time I devoted to researching and writing about women of 'olden times.'

Introduction

TRADE unionism in Britain began during the eighteenth century with societies of journeymen. Since the journeymen were usually of the same skilled trade—hatters, printers, woollen workers—their societies were known as trade unions. By gaining control over the initiation of apprentices and providing friendly society benefits for sickness and burial, they resembled the guilds of the middle ages. Under the law of Masters and Servants, if these unions went on strike they could be prosecuted for breach of contract, a criminal offence punishable by imprisonment. The development of trade unionism in Britain during the nineteenth century reflected this contradictory attitude towards its value to society.

During the period following the French Revolution, when the government feared that unions might promote insurrection, the Combination Acts of 1799 and 1800 made trade unions illegal. The Acts were repealed in 1824, permitting unions to exist as long as they limited their activities to the determination of wages and hours and refrained from the use of violence, threats, intimidation and obstruction. But trade union legality received a jolt with the prosecution of the Tolpuddle Martyrs in 1834 under statutes of 1797 and 1819 which forbade illegal oaths. The enforcement of the law of Masters and Servants, which prohibited strikes that prevented completing commissioned piecework, further inhibited the growth of unions from 1840 to 1867 when it was repealed. Nevertheless, throughout the period unions grew in size and benefit funds increased, for trade unionists believed they were protected under the Friendly Societies Acts. This illusion was shattered by the Hornby v. Close decision in 1866, which held that unions were illegal since they were in restraint of trade. Not until the Trade Union Act of 1871 did unions receive the legal status that they had believed was theirs in 1825, although the Criminal Law Amendment Act of 1871 still prohibited unions from coercing workers by violence, intimidation or obstruction. The limits of industrial disputes were finally clarified, at least until 1895, by the Conspiracy and Protection of Property Act of 1875, which formally legalised picketing, while penalising 'watching and besetting'.[1] It is against this background that the early attempts of women to join with men in forming trade unions must be considered.

With the exception of domestic service, the main source of employment for women during the nineteenth century was the textile industry. Originally, like most pre-industrial employments, weaving was a home or domestic industry in which the whole family participated, but the introduction of machinery gradually replaced the home with the factory.[2] The process was slow. Until 1850 fewer than half of the textile workers of all ages and both sexes worked in factories.[3] This figure grew to seventy-five per cent by the 1880s. Officially the total number of women in the textile industry did not exceed the number of men until 1847, but these figures are misleading. Women outnumbered men in all sectors of the textile industry except woollens for most of the nineteenth century. The reason for the confusion is the number of workers employed in out-work or domestic industry as against in-work or factory industry. In 1833, 5,000 women were working in cotton factories as compared with 60,000 men.[4] In 1847, roughly a quarter of these women were married.

With these facts in mind it should come as no surprise that the history of British women's trade unionism began in the textile industry and dates at least from 1747, when women were included in the Worsted Small-ware Weavers' Association of Manchester of the Lancashire worsted industry. These women paid the same dues and received the same strike pay as men.[5] All-women unions were born thirty years later, in 1788, when the women hand-spinners of Leicester formed the famous 'sisterhood' which numbered 18,500 and displayed Luddite sympathies.[6] They protested against the introduction of machinery, which by doing away with the existence of spinning at home limited their individual freedom and forced them into an 'immoral' environment. For some, working in a factory had the same connotation as going to the poor house.[7] In 1811 the women lacemakers of Loughborough organised a 'combination' or union 'to dictate to their employers and to raise the price of their wages'. They also sent organisers to neighbouring towns to raise funds and create other associations. This was enough to alarm the parson magistrate, who warned them that they were violating the Combination Acts.[8]

In the brief survey that follows of women in trade unions from 1800 to 1874, the year when a co-ordinated attempt to encourage the growth of a women's trade union movement took place, five major factors should be noted: (1) the difficulty of organising women, (2) their position in the work force, (3) their relation with male trade unionists, (4) their relation with employers and (5) the impact of the women's rights movement. As the Industrial Revolution progressed, bringing with it changes in technology, women who had been employed as early as the Middle Ages as journeywomen in various crafts had to adjust to the new forms of industrial organisation. In the cotton industry women weavers were more difficult to organise than men. With wages that averaged only 6s. a week they had reason for militancy and in both 1808 and 1818 took part in strikes. At Stockport, during the strike of 1818, the girls dunked blacklegs (i.e. black sheep who strayed from the flock) under a pump. In Manchester women were admitted into the Spinners' Union and drew strike pay, but in 1829 the Cotton Spinners of the United Kingdom passed a resolution expelling them because they violated trade union rules.[9] The federation did offer its help to secure equal pay rates and urged the women to organise, but their efforts failed.

This was not an uncommon pattern in a number of industries where women competed with men during the nineteenth century. The wives and daughters of male members were, on occasion, admitted as members of trade unions. This was true of the General Association of Weavers in Scotland, who permitted members of their own families into the union. Yet during strikes, in order to gain food for the family, the female members might be driven to scab. The unmarried men and those husbands whose wives did not work usually retaliated by expelling the women. Faced with the fact that women in some industries (cotton especially) were indispensable, however, they tried to get women to form separate unions so that they would not drive men from the industry by accepting lower wages. This separate but equal ploy rarely worked and was usually an experiment in equivocation.

Women could be discriminated against not only by male workers but by employers. In Scotland, for example, although the male Glasgow Scottish Spinners tried to bar women from the spinning rooms and intense struggles took place between the unorganised, underpaid women and the men's unions, the union did advise women on piece-rates and in the early thirties conducted an equal pay campaign. This effort failed when the employers decided that women spinners turned out work that was inferior both in quality and quantity.[10]

In the cotton industry, after the introduction of the power loom, women who were especially skilful in this process were difficult to organise. At first, men handloom weavers declined to work in factories utilising the power loom. Since the majority of the labour force was thus composed of women and children wages were correspondingly low, and low-paid industries were usually more difficult to organise than better-paid industries.

By the 1830s women worked in almost all departments of the cotton, jute and silk factories. They also began to be employed as weavers in the worsted and woollen mills. The presence of women in the textile industries presented male trade unionists with a major problem. A number of solutions were tried. In Bolton the Association of Cotton Spinners admitted women, but only in the piecers section. The male spinners of Yorkshire in 1842 urged through the Yorkshire Short-Time Committee that the proportion of women workers to men should be limited and married women forbidden to work during the lifetimes of their husbands. In the long run neither solution worked and although spinners' unions had long generally excluded women entirely, by 1847 women textile workers outnumbered men.[11]

The most notable role played by women in trade unions during the 1830s resulted from their membership in the Grand National Consolidated Trades Union of Great Britain and Ireland when it was formed in 1833-34. It included a few women's lodges, such as the Lodge of Female Tailors and the Grand Lodge of Operative Bonnet Makers. The 'Ancient Virgins' also took part in the Oldham riots, which featured a demand for a ten hours day.[12] After the demise of the Grand National Consolidated Trades Union the evidence of women in trade unions becomes scanty; however, one more event is worthy of note. In 1834 T. Roberts of Edinburgh tried to organise the seamstresses there and although he failed his efforts led Tom Hood to write 'Song of the Shirt', which probably did more than any single piece of writing to inspire middle class efforts to help working women over the balance of the nineteenth century.[13]

One industry for which more data is available is the printing trades, where trouble had been brewing since 1825 when the London Union of Journeymen Bookbinders protested against the Society for Promoting Christian Knowledge for unfair wage reductions. In 1834 they again supported 200 women folders and sewers against a reduction in wages by the British and Foreign Bible Society. It was claimed that their wages were so low that some were forced into prostitution.[14] The employers claimed that the women earned 8s. to 10s. a week while men earned 30s. a week. On the other hand, the union's secretary, Mr Dunning, claimed that the women averaged 5s. 11d. a week. A settlement gave the workers from 7s. 6d. to 15s. a week for a ten hour day. In 1849, however, the dispute erupted again and a strike was called by the employees of a Miss Watkins, who had a monopoly for binding the works of the Bible Society. They demanded wages equal to those paid by the Society for Promoting Christian Knowledge. Their leader was the youthful, energetic Mary Zugg, who commanded great respect and affection from her followers. Though the strike was supported by the men of the London Union of Journeymen Bookbinders to the tune of £650 collected by the strike committee, it failed.[15] Miss Zugg faded into obscurity and died of consumption in 1861.

For the most part during the hungry forties joint efforts between male and female workers to form unions were unsuccessful, and even when the cotton weavers' association became firmly established during the 1850s and 1860s women were difficult to organise and proved a liability during strikes. At Preston in 1853-54 at a lock-out which included 18,000 operatives many of whom were women, the latter were condemned by Charles Dickens in his 'Mill in the Hydes', later printed in his *Household Words*, for failing to give money to the strike fund.[16] Aside from these and other scattered examples of women's participation in trade unions before the 1850s, as well as their membership in Friendly Societies founded exclusively for women and female auxiliaries such as the Female Foresters, Female Druids and Female Rechabites, etc., it is difficult to gauge the extent of their participation in the embryonic trade union movement—the TUC was not founded until 1868 and government statistics are not reliable.[17]

Nevertheless, it was in the textile industry that the first sound trade union including women was formed, in 1854, an organisation of powerloom cotton weavers, the Blackburn Powerloom Weavers' Association. Eventually in 1866 a standard list was established by the Preston and Blackburn employers and employees. The North-east Lancashire Amalgamated Weavers Association was formed in 1858, and in these unions women were from the first admitted to membership equally with men and received equal piece rates. They paid the same levies, received the same benefits as men, and by 1876 numbered 15,000 or one-half of the membership.[18] In 1891, 40,300 or sixty-two per cent of its 65,000 members were women. District lists of prices were negotiated, established and maintained with the help of the women who gave them solidarity. Women were often recruited by family pressure and unions barred from office families who had members eligible for membership but who had not joined. The question of competition from separate organisations of men's and women's weavers never became a problem. In union there was strength for both men and women. Successful trade union-ism for women can then be claimed to begin during the 1850s and 1860s, while a coordinated effort to form separate trade unions by women would not take place until 1874.

While women found both jobs in industry and acceptance in the unions in Lancashire, societal changes caused by industrial-isation put their sisters in other parts of Britain in a confused and contradictory situation with regard to their role in home and industry. On the one hand there was the mid-Victorian goal of liberating the materfamilias from daily labour. On the other, there was the reduced opportunity for finding husbands caused by the over-emigration of men. Thus, when women in nineteenth-century Britain started to re-define the role of their sex in society, a part of the process was the question of work.

Between 1851 and 1881 adult women comprised roughly one-third of the population. Of this number, forty-two per cent be-tween the ages of twenty and forty were spinsters in 1851 but only one-fifth were employed.[19] The major field of employment for women was domestic service, a field which increased in numbers until 1911. In 1851 the figure for England and Wales was 971,000 and in 1881 it was 1,545,000. As Eric Richards says, 'Domestic service was clearly the prime resort of unmarried women over the entire period. Apart from domestic service, textiles, stitching and washing there was little else open to women of any class in England before the final decades of the century.'[20]

The movement to find increased employment opportunities for women began with the agitation that preceded the introduction of the first Married Women's Property Rights Bill in 1856 by a committee led by Barbara Leigh Smith (later Mme Bodichon). This in turn led to the founding of the *English Women's Journal* in 1858 by Miss Smith and Bessie Rayner Parkes (later Mrs Belloc). Though a satisfactory bill was not passed until 1882, the so-called Langham Place Circle moved into other problem areas and next founded the Society for Promoting the Employment of Women in 1859, with the Earl of Shaftesbury as its President. It later became affiliated with the National Association for the Promotion of Social Science,[21] whose purpose was to find jobs for women who wished to be independently employed.

Another landmark in the movement for equal rights for women was the campaign, organised by Mme Bodichon and Emilia Boucherett, which led to the presentation of the first women's suffrage petition presented to Parliament by John Stuart Mill in 1865. Despite Mill's efforts at amendment, the 1867 Reform Bill again excluded women from the right to vote. As part of the work of the Society for the Employment for Women, Miss Boucherett and Helen Blackburn, as co-editors of the *Englishwoman's Review* (the successor of the *English Woman's Journal*), founded the Victoria Press utilising women typesetters and managed by Emily Faithfull.[22] In 1891 Miss Boucherett and Miss Blackburn founded the Women's Employment Defence League, which became the Freedom of Labour Defence Association in 1897.

The early feminists often invoked the theory of laissez-faire and free contract to argue for the employment of the most capable person irrespective of sex. At times Barbara Bodichon even called upon employers to hire women workers instead of men because women workers could be paid only half of what was expected by men.[23] Since most employers were already probably well aware of this fact, it is little wonder that working men feared competition from women. The Langham Place Circle also felt compelled to protest against being squeezed out of employment by what humanitarians regarded as beneficent legislation that restricted the hours of work of women and children. Such legislation as the Ten Hours Act of 1847, by making a special case of women, inferred that they were unequal to men. The FLDA had as its purpose the protection of 'workers especially women workers, from such restrictive legislation as lessens their wage-earning capacity, limits their personal liberty, and inconveniences their private lives'.[24] Their emphasis on individualism would cause the Fabian Socialist, B. L. Hutchins, to regard them as the right wing of the Women's Rights Movement.[25]

A major manifesto of this movement appeared in 1859 with Harriet Martineau's *Edinburgh Review* article on 'Female Industry', which first called attention to the problem of redundant women. Using the census for 1851 it pointed out that there were 500,000 more women than men in Britain, including single women who could not hope to marry and be taken care of and widows whose husbands might not have provided for them.[26] As a matter of fact, women had been involved in the economy in greater numbers before 1820 than during the period 1820-70. Two periods of unemployment in 1857 and 1866 caused by economic down-turn created a dual crisis—to the problem of what to do about superfluous women was added the problem of what to do about unemployed men.[27] Not surprisingly, each group sought solutions at the expense of the other. Jessie Boucherett argued that men had not emigrated as much as they ought to, forcing wages down so low in all trades not protected by unions that women had to go to work to feed their families. Thus the previous women's labour market had been invaded from two sides: men moving into women's occupations and women forced to work to make ends meet. Her solution was increased male emigration and technical education for women to enable them to compete in the job market.[28]

Over the next half century the problem would be solved mainly by increased employment opportunities in secondary industries caused by an increase in the per capita income of the

majority of the population. Between 1861 and 1911 the increase
of male workers in England and Wales was seventy-seven
per cent, while for women it was forty-four per cent. The number
of workers in middle class occupations—teacher, nurse, shop
assistant—increased by 192 per cent for men and 307 per cent
for women.[29] Engineering and food processing also provided
increased opportunities for female manual labour. The greatest
employment for women was in the non-manual fields, and the
Society for Promoting the Employment of Women Workers
also agitated to keep open and improving the conditions of labour
of their sisters in these trades. To bring up the level of income
of women workers so that men would not have as much to fear
from female competition, trade unionism was one method they
advocated.

The early years of the 1850s witnessed both a healthy industrial
economy and a corresponding growth in trade unionism. The
formation of the Amalgamated Society of Engineers in 1851
typified the strengthening of older unions. These so-called 'New
Model' unions were characterised by restriction of membership
to apprenticed craftsmen, payment of high subscriptions and
friendly benefits. They preferred negotiation to strikes in their
efforts to shorten the working day, increase wages and regulate
work rules. Success was common during the prosperous fifties
but there were occasional strikes. The 'New Model' unions were
sometimes aided by benevolent capitalists or 'New Model'
employers such as M. T. Bass, Liberal MP for Derby, who helped
found the Amalgamated Society of Railway Servants in 1871
and who in other ways aided trade unionists.[30] 'New Model'
unions spread to the iron founders, carpenters and bricklayers;
but in mining, cotton, cabinet-making, tailoring, boot and shoe-
making, district unions remained strong. In the cotton industry
a loose federal structure was adopted. Among the weavers,
according to H. A. Turner, there was already a strong development, from the 1850s, of 'mass' unionism associated with the
'New Unionism' of the 1880s and 1890s.[31] Cotton unions did
co-operate with each other in securing the passage of factory
legislation and thus aimed at economic gains through political
means rather than industrial action. The textile unions of weavers
which admitted women, discussed earlier, come under this classi-
fication.

It is in the early 1870s that we can discern the growth of fore-runners of the 'New Unionism' of the 1880s. Lower paid, less skilled workers formed unions among railwaymen, seamen, car-men, dockers, agricultural labourers and gas workers. Among women trade unionism also began to grow, the Edinburgh Up-holsterers, Sewers Society, which included women, was founded in 1872 and George Odger, of the Ladies Shoemakers Society, proposed a motion (which was carried) that women be admitted on the same terms and given the same rights as men during the National Union of Boot and Shoe Operatives Conference. Never-theless, while British women's trade unionism had its main strength in the textile unions formed in the 1850s, the Women's Protective and Provident League, founded in 1874, provided it with the means for later growth and amalgamation. The unions affiliated to the WPPL and its leaders displayed many of the characteristics of the 'New Model' unions but by its appeal to lower paid and less skilled workers it also owed something to 'New Unionism'. This will be shown by examining the WPPL in greater detail.

I

Emma Paterson and the Women's Protective and Provident League

IT WAS in July 1874 that the Women's Protective and Provident League was founded by Emma Paterson (née Smith). Although the League was not a trade union itself, its purpose was to foster trade unionism among women and, given its limited resources and the spirit of the times, it did as much as was possible. As a result, the Webbs in their *History of Trade Unionism* regarded her as 'the real pioneer of modern women's trade unions'.[1] Mrs Paterson was born in 1048, the daughter of a headmaster at a school in East Ham, who in 1843 was attached to St George's, Hanover Square. As a young girl Emma was his constant companion and regarded by her friends as something of a bookworm. She later helped her father teach school and became apprenticed to a bookbinder.

When she was sixteen, her father, who only earned £60 a year, died of typhoid fever, leaving his family in fairly straitened circumstances. Emma and her mother tried to establish a school but were unsuccessful. Disliking both teaching and being a governess, at the age of eighteen she began work as an assistant to the clerk of the Working Men's Club and Institute Union (WMCIU). Founded in 1861, the WMCIU was part of the effort during the middle decades of the nineteenth century to bring about a reconciliation of employers and working men. Its founders included Rev. Henry Solly, Hodgson Pratt, Auberon Herbert and Thomas Paterson. By the time Thomas and Emma Paterson were married in 1873, there were 245 clubs in the organisation. Many of its patrons (Rev. S. D. Headlam, S. S. Taylor and Frederick Verney, etc.) later served in the same capacity with the Women's Protective and Provident League (WPPL). The paternal influence of aristocrats, clergymen and members of the middle classes was an important factor in shaping the aims and methods of operation during the early years of both organisations.

Mrs Paterson had mastered her job so well that in July 1867 she had been appointed Assistant Secretary. Her association with Pratt, Herbert and Paterson introduced her to both secularism and an individualist brand of positivism. Intellectually this meant she believed in understanding the world through laws derived from nature and mathematics and that this positivist stage of knowledge superseded earlier theological and metaphysical periods. Positivism revered scientists, captains of industry and other great men. Through her work she was introduced to the aristocracy of labour, the London 'Junta' (George Howell, Robert Applegarth, Edwin Coulson, Daniel Guile and George Odger). Later these contacts helped her trade union work to some extent.

Thomas Paterson worked as a cabinetmaker and wood carver. He was a self-educated intellectual, who spent his spare time at the British Museum reading philosophy. As a Scot, Paterson was raised a Calvinist, but as a result of his reading he became a positivist.[2] His opinions had a lasting influence on his wife; she never became a socialist or a militant foe of capitalism. At the same time, even though her manner was usually kind, 'gentle Emma' could have a sharp tongue if well-meaning but incompetent middle-class volunteers got in her way. Frederick Rogers probably best described the secret of her success when he wrote in 1913 that, 'Without either physical attraction or charm, the quiet, shrewd little woman exercised an influence on the labour movement which no other woman has equalled since her day, and its secret lay in her entire sincerity and absence of pose.'[3]

After five years employment with the WMCIU Emma resigned to become Secretary of the Society for the Promotion of Women's Suffrage Association in 1872; but was soon dismissed by its leaders because 'her physique was too weak and her speech contemptible'.[4] Pressure groups during this period put a high priority on the speaking voice of their leaders. Weak though her physique was (she had diabetes), over the next fourteen years she displayed hidden reserves of energy. Even so, during 1872 she used part of her time assisting Emily Faithfull's efforts to aid women bookbinders made unemployed by the debate in parliament in 1871 over the revised prayer book;[5] while the men were able to receive £2,500 from their unions, the women, who were not unionised, had only their savings to rely on. The incident showed her the need to do something to aid working women.

These efforts were temporarily interrupted in July 1873 when Emma, aged twenty-four, married Thomas Paterson. Their honeymoon was spent in a manner later emulated by that equally serious minded couple, Sidney and Beatrice Webb, studying trade unionism. The Patersons journeyed to America and while in New York were inspired by the structure of the successful Women's Typographical Society and the Female Umbrella Makers Union. Unlike the textile unions in Lancashire, these had women officers who managed their own sickness benefit fund. Upon their return to England the couple decided to see if a similar organisation could help the women bookbinders. To stir up interest she wrote an article, entitled 'The Position of Working Women and How to Improve It', for the April 1874 *Labour News*, urging the cooperation of all sympathisers and sketching a constitution for a Central Association to which local branches of different trades might affiliate. It objected to the fact that women were often paid half of male wages and that while unskilled men received 18s., most skilled women were paid only 17s. a week. This caused men to resent the employment of women workers because they feared the wages of the industry would be lowered and as a result men initiated the campaign to limit factory hours not from altruism but selfishly to limit the employment of women. While not denying that a reduction of women's working hours was desirable, she claimed the result was oppression rather than protection. A better course of action for women would be to seek improvements through trade unionism as men had done and make government interference unnecessary. In addition to higher wages and shorter hours, other benefits offered by trade unionism were sickness insurance, unemployment benefit, educational programmes, emigration clubs and job registers.

Mrs Paterson urged working men either to admit women to their unions on equal terms (women in the cotton trades were unable to make their weight felt because they paid only half as much dues) or aid them to form similar societies. The plight of women could not be blamed on employers alone since many were just and would gladly pay women more, but were powerless to do so unless their workers unionised—for if they paid wages

higher than their competitors they would be forced into bank-
ruptcy by the competition of their less humanitarian competitors.
She concluded by targeting four industries with a sufficient
number of women to support unions: straw plait workers—
45,270; tailoresses—38,021; earthenware workers and bookbinders—7,557.

These ideas would remain Mrs Paterson's philosophy of trade
unionism for the rest of her life. In analysing her thinking about
the reason for male trade unionists favouring restrictive legislation for women it should be noted that men in fact benefited in
two ways: (1) by reducing the advantages of employing women
and (2) as the men would later admit, they hid behind the petti-
coats of women to reduce their own hours of labour. Nevertheless, the reduction of the hours of labour by means of legislation
was a more rapid method of improving working conditions at a
time when unions in the cotton industry were rather fragile
amalgamations. Male self-interest tried to prevent the employment of women and eliminate the advantages of docility and
lower wages that they offered employers.[6]

On 8 July 1874 a conference, chaired by Hodgson Pratt, was
held to discuss Mrs Paterson's proposals. An Executive Committee composed of representatives of women's rights, trade unionist,
positivist and Christian Socialist groups, was named. It was
decided to call the organisation the Women's Protective and
Provident League. Mrs Paterson preferred the word league to
union because it sounded less aggressive and reminded her of the
Anti-Corn League and other victorious movements. The Committee was particularly anxious to avoid antagonising employers
since many were friendly to the need for some kind of women's
provident organisation. The League's objects were: (1) to protect
trade interests of members by endeavouring where necessary to
prevent the undue depression of wages and to equalise the hours
of work, (2) to provide sickness or unemployment funds, (3) to
serve as an employment bureau, and (4) to promote arbitration
in cases of disputes between employers and the employed.

Some time in August of the same year Mrs Paterson read a
paper at the Social Science Congress held in Bristol suggesting
the formation of a general trade union or one that included
members from all occupations. The result was the formation of
the National Association of Working Women. While it con-

tinued as an independent group there, for a number of years, on her return to London she decided that a federation of various societies was better than a national organisation. It was decided to use the bookbinders' society as a prototype female union since most men's unions with the exception of the textile unions barred female membership.[7] At the next meeting of the WPPL, held 12 September, 300 women bookbinders were present to assist in the formation of the Society of Women Employed in Bookbinding. Its rules became a model for subsequent unions. By October 1875, £80 was raised from subscriptions and entrance fees, enabling the initiation of sickness and unemployment benefits. Three-fourths of the payments were to single women and widows. Mr H. R. King, Secretary of the London Bookbinders, provided assistance to the young organisation. Within the next year four other societies were founded in upholstery, dressmaking, shirt and collar making and hatmaking. Something of the excitement of these early days can be gathered from a letter written after Mrs Paterson's death by one of the oldest members of the Bookbinders' Union, in which she recalled :

> We had a rare time of it for three months—we had her all to ourselves every Monday night, I never missed once—used to long for them. . . . I think all caught her spirit, entered heartily into her plans and were all ready to do her bidding. When she spoke in public we were all proud of our Mrs Paterson.[8]

In 1876 Mrs Paterson founded her own press, the Women's Printing Society Ltd, with women as compositors and printers. As part of its recruiting campaign, the WPPL began publication of a monthly, the *Women's Union Journal*. In retrospect its publication must be considered a luxury in view of the League's sparse income.[9] The sale price covered only one-third of its cost and it devoured roughly forty per cent of the League's income from 1874 to 1880. In spite of its meagre funds, in February 1875 the WPPL, with the help of Rev. F. Wills and William Rogers, established the Society of London Sewing Machinists. The impetus for its 400 members to organise was to prevent wage reductions and for a while the society seemed to thrive, but then fell to pieces. Similarly, the feather and flower workers in Clerkenwell were also organised with short-lived success. Other unions—shirt-makers in Bermondsey, boot and umbrella makers in N. London, laundresses in Notting Hill and Hampstead, tailoresses in Soho and Whitechapel—were also created.[10] Once established, these organisations were independent and did not receive financial aid from the WPPL; as a consequence these marginal unions required constant resuscitation. One of the major obstacles faced by the struggling London unions was the difficulty in paying subscriptions to the WPPL's Central Office because of the distance involved.

The strength of a branch depended on finding a good Secretary. Once the Society of Women Bookbinders was on its feet, Mrs Paterson entrusted Miss Eleanor Whyte, a working bookbinder, with the job of Secretary and under her able stewardship the union prospered at least until 1909. Another excellent lieutenant was Jeannette Gaury Wilkinson (1844–86), an upholsteress who at the age of seventeen became a protegée of J. H. Levy, Secretary of the Vigilance Association for the Defence of Personal Rights. She studied at Birkbeck Institute, became a teacher and served in that capacity from 1876 to 1882. She too was a secularist in religion and a radical individualist in politics. Miss Wilkinson became connected with the WPPL a few months after the Society of Upholsteresses was started in 1875. A speaker of tact and power, she represented the union nine times at the TUC.[11]

The WPPL also formed unions outside London at Dewsbury and Leicester. In February 1875 the Dewsbury, Batley and Surrounding District Heavy Woollen Weavers' Association staged a successful strike which featured a protest demonstration of 9,000 against a shift from piece-rates to time-rates, while in Leicester, after their organisation, women in the hosiery trade secured a twenty-five per cent increase in wages. They originally earned 5s. to 7s. per week. In Leicester, the employer retaliated by sending his work to the countryside, whereupon unions were established in twenty-seven of thirty-seven surrounding villages and wages were maintained at between 7s. to 9s. per week.[12] In Glasgow, a Benefit Society for Glasgow Working Women was established by Henry Wright, Secretary to the Glasgow Branch of the Scottish Association of Operative Tailors. Mrs Paterson and Miss Simcox also assisted in organising societies in Manchester, Oxford, Sheffield and Portsmouth.[13]

One of the WPPL's more publicised agitations took place in

1879 when 1,500 Royal Army clothing workers in Pimlico, who had earned as much as 30s. to 36s. per week by taking work home to do at night, were discharged as the result of a government economy move. They were told that they could be re-hired with a fifteen per cent reduction in piece work rates and withdrawal of home work. At the suggestion of Henry Broadhurst, Parliamentary Secretary of the TUC, Mrs Paterson, Hodgson Pratt and Rev. Steward Headlam organised a meeting on 16 April at the Westminster Democratic Club. Eventually a deputation of 1,000 was sent to House of Commons where A. J. Mundella championed their cause and a Committee of Enquiry was appointed.[14] As Frederick Rogers recalled, Mrs Paterson was skilled in such endeavours:

> No Parliamentary Whip ever knew better 'who was who', in the political world, who would help a cause for love, and who for popularity or other secondary reasons . . . who among the working classes, who is honest, who is both honest and influential, who is only influential, and who is neither one nor the other.[15]

The Parliamentary Enquiry was probably the first launched by the direct demand of women workers themselves and resulted in the formation of a Pimlico Branch of the London Tailoresses' Union with 140 women members, on 18 April 1879.[16] But the efforts of the Tailoresses to secure their aims were frustrated over the next two years by a combination of economic circumstance, Liberal political chicanery, and the maze of bureaucratic red tape.[17]

While the WPPL organised these single trade unions, it favoured forming mixed societies and did so wherever men agreed to it. Women were admitted to the National Union of Operative Boot Riveters and Finishers in Leicester, the Amalgamated Clothing Operatives, the London Compositors, the Printers Warehousemen and Cutters, the London Cigar Makers, the Steel Smelters, the Tin and Steel Millmen, the Chain Workers and the Sheffield Hand File Cutters.[18]

Between 1874 and 1880 the WPPL's activities suffered from a shortage of funds. Its funds were derived strictly from subscriptions and it was not self-supporting. In its early days substantial personal and monetary aid was given by Christian

Socialist ministers. Faced with a £90 deficit in 1879 the League was rescued by Rev. Stopford Brooke who raised £55 preaching a sermon to his large and influential congregation, while the balance was covered by a concert which Mrs Brassey, daughter-in-law of the famous railroad contractor, sponsored.[19]

The WPPL took great pains not to offend Model Employers by constantly emphasising that it was not a strike agitating organisation, but Mrs Paterson was less gentle in her treatment of clergymen. At a meeting held 15 March 1879 at St Paul's Churchyard she thanked the clergy for the use of schoolrooms for meetings but chided them for the practice of starting meetings with prayer and closing them with hymns. Parochial work societies manufacturing cheap needlework that undercut shopkeepers were also condemned by Miss Simcox. Instead, she urged self-supporting national workshops like those advocated by Louis Blanc in Paris in 1848, where the state was the only employer, and which were preferable to socialism. Co-operatives offered another solution for women in the sweated 'needle' trades of the East End, and in 1876, she and Miss Hamilton helped establish and manage the Co-operative Shirt Makers' Association, which to avoid antagonising shopkeepers used the name Hamilton and Company.[20] Under the Association each worker with her individual sewing machine in her own home became her own employer and thereby combined the best of the domestic system and modern technology while eliminating the middleman.

The WPPL provided a variety of benefits for its members, including the Women's Halfpenny Bank established in 1878 with 230 depositors. It granted loans at five per cent interest to depositors and members of women's unions. A reading room, an employment register where women could find a warm place to rest while looking for jobs, and a circulating library of over 1,000 books, were all available for members' use. The employment register and reading room were popular, but most working women had little inclination for reading after long hours of eye-straining work. The League also organised frequent joint excursions for unions to Epping Forest, and Lady Goldsmid arranged to furnish seaside houses or rooms to members at 3s. to 4s. a week. A Women's Union Swimming Club, organised at St Pancras Baths in November 1878, attracted over two hundred women weekly at a price of two pence.[21]

In 1875 the WPPL began to make itself felt at the annual
TUC Conference; but a year earlier the National Union of
Working Women from Bristol became the first women's union
to be admitted, even though its representative was a man, H. M.
Hunt. He was seated only after some opposition since as one of
the delegates explained, 'the next thing they'll be wanting to
represent themselves'.[22] The first women delegates were admitted
to the Eighth Annual TUC Conference at Glasgow in October
1875, with Mrs Paterson representing the Society of Women
Bookbinders and the Society of Women Upholsteresses and Edith
Simcox representing the Society of Women Shirt and Collar
Makers. Their personal acquaintance with many of the TUC
leaders probably facilitated their admittance without opposition.
Miss Simcox (1844–1901) served as Mrs Paterson's chief lieutenant and was a supporter of women's suffrage, a contributor
to the *Nineteenth Century* and a revisionist Socialist. Even so,
at the TUC Conference in a paper on the 'Organisation of
Women's Labour', calling for equal pay for women and criticising the ineffectiveness of the factory inspection, she condemned
legislation that reduced wages by a reduction of hours.[23]

Mrs Paterson also risked the male delegates' wrath by
announcing that long hours were preferable to legislation, if by
giving women a false sense of security, legislation obscured the
need for organising trade unions. She claimed men had been
able to get shorter hours by unionism than women had by legislation. Henry Broadhurst, Parliamentary Secretary of the TUC
dissented, contending that shorter hours should be achieved either
by unionisation if possible or, if not, then by legislation. He
patronisingly assured Mrs Patterson that he understood her
impatience with restraint, a trait natural to women. At any rate
he felt that the improved condition of working men had caused
married women to drop out of the labour market and thus raised
the wages of other women. He concluded by saying that the
factory was an unsuitable place for women and that wives should
be in their proper place—at home.[24] Proceedings reached a
dénouement when George Shipton, of the London Trades Council, made and John Kane seconded a resolution pledging assistance in the promotion of a self-relying women's trade union
movement.

At the 1877 TUC Conference a separate women's meeting
B

was held where problems of special interest to women's trade unionists were discussed, a forerunner of the Annual Women's Conference in 1921. Mrs Paterson appreciated the respite it gave to trade unionists of both sexes interested in the welfare of women workers. As she said, at least here discussion could proceed without men making silly puns or howling down women, as gentlemen 'in another place' did. She condemned Broadhurst's charge that women couldn't form unions because their wages were too low to pay dues, explaining that he had taken a similar attitude towards low paid men, and compared him with the socialists who produced similar arguments against the usefulness of trade unionism. Mrs Paterson continued to oppose restrictive legislation and expressed consternation that some members of the TUC displayed great indignation when Mr and Mrs Fawcett had charged that men were trying to legislate women out of work, but the 1877 TUC Conference did exactly that.[25] It passed a resolution to prohibit women from working in the chain and nail industry, which used a spring-tilted, foot operated, twenty-pound hammer called the 'oliver'. Since the industry was gradually being moved into factories, the TUC hoped to reduce the number of competing domestic workers who were a barrier to working-class organisation, but the WPPL, motivated by a romantic desire to maintain cottage industry and preserve women's jobs, opposed this action in 1877, and again in 1882 and 1887.[26]

The WPPL continued to champion women's rights at the 1878 TUC Conference. When Thomas Birtwistle of the Accrington Power Loom Weavers made a motion to 'appoint a considerable number of practical working men as assistant sub-inspectors', Mrs Paterson asked that this be amended to include 'practical working women'. Later Broadhurst accused women of trying to sabotage the future Factory and Workshops Consolidated Act of 1879. He artlessly claimed that this justified his fears that women's representation at the Congress was a mistake because swayed by emotion they might vote for things they would regret in more rational moments.[27] George Potter then moved that the word "persons" be substituted for "men and women", whereupon Birtwistle agreed to the use of practical workers and this wording was carried by a vote of forty-six to thirty-three.[28] It was not until 1893 that the first woman actually was appointed.

During the course of the Conference Mrs Paterson took time

to attend a meeting of the cotton operatives at the Great Western
Cotton Works at Bristol, mostly women, who although unorganised had been on strike for six weeks in the face of a five per cent
wages reduction. The reduction was caused by the use of faster
machinery in Lancashire placing the Bristol plant at a disadvantage. Realising that without organisation and accumulated funds,
a prolonged struggle would end in failure, male representatives
of the Cotton Operatives Unions of the North of England tried
unsuccessfully to get the Bristol workers to accept the reduction.
It was only through Mrs Paterson's efforts that the women came
to see the groundlessness of their fears that the men's advice was
not disinterested, and returned to work, low as their wages were,
to organise for a future struggle.[29]

Between 1879 and 1886 Mrs Paterson attended every TUC
Conference with the exception of the Manchester Conference in
1882 which she missed because of her husband's death. Because
of a shortage of funds, the WPPL could not afford organising
trips to the provinces but took advantage of TUC Conferences
to do organising work in the cities where the meeting was being
held—at Edinburgh, Dublin, Aberdeen and Nottingham. At
each she and her nine colleagues fought against restrictive legislation. At Nottingham, in 1883, when one of the women delegates
complained, 'If women were not allowed to earn a livelihood
what must they do', the male delegates shouted with derisive
laughter, 'Get married!'[30] As long as the WPPL adhered to the
policy of opposition to restrictive legislation, the cause of women's
trade unionism was hampered; yet although this policy was
unpopular with male TUC delegates, Mrs Paterson was respected
for her courage in expressing her views.[31] Several times her name
was proposed as a member of the Parliamentary Committee or
Executive of the TUC, and at Hull, the year of her death, she
just missed election—remarkable since usually the larger and
wealthier unions gained seats.[32]

When Mrs Paterson was not attending TUC Conferences,
serving as Secretary of the Vigilance Association for the Defence
of Personal Rights, attending women's suffrage meetings, working during Parliamentary and School Board Elections and helping
to found Co-operative Societies, she spent her time furthering
the interests of women workers in other ways.[33] In 1881 she
arranged for a conference presided over by Lord Shaftesbury

to advocate the appointment of women as factory inspectors.[34]

Following her husband's death in October 1882, Mrs Paterson was again plunged into poverty, for a period living on a budget of 6d. a day after having spent her savings on some of the societies she was interested in. She was finally forced to accept a small salary from the printing society for proof reading. This became more difficult after 1883 when her eyesight began to fail as the result of diabetes. Her mother's death further complicated matters since she had done much of the WPPL secretarial work as well as housework for the Paterson family.

As the WPPL struggled during the unfavourable climate of the 'Great Depression' to prevent legislative restrictions limiting employment opportunities for women, many of the economic assumptions of the previous century began to be questioned. One arena where the debate took place was the Industrial Remuneration Conference of 1885. Seldom during the nineteenth century had such a broad spectrum of social opinion been assembled in Britain, from socialist to extreme laissez-faire, to discuss the problems dividing them. Sir Charles Dilke presided at the Conference and four WPPL members represented their unions and the London Trade's council. Mrs Paterson challenged the statistics of Sir Robert Giffen's *Progress of the Working Classes*, which demonstrated that the overall standard of living in Britain had improved under capitalism. She disputed these findings because they did not cover women workers except those in weaving, and she pointed out that according to Leone Levi the number of wage earning women, including 1,300,000 domestic servants, was 3,800,000 earning a weekly average of 13s. 8d.[35] She assumed that Giffen had probably consigned the women to his category 'residium still unimproved'. Mrs Paterson condemned the Factory Acts but this time for being inadequate in regulating the hours of women's work. As they stood, they provided that in seasonal trades women could work fourteen hours a day for forty-eight days in a year and legalised employment in workshops until four o'clock on Saturday afternoons. Thus while men enjoyed a half day off work on Saturday, women in the dressmaking, millinery and tailoring establishments were still without a Saturday half-holiday.[36] To improve matters both trade unionism and suffrage were necessary in order to provide them with the power they so obviously lacked: within the last ten years deputations of working women seeking changes in the Factory Acts and the appointment of women factory inspectors had been refused by the Home Secretaries of both the great political parties, Sir Richard Cross and Sir William Harcourt.[37]

Miss Simcox, in her paper 'Loss or Gain of the Working Classes during the Nineteenth Century' agreed with Giffen that there had been gains but argued that the lion's share had gone to capitalists, with larger capitalists benefiting more than the smaller, while on the other hand the worker had become poorer in relation to his wants. While not supporting a social war, she advocated a revolution in the minds and consciences of the community resulting in a radical reformation of the theory and practices of the economic world.[38]

The Conference was not without its casualties; Mrs Ellis, of the Huddersfield, Dewsbury and District Power Loom Weavers, who had also criticised Giffen's figures and the current quality of textiles, returned home to find herself dismissed by her employer for having taken leave from her job for three days, in spite of the fact that she had secured a replacement.[39]

After participating in the Industrial Remuneration Conference, the League supported the efforts of the Personal Rights Association, the Liberty and Property Defence League and the Society for the Employment of Women, in defeating attempts by Thomas Burt and Broadhurst to exclude women from working at the pit-heads (on the surface) at coal mines. These 6,000 so-called 'Pit-Brow' women were employed moving coal tubs. Women had been prohibited from working below ground since 1872, now an amendment to the Mines Regulation Bill of 1886 aimed at 'liberating' these jobs for men through 'aggressive philanthropy'. Meetings of the 'Pit-Brow' women were held at Wigan, Bryn and St Helen's, where they declared they were healthier and happier outside near the mine than in some dingy factory. A healthy looking, bright-eyed, ruddy-cheeked deputation of pit-brow women accompanied Josephine Butler to protest to Home Secretary Henry Matthews. A month later the amendments were killed in the committee stage by a group of MPs that included Charles Bradlaugh.[40] WPPL action could not help but antagonise male TUC opinion; on the other hand, jobs were jobs.

In October 1886 the WPPL held a conference to consider

suggestions for extension of its work. Since its foundation, of ten societies formed in London, four had failed, one was struggling, but five were thriving. These six had funds of £475 after paying out £750 in out-of-work, sickness allowance and working expenses, but their total membership was only 600–700 members. In the provinces twenty-one societies were founded, but only nine had survived with a total membership of 1,800. In addition, there were 30,000 women in textile unions.[41] Out of three million women employed in industry this seemed meagre but Mrs Paterson rationalised that there were probably fewer than 1,000 men in unions after they were formed in the eighteenth century. To improve the League's performance she urged establishment of new local branches in different suburbs of London and the provinces. In response Rev. Headlam and Adolphe Smith urged that :

The League ought to stress its Protective-Trades-Union-element as distinct from the Provident element, and further, for the League to use its influence to support such political action of an economic description as will bring about a better distribution of wealth.

Headlam had been bitten by the ideas of Henry George in 1882 and became a champion of taxation of land rents. His thinking was symptomatic of the ferment among some of the intelligent-sia and working classes who in the mid-1880s began to feel that New Model Unionism was not enough—more radical changes were necessary. New Unionism and socialism were other altern-atives.[42] After some further discussion the meeting was adjourned until October to decide upon the motion.

At the October meeting Rev. Headlam again espoused Georgite doctrines until Hodgson Pratt, the Chairman, ruled him out of order. Mrs Paterson then read a letter from J. H. Levy agreeing with the first half of the motion but denouncing the part after the word 'element' as socialist. Miss Simcox, who personally and publicly espoused socialist views, also reacted negatively because she felt that mixing political agitation with the promotion of trades unionism would dry up the sources of the League's funds. Instead she proposed changing the part after the word 'element' as follows :

and further for the League to use its influence to support all other modes of action of an economic description which may tend to bring about a better distribution of wealth.[43]

Miss Simcox explained that by her amendment she meant co-operation and other improved forms of industrial organisation. Headlam acquiesed in Miss Simcox's amendment and the resolution was carried by a vote of nine to five.

Next a motion was made to hire a full-time, paid organising agent with a yearly salary of £100 and to offer the post to Mrs Paterson. She was offended and rejected the offer, suggesting consideration be given to discontinuing the League and turning its work over to the Women's Trades Council, a body of union women supported by union funds which might receive more active consideration from leaders of men's unions than had been offered to the League. In view of the resolution committing the League to new modes of action, Mrs Paterson said she could not say whether she would remain Secretary. She was also afraid that a 'mechanical' organiser might be hired, and urged greater personal commitment by those present. Nevertheless, the motion to hire a paid organiser was adopted.

With all due respect to Mrs Paterson, some of the vigour must have gone out of the League. Both Miss Wilkinson and Mrs Paterson had been ailing since 1883, but Mrs Paterson recuperated to some extent in the Channel Islands and Carlsbad from January to September 1886. Miss Wilkinson, however, died in August. In November 1886 Mrs Paterson was examined by Mrs Garrett Anderson and then went to visit a friend at Tunbridge Wells, where she died at the age of thirty-eight, while reading proofs of the *Women's Union Journal.*

In assessing the accomplishments of the League while Mrs Paterson was its mentor, we should recall the number of obstacles it faced. For one thing, it was difficult to build unions from members who lacked sufficient time, education or money to manage union affairs. There even appears to have been a shortage of middle-class women willing to spend a few hours a week training a secretary chosen from the working-class trade union members, although some men like David Schloss, the economist who served a five years' stint as Treasurer of the East London Tailoresses, filled the void.[44]

Another reason for the League's unsteady take-off was the turbulent economic air encountered soon after it was launched. The so-called 'Great Depression' of 1873–96,[45] also retarded male trade unionism. The number affiliated to the TUC declined from a peak of almost one million in 1874 to less than half that total during the years 1879–84. As Pelling said of male trade unionists during this period, 'Action meant expense, and their funds were of lilliputian proportions.'[46] This led to increasing sectionalism within the movement as a whole. As a result when it came to financial aid for the WPPL, the TUC believed in self-help. Given the economic climate, their myopia is understandable; however, at times both mine unions[47] and cotton unions[48] gave token financial and hearty moral support. If the sources of aid from trade unionists were atrophied, other trade unionists complained that the League perhaps repelled potential members because it was looked upon as a goody-goody society tainted with an air of patronage and in the mid-1880s there was a tendency amongst some workers to escape from a dependence upon paternalism.[49] Both of the League's unpaid organisers, Miss Wilkinson and Miss Simcox, denied this, maintaining they had never heard the League spoken of as a middle-class-patronised affair[50] and, indeed, Miss Simcox observed that in her experience women were afraid that unions would go too far rather than not be progressive enough.

Finally, while the League received great moral support and some financial aid from a number of friends of the labour movement who spoke at its meetings, such as George Howell, Auberon Herbert, William Morris, Thomas Brassey and the Countess of Portsmouth, it lacked the funds to carry on a dynamic organising campaign. The Great Depression contributed to this state of affairs. The profit squeeze caused New Model Employers to feel less beneficent. Talk of socialism frightened many Liberals into feeling that there were limits to aiding movements threatening their status and pocketbooks.[51] An effort in 1882 to raise a special fund of £250 for an organising campaign in the provinces produced only twenty pounds and had to be cancelled.[52] The League's Council realised that its budget, averaging £110 a year, was insufficient, but part of the responsibility was the Council's itself—in 1886 only five of its forty-two members contributed to its funds.[53] What was needed was a financial angel.

2

League into Union:
The Era of Lady Dilke 1886-1903

WITH the death of Emma Paterson, leadership of the WPPL for the rest of that century passed to Lady Emilia Dilke. She had been a member of the League since 1875 and from 1886 to 1904 contributed approximately one hundred pounds to it annually and covered any special deficits if they occurred.[1] Lady Dilke was the daughter of Henry Strong, an ex-Army officer who had served in India, and who had subsequently become manager of an Oxford bank. After the death in July 1884 of her first husband, Mark Pattison, Rector of Lincoln College, she married Sir Charles Dilke in 1885. Dilke was the most popular of the London Radicals, but his political career was crippled by a lurid divorce trial in 1885. Their marriage helped his tarnished reputation. Dilke's fortune enabled his wife to serve as the WPPL's financial angel.

Lady Dilke's intellectual odyssey took her from Puseyism to Positivism to Radical Liberalism. She was a close friend of John Morley, editor of the *Pall Mall Gazette* and an early supporter of the Women's Suffrage Society, where she came under the influence of Mrs Fawcett. Throughout her life Lady Dilke was both an artist and an art critic.[2] Her keen wit, charming manner and excellent speaking voice enabled her to serve as an able 'general' during the second stage of the drive to expand trade unionism among women.[3] She did not allow her upper class origin to hamper her mission and impressed workers as she climbed over bales of rags in a warehouse to learn about rag-sorting. Lady Dilke also appealed to the aristocracy of employers in Manchester by insisting that even though their factories were good places to work, they should not rest until they caused others to emulate them.[4]

In addition to her organising efforts, she publicised the cause of working women by her speeches and articles. Their main theme was that 'the secret of England's industrial greatness' was its dependence upon the women and girls who formed an unlimited supply of cheap labour. This kept both male and female wages low. While not a militant, she was not above warning the smug and complacent that if something was not done an avenging angel would appear bringing not peace to the world but a sword.[5] Women could overcome their weakness by trade unionism which, through its control over the labour market, would cause improvement. However, before the necessary leverage, usually assessed at fifty per cent of the work force, could be exercised a great deal of work was required. As of 1870 there were 47,832 women in trade unions affiliated to the TUC of whom 5,116 were in single-sex women's unions, while another 10,000 were in societies not sending delegates to the TUC, a total of 57,800 out of a possible 3,000,000.[6]

In the formidable task before her, Lady Dilke was aided by her niece, Gertrude Tuckwell, whose belief in social reform was derived from her father Rev. William Tuckwell, Lady Dilke's brother-in-law. As Rector of Stockton in Warwickshire, he demonstrated his commitment to land reform by dividing his own glebe into allotments and leasing them for one pound an acre. Later as a master at New College, Oxford, he became a very radical opponent of the wealthy. After coming to London in 1883, Miss Tuckwell served as an elementary school teacher for six years in a poor section of Chelsea. Unable to stand the changes made by the Chairman of the London School Board, who was a champion of individualism and the Church of England, she left teaching in 1889 to edit the *Women's Trade Union Review* and serve as secretary to Lady Dilke.[7]

The Dilke Era saw some profound changes in WPPL policy. As Miss Tuckwell said :

> She found in the WPPL a little close corporation, full of sex antagonism and opposition to legislative protection but under her sway these limitations gradually disappeared, and the women's trade union movement became an integral part of industrial progress.[8]

While this verdict is true, it has the benefit of hindsight, for Lady Dilke was herself committed to the early laissez-faire policies of the WPPL, having condemned in 1877 a Factory Act Amendment Bill sponsored by R. A. Cross, Home Secretary, as an example of Tory sentimentality.[9] Eventually under the influence of Sir Charles Dilke this attitude was to change. Dilke in 1885 co-authored with Joseph Chamberlain the 'Unauthorised Programme' proposing socialist ideals for radical liberalism.

Following the death of Mrs Paterson, Edith Simcox served as acting Secretary of the WPPL until February 1887 when Clementina Black (1854–1922) became permanent Secretary. The author of a number of social investigations and novels including *The Agitator*, Miss Black, the daughter of the town clerk of Brighton, was also one of the original members of the Women's Industrial Council, Vice-President of the National Anti-Sweating League and a non-militant suffragette who drew up the 1908 Suffrage Declaration.[10] She led the League between 1886 and 1888 in the formation of a Consumer's League which aimed at uniting consumers to pressurise employers who paid low wages. It held a conference to deal with three causes of low wages, German competition, the Jewish 'sweater' and freaks of fashion. One outcome of the conference was the publication in November 1887 of a 'white list' or a list of employers who paid fair wages—which were described as follows :

> Upholsteresses not less than fifteen shillings weekly. Dressmakers and milliners not less than sixteen shillings weekly. Printers not less than thirty-six shillings weekly.[11]

The idea spread and while London was too large and impersonal for the system to work, the Oxford and Leeds branches seemed more successful.[12]

The Consumer's League also indirectly contributed to the initiation of the 1888 London match girls strike, a forerunner of the London dock strike and New Unionism of 1889. As early as October 1885, discontent smouldered at the Bryant and May match factory. At that time the *Reformer* reported a strike caused by low wages and to protest the danger of the disease, phossy-jaw, caused by inhaling the chemical phosphorus. In 1887 Walter Besant, Annie Besant's brother-in-law, wrote *The Children of Gideon*, influential in bringing attention to sweated labour and women's working conditions. It disclosed that shareholders of a large match manufacturing firm received a dividend of twenty-two per cent on the work of women and children whose wages were 4s. to 9s. a week.[13] In June 1888, Miss Black, at a meeting of the Fabian Society, gave a lecture on female labour urging support of the Consumer's League and mentioning conditions at Bryant and May. After the speech, it was decided to boycott the purchase of Bryant and May matches. Mrs Besant and Herbert Burrows then visited Bryant and May's factory and interviewed three of the girls.[14] They complained of bullying foremen, irregular lunch hours and the need for a separate lunch room and adequate washrooms, but their greatest grievance was their fury at having to contribute funds to erect a statue of Gladstone.[15]

Following this, Mrs Besant wrote an article in the *Link* calling the shareholders' attention to the wretched wages and working conditions that enabled them to earn such high dividends. The company reacted by firing the three girls and threatened libel action against Mrs Besant. As a result a mass meeting was held at Mile End Waste and after hearing speeches by Mrs Besant, Miss Black, Rev. Headlam, John Burns and others, 1,400 workers voted to strike. The company then responded by threatening to import blacklegs from Glasgow or move their operation to Sweden.[16] The WPPL assisted the strikers by collecting £400 in strike funds and urged the formation of a union. Pressure from middle-class newspapers like the *Financial World* and *Times*, advising Bryant and May to improve conditions and timely arbitration by George Shipton, of the London Trades Council at the behest of the WPPL, resulted in a settlement. It included better wages and the abolition of fines and deductions.[17] Mrs Besant became President of the Executive Council of the newly-formed Matchworkers' Union and Edith Simcox was appointed to represent them at the International Trades Union Congress in London in November.[18] While Mrs Besant deserves the lion's share of the credit for the match girls' victory, the role of Miss Black and the WPPL were also important. The union, formed with 700 members, was in 1888 the largest single all-women's union in England.[19]

The match girls' strike resembled New Unionism with the publicity and aid it received from socialist leaders and its example spread to the provinces in Liverpool and Bristol.[20] In Liverpool, during the crest of the trade cycle of 1889, a number of women's trade unions were established as the result of the news of the match girls' strike and the House of Lords Report investigation of 'sweating'. The Liverpool Trades' Council also helped trigger this growth by aiding in the formation, on 22 January 1889, of the Women's Industrial Council of Liverpool. Led by Mrs Jeannie Mole, its Secretary, it helped form unions among women cigar-makers, book-folders, upholsteresses, marine-sorters and coat-makers. A native of London, Mrs Mole was a wealthy woman but as the result of reading Carlyle and Ruskin and seeing the slums of that metropolis became a socialist. In the summer of 1890 the newly-formed Coat-Makers' Union, composed of 300 girls, staged a three weeks strike that led to a reduction of hours. The Liverpool Trades' Council collected £70 to support the strike. In October of the same year the Trades Council ceased meeting in a public house, admitted its first woman delegate and began to hold its meetings in the Free Church Hall. During its Annual Conference, in 1890 held in Liverpool, the TUC gave special attention to organising Liverpool women in trade unions. New unions were started among laundresses and sack and bag makers; however, most of these soon collapsed in the economic downturn of 1893, except the upholsteresses' which amalgamated with the male Amalgamated Union of Upholsterers.[21]

While the match girls' strike had a brief impact in Liverpool and Bristol, did it have a lasting effect on women's trade unionism, or was 'the match that fired the Thames' a light that failed? As we have seen, the union extinguished itself by 1903 and little growth took place between 1888 and 1903. Why? One cause was that Mrs Besant did not remain on the scene to become the female version of Ben Tillett or John Burns—someone who could organise women at the factory gates. Mrs Besant drifted off into theosophy. Complicating matters was the role played by Miss Black who resigned as Secretary of the Women's Trade Union and Provident League[22] (hereafter referred to as WTUPL, the new name adopted by the WPPL), to join the newly-organised Women's Trade Union Association (hereafter referred to as WTUA). Launched with high hopes on 8 October 1889 at a meeting presided over by the Bishop of Bedford, after the successful dock strike, it had the active support of a diverse group including H. H. Champion, John Burns, Ben Tillett, Tom Mann, B. Cooper, Chairman of the London Trades' Council, Lady Sandhurst and Sydney Buxton. The WTUA appealed for

£2,000 to fund its activities and quickly raised £300. Miss Black favoured amalgamation of the WTUA and WTUPL, but the older WTUPL turned a cold shoulder on the WTUA and, while wishing it success, preferred that new recruits join its ranks.[23] The zenith of its success was reached in 1890 when it organised members in the rope-making, confectionery, box-making, shirt-making, umbrella-making and brush-making industries in the East End, but even that year it failed to make much headway outside of London. Some trade union leaders, Kier Hardie for example, gave support, even though he had mixed feelings, because he recognised the necessity for organising women to safeguard male unionism; however, he confessed to a belief that in the future all women would return to domestic life.[24]

During the first year of WTUA's existence, Miss Black, in tandem with John Burns, seemed able to work the same magic they had wielded during the match girls' and dockers' strikes. Their activities at the Allen Chocolate Makers strike typified many of the ingredients present in early efforts to unionise women. First, Miss James, a former confectionery worker and a WTUA organiser, met on 10 July with twelve workers and heard complaints by a girl who complained of being dismissed after she refused to pay a fine for laughing. Following this ninety of the girls came out on strike and girls in other industries offered to join the strike, but were advised to bide their time. Meanwhile Burns and Black appealed for funds, provided food for the strikers, stationed pickets, helped the girls draw up demands and applied to the employer for an interview. Since the WTUA rules forbade use of its funds to support strikes, money was raised among London unions at Woolwich and the docks; £7 were garnered from collecting boxes and £5 were gathered by Mr Burns at the County Council.

The pattern of events at Bryant and May was repeated. The rumour spread that the Company would close; public opinion and the police were friendly. Eventually Mr Allen dealt directly with the girls in the union, conceded their demands to reinstate the girl dismissed, granted an improved lunch schedule, abolished fines, except for lateness, and everyone parted on friendly terms.[25]

The strike was successful; but while it might have been manipulated to galvanise a simultaneous walkout in many related industries in the East End, with demands for pay increases during a period when there was great sympathy with labour questions, it wasn't. New Unionists acted no differently than the WPPL had; in fact soon there was a loss of momentum. In 1892, a year before a down-turn in the economy took place, the WTUA reported to its Third Annual Meeting that in no year had it exerted greater efforts and in no year were direct results smaller.[26] By 1893 the WTUA retreated to a more passive policy of advising men not to exclude women from work and to welcome them into their unions.[27] The 'spark' ignited at Bryant and May grew dim and in 1897 the WTUA merged with the Women's Industrial Council. This organisation, with Miss Black as its President, was established in late 1894 by some leading Fabians and the British Economic Association. For the next twenty years it would serve as an important agency for the collection and publication of information on women's work, reporting abuses to factory inspectors, educating women and girls in social and industrial questions, and advocating technical day schools and infant care schools.[28] Meanwhile, the Match Girls' Union led by Herbert Burrows fought on gallantly[29] and after the WTUA collapsed in 1897 it affiliated with the WTUL. In 1902 it staged a wild-cat strike against Bryant and May over the introduction of new manufacturing procedures[30] and following its failure the union was wound up in 1903.

The year 1889 not only saw the birth of the WTUA but also saw the WPPL change its name to the Women's Trade Union and Provident League. This was done to discourage numerous visits from people who came to its offices to complain against bad husbands and servants.[31] The League dropped the word provident from its title in December 1891.[32] After the unemployment riots of 1886 the number of new contributors to the League increased, by thirty-eight in 1887, and another thirty-six in 1888, making a total of 360 and bringing its income to £285 so that its accounts showed a modest balance.[33]

Outside of London the years 1888–89 were years of chequered growth. In June 1888 an effort to organise the saddlery trade in Walsall failed.[34] In September, at Leeds, where, aided by Emma Paterson, she had earlier formed an unsuccessful union of tailoresses, Miss Isabella Ford led a strike of weavers assisted by the local trades' council. Three sisters interested in women's rights, Isabella, Bessie and Emily, were all active in the ILP. Bessie secured publication of the poems of Tom Maguire, the Leeds socialist poet, and Emily helped organise the Leeds Tramway workers. The three sisters grew up during the cotton famine of 1860–65, affording their parents a good opportunity to indoctrinate them thoroughly with sympathy for the underdog. Her father would question Isabella as follows : Father, 'What is an operative, Baby?' Child, 'A starving creature.' The September 1888 strike at Wilson's and Sons resulted from the workers' efforts to resist a reduction of 3s. a week. Miss Ford with the help of Allen Gee, Secretary of the West Riding Power Loom Weaver's Association, participated in forming a union of two hundred called the Society of Workwomen. While the settlement reached only succeeded in limiting the reduction to 2s., it did abolish fines. Eventually the small society grew to 2,000 with the addition of tailoresses. Later because of dissatisfaction with their wages, averaging 11s. a week, and because of discontent with arbitrary deductions, the Society of Workwomen staged another strike. The League and the Leeds Trades' Council raised £800 for a strike fund and helped rally 5,000 workers in the town square; but the firm refused to negotiate and the sympathies of the general public were untouched. Defeated, the Society of Workwomen then lapsed into oblivion. This was not the end of Miss Ford's struggle in behalf of trade unionism. As a member of the Leeds Trades' Council she continued her efforts and later became very active in the suffrage movement. In other areas, attempts to recruit members for a weaver's union during the TUC Conference at Bradford produced meagre results, as did endeavours by Trades' Councils in Manchester, Dundee and Glasgow.[35]

The shift to economic intervention within the WTUL was symbolised during this time by the passage of the first Equal Pay resolution at the Trade Union Congress in 1888. Initiated by Clementina Black and seconded by Richard Juggins, of the Chain-makers and Strikers Association, the resolution's unanimous approval was due mainly to the fact that many of the men hoped equal pay would cause employers to refuse to employ women.[36] Meanwhile a conflict occurred between the League and TUC as a result of Edith Simcox's rejection as a representative of the Shirtmakers at the TUC Dundee Conference in 1889. The reason given was the 'feeling that Miss Simcox was not the class of person whom they desired to see in the Congress';[37] however, the *Manchester Guardian* concluded that the real reason was her enthusiasm for the International.[38] It is little wonder that because of this rebuff and her dissatisfaction at the personal squabbles within labour circles, Miss Simcox soon became disenchanted, retiring to write about primitive civilisations.

About this time a turnover in the League's leadership also took place. J. W. Overton, editor of the *WUJ*, died 30 October 1889. A long-time positivist and journeyman coppersmith, he typified 'Old Guard' WPPL attitudes. Just before his death he wrote a scathing denunciation of the 'socialist' New Unionists, and rejoiced in the work of captains of industry and New Model Unionism.[39] After Overton's death, the monthly *WUJ* was replaced by the quarterly *Women's Trade Union Review*. Miss Black's resignation led to the appointment of Miss Emily Routledge, half-sister of the publisher Edward Routledge, as Secretary,[40] and the post of Assistant Secretary was filled by Emilie A. Holyoake, daughter of the famous co-operator Jacob A. Holyoake. In 1893 she replaced Miss Routledge but resigned the position upon her marriage in 1894.[41] The League's new Treasurer was Miss May E. Abraham, newly arrived in England from Dublin in 1887 and, although inexperienced with working-class problems, she was enthusiastic and proved a born organiser and agitator.[42] Miss Abraham replaced Marian Hatchard as Treasurer. Miss Hatchard had served in the post for only a year, resigning following her marriage. Matrimonial losses caused a lack in continuity in the League's leadership, a factor that made recruiting even more difficult. Miss Abraham's later acceptance of a civil service position exemplified another way in which the League lost some of its most gifted leaders.

Besides personnel changes during the nineties, another significant shift occurred during the discussion at the TUC Conference of the amendment of the Factory and Workshops Act of 1891. The decision to support the regulation of laundry hours marked a change in the League's earlier laissez-faire policy. But as Lady Dilke said at the Bristol TUC of 1898, it was suicide to put sex against sex. There were 185,246 women employed in the laundry industry in 1891, and they often worked fourteen to sixteen hours a day. No one could claim that shorter hours in the industry would hurt the chances of either women or men to find employment. To exert pressure for passage of the amendment, an Amalgamated Society of Laundresses was formed out of the remnants of earlier societies and it soon had 3,000 members and eight branches in London and Brighton. The London Trades' Council helped organise a giant demonstration in Hyde Park where it was claimed that at least 66,000 workers favoured regulation. Not all League members followed Lady Dilke's lead; Ada Heather Biggs and some of its laissez-faire elements, members of the Women's Employment Society, organised a special pressure group, the Woman's Employment Defence League, in opposition.[43] With the aid of the Irish Party in Parliament which withdrew support because of the prospect of the inspection of convent laundries, the Amendment was defeated or emasculated in 1891, 1895 and 1901. Lady Dilke and the WTUL condemned the WEDL for its stand, and to prove her point Lady Dilke used the textile industry as an example of beneficial legislative interference; there restricted working time set the standard of work for the entire trade.[44] By 1893 few laissez-faire purists remained on the WTUL General Committee.

The League, in 1893, had two advisor or policy making groups : (1) a General Committee composed of a certain number of members, usually those interested in labour conditions or labour representatives in Parliament, elected at the annual meeting and including as *ex-officio* members all secretaries of affiliated London trade unions, and (2) a Committee of Counsel composed usually of male secretaries of unions that had female members, and other members elected from these unions at the annual meeting. Unions could affiliate with the League at the rate of 2s. 6d. per 250 members. This entitled the union to an annual visit from a League organiser for a single meeting or for a week's organising effort during which the member union provided hospitality. If a second week was required an extra fee of 15s. was charged and train fare had to be paid if more than one visit was made in a year. It is useful in contemplating the League's possible expansion to remember these financial realities.

With these limitations in mind, the League decided in 1892 to alter its tactics for organising outside of London. The past practice of intermittent tours, usually creating fragile unions that often withered and died, had proved unsatisfactory. Each year the League enrolled hundreds of members knowing perfectly well that if half were retained it was a good year.[45] Two remedies were possible: devoting long periods of time to one area (difficult because of the League's limited staff) or revisiting areas on a scheduled basis. So began the practice of two annual tours—in spring and autumn—to form new unions and strengthen old ones.

The time was especially ripe among the textile operatives. In 1889 the WPPL, on the suggestion of Lady Dilke, successfully made a bid for the affiliation of a number of textile unions. Here improvements in machinery caused the proportion of women workers to increase in the last half of the nineteenth century.

In 1861 there were 131 women employed for every 100 men; in 1871, 148 women for 100 men and in 1881, 164 women for every 100 men.[46] Many of these women were mothers who went to work because they wished for or needed extra money to raise their standard of living. For instance, in Preston over sixty per cent of the married women workers were employed for these reasons.[47]

In discussing textile trade unionism, a number of divisions should be kept in mind. First, material—cotton, wool, linen, silk; second, geographic area   Lancashire, Yorkshire, Northern Ireland, Scotland; and finally, the type of manufacturing process —hand-loom weaving, power-loom weaving, spinning, dying, carding, blowing, etc. Changes did not occur uniformly in each of the above and must be dealt with separately. Women in textile unions formed the majority of women in trade unions during the nineteenth century, and a separate book would be required to cover their history adequately. The following account covers those events which the WTUL considered significant.

As machines were introduced in the textile industry, the distinction between men's work and women's work decreased and more women came to replace men, often doing their work at half pay. In the West Riding area an employer actually paid men £2 to quit so that he could fill their jobs with women at thirty-five per cent of the rate paid men. When one of the men was asked how he got even with the women, he replied, 'I married one.'[48] In the cotton industry, spinners' unions had successfully barred women, limiting their employment to helpers or piecers until the introduction in 1880 of ring spinning which became a woman's job. The ring spinners found a home not in the spinners' unions but in the newer Cardroom Operatives' Unions.[49]

In the Lancashire cotton industry the proportion of female weavers gradually increased during the nineteenth century and since their influx was hard to stop, it was decided to organise them before things got worse. Textile unions requested WPPL aid. A male textile official telegraphed League headquarters, 'Please send us an organiser for the women must be organised or exterminated'. During the 1890s the League placed its highest priority in this area, in effect doing whatever was possible there, rather than devoting its energies to the more difficult task of recruiting in sweated industry or in small workshops in Birmingham or Cradley Heath.[50] Lady Dilke contributed £72 annually to hire a paid organiser to help recruit textile workers exclusively.[51]

Cotton trade unions, before their amalgamation, were centred on a town and its surrounding districts, such as Preston, Burnley or Blackburn. In 1858 the North Lancashire Power Loom Weavers Union was formed (it was also known as the East Lancashire Amalgamated Power Loom Weavers and generally considered to be the 'First Amalgamation'). As H. A. Turner pointed out, trade unions could attempt to control the supply of labour, so that its price would be raised automatically or they could try to fix its price, leaving supply and demand to adjust themselves. New Model craft organisations emphasised the first method, while non-craft workers, the New Unionism of the 1880s, stressed the second. The early weavers' amalgamations in the 1850s anticipated the dockers' and gas workers' unions by over forty years, while the Spinners' unions' preoccupation with control of entry made them resemble the New Model craft unions of the 1850s.

The new cotton textile amalgamations were not as conservative as portrayed by the Webbs. Shortly after it was formed the 'First Amalgamation' supported a twenty-nine week strike of the Padiham weavers and there were frequent local strikes in the 1860s. In 1878 a 'Great Strike' of 100,000 North Lancashire operatives against a wage reduction took place and was defeated after nearly two months, and during the 1880s a whole crop of major strikes and lock-outs took place in the cotton industry. A dispute in 1884 in Blackburn over wage revisions made evident the need for an even larger amalgamation and resulted in the birth of the Northern Counties Weavers' Association in 1884.

The growth of trade unionism and the frequency of industrial disputes are usually affected by the economic health of the related industry. During the nineteenth century, exports of cotton from Britain increased during each decade by at least sixty-three per cent until 1865–1874, when the rate of increase began to decline until 1895–1904, when it fell to six per cent.[52] Britain's share of the world cotton export trade also began to decline after 1884.[53] It was no surprise that when the boom of the eighties came to an end in November 1892, employers and employees were at odds over whether a five per cent cut in wages or working short-time was the best way to cope with the reduction in the demand for cotton products. The result was a lock-out that lasted from 7 November to 27 March 1893. Forty thousand spinners and twenty thousand weavers were put out of work and £2,000,000 were lost in wages. Capitalists were blamed for over expansion and the operatives urged the manufacturers to adopt a policy limiting production.[54] Industrial peace was reached in the vaguely worded Brooklands Agreement, named after a country inn outside of Manchester, by representatives of the Federation of Master Cotton Spinners' Association, Operatives Spinners' Amalgamation, Card and Blowing Room Operatives' Amalgamation, and the Amalgamated Northern Counties Association of Warpers, Reelers and Winders, who signed the document providing the spinning section of the industry with a centralised mechanism for negotiating disputes. The parties agreed to avoid future strikes and lockouts as inimical to their interests, and raises or cuts were limited to five per cent a year.[55] The 1893 stoppage had a devastating effect on some of the unions, with the Oldham Operatives being left with a £20,000 debt.[56]

The Brooklands agreement provided for the first time central and systematic machinery for negotiating with the employers in the spinning section of the industry. This, taken together with the Uniform List of weaving wage rates drawn up by the Cotton Weavers in May 1892, led to a period of industrial peace in the industry from 1895 to 1900. During this time the number of trade union members increased and by 1900 there were 109,000 members of weavers' associations, with the Northern Counties Weavers' Association alone containing 47,000 members (26,000 of whom were women). Two-thirds of the 14,000 members of the Card and Blowing Rooms Amalgamated Association at Manchester were women and girls. The Bolton and District Power-Loom Weavers' Association had an even larger proportion of women to men, 58,000 to 580. In 1900 three-fifths of the country's female trade unionists were in the cotton industry and by 1910 there were 150,000 or three-quarters of all unionised women.[57]

What made women textile workers so willing to join unions? First, twenty per cent of the women in the Lancashire textile industries were married and League organisers were unanimous in their opinion that married women were the easiest to recruit. Secondly, there was male trade-union pressure in the factory and in the home, and coercion in the factory usually took the subtle form of dilatoriness or ineptitude from the male trade unionists in charge of tuning the recalcitrant workers' machines.

Coercion or pressure in the home was also easily exerted because textile towns like mining towns were close-knit, isolated communities, and influence was exerted by the door-to-door collection of union dues and neighbourhood social pressure.

As trade unionists, women in the textile industries were less active than their male counterparts and did not attend evening meetings because of their domestic duties. They consequently deferred to men and played small part in shaping policy. Women paid their dues, reported their grievances to men officials, shared increases in wages and awaited their benefits from accident or sickness. There were no women secretaries among the local unions in the weaving trades and no woman held a place on the general council or central committee of the Northern Counties' Amalgamations. Exceptions elsewhere were usually unmarried women or those who had other members of their family to carry on domestic duties at home.[58] After a long day's work, there was little time left to get proper food prepared and keep the home tidy and clean, much less to receive impressions of any better conditions. Even so, within unions enrolling a majority of women, Lady Dilke seemed content to allow men to be the leaders because women were 'slack' officials and did not understand 'working up' a union.[59] One of their major faults was the 'tendency of women's trade unions to strike, before they were in a position to carry it to a successful conclusion'.[60] Overall however, the women made good trade unionists during the nineties; they did not scab and they followed the dictates of their leaders.

During the nineties, the cotton trade unions displayed an ambivalent attitude towards government regulation. Since 1871 the Factory Acts Reform Committee had served as a pressure

group to obtain improvements in working conditions by legislative means. This Committee was reorganised in 1883 and
again in 1889 as the United Textile Factory Workers' Association
which campaigned for a 48-hour Bill and more factory regulation. It also gathered 200,000 signatures for a petition against
'steaming' (this was the practice of using steam in the weaving
sheds to prevent breakage of material). It succeeded in obtaining
the passage of the Cotton Cloth Factories Act of 1889 which
limited the maximum humidities allowed.

Demands by New Unionists during 1889 and 1890 for a
statutory eight hours' day led the President of the Weavers'
Amalgamation, David Holmes, to give the proposal his backing,
in spite of the fact that neither he nor the leaders of the spinners'
and card-room amalgamations really wanted a bill. They later
voted against a resolution in favour of an eight hours' day in
1890 and 1891 at the TUC because it would prejudice Britain's
competitive position in the world export markets. Both Thomas
Birtwistle, the Weavers' representative on the Parliamentary
Committee of the TUC, and James Mawdsley of the Spinners'
Amalgamation, shared Holmes's position. By 1892 as market
conditions worsened, the cotton unions shifted again to support
statutory reduction of hours in the hope of restricting over-
production and avoiding a lock-out. An improvement in demand
for cotton goods in 1894 caused the unions to once again withdraw their support for an eight hours' day. Historically, one of
the principal purposes of the combination of textile operatives
was to restrict working hours. Campaigns by the workers during
the earlier part of the nineteenth century were conducted in the
name of protecting women and young workers, but as H. A.
Turner argues, it would be wrong to regard this as the Webbs
did—'as hiding behind the skirts of the women'. Instead, this
policy was necessary in order to gather public sympathy, and
also because women had a lesser capacity to resist exploitation
and this made it difficult for men to enforce the reduction of
their hours by direct action.[61]

In the woollen industries women trade unionists during the
1890s lagged behind their sisters in the cotton unions because
male trade unionists in the woollen industries, mainly the West
Yorkshire Power-loom Weavers (who in 1900 would change
their name to the General Union of Textile Workers), encoun-

tered greater obstacles. These included the virtual closing of the American market by the McKinley tariff, competition by German goods within England, a proposed French tariff, labour-saving machinery and competition from married women who were forced to work to supplement the reduced wages of their husbands. Improvement in machinery made wool weaving a light occupation, and thus weaving and spinning in the woollen and worsted industries increasingly became a women's and girls' job. In Bradford there were five women weavers for every one male. Women's wages came to be considered as subsidiary rather than the main source of a family's income. Unmarried women workers had the effect of bringing down wages to their subsistence level. A surplus of women workers was both the cause and the effect of a weak bargaining position. Life for both the employer and his employees was also complicated by seasonal and demand fluctuation for the product.[62] As a result, weekly wages in Yorkshire woollen mills were usually 5s. to 10s. less than in Lancashire cotton mills. There was little collective bargaining anywhere in the industry and their failures and disappointments made the leaders of the General Union exceedingly cautious.[63]

The problems were typified by the strike at Samuel Lister's Manningham Mills at Bradford, caused by the company cutting wages by twenty per cent. Although the mills had not been organised, Ben Turner, Allen Gee and W. H. Drew 'organised a massive and unprecedented display of unity in an industry where, in the past, workers had been neither militant nor united'. A strike committee, aided by Lady Dilke, with over half its members women, made collections and staged marches but in spite of a four months' struggle the operatives were defeated.[64] Even though Bradford was a stronghold of the ILP, had a strong Labour Church Movement, and possessed an energetic local Secretary, Julia Varley, the League was unable to make much headway there as late as 1901.[65]

During the League's autumn tours in the 1890s efforts were again made to unionise the linen workers of Belfast, where as early as 1874, from 6 July to 27 August, forty thousand mill workers went on strike. Life in the mills was described in 1911 by a woman worker to James Connolly:

. . . I was just turned eight when I began . . . Worked in steam making your rags all wet, and sometimes up to your ankles in water. The older you got the more work you got. If you got married you kept on working. Your man didn't get enough for a family. You worked till your baby came, and went back as soon as you could, and then, God forgive you! You counted the years till your child could be a half-timer and started the same hell of a life over again.[66]

Conditions in the steaming sheds of the linen mills where jets of steam were used to prevent fibres from cracking resulted in an average life span for carders of thirty years.[67] The Autumn 1891 tour conducted by Misses Abraham and Routledge, resulted in the formation of three new unions among Spinners, Preparers and Reelers; Weavers, Warpers and Winders; and Warehouse Workers. These would be strengthened during the 1893 TUC Conference held in Belfast by Miss Tuckwell and Lady Dilke and the male trade unionists in attendance at the TUC Conference. Some of the more active were Thomas Lord of Nelson, Kier Hardie, David Holmes, President of the Northern Counties Weavers' Association, and Ben Tillett. The latter, who was enthusiastically received by the girls, reminded them of the earlier attempts and failures to organise unions in Belfast and hoped that this time they would prove deserving of the help given them; trade unionism was more than play or music hall jollity. Aid was also given by the Belfast Trades' Council but the main spark was provided by a local organiser, Mary Galway, who later became Secretary of the Textile Operative Association of Ireland, numbering 1,000 members of whom ninety-five per cent were women. Greater efforts by the League were cut short when the Committee of Counsel advised postponing a great part of the tour due to a shortage of funds. The effort had cost the League the princely sum of £30.[68]

In 1896 organising attempts, with the aid of £20 contributed by the Belfast Trades' Council, were renewed;[69] and shortly thereafter the Truck Act of 1896, requiring employers to post a list of all rules and regulations on fines and penalties, led to a strike on 19 January 1897. The agitation resulted in a doubling in the union's membership. Eventually 8,000 workers participated in the strike. The negotiations between the employers and the workers, led by Misses Galway and Cockbill representing the Belfast Trades'

Council, resulted in mutual concessions over the disputed points, but by 1900 membership had dwindled to 800. One of the reasons was the ability of employers to exploit the divisions between Catholics and Protestants. Miss Galway was unable to obtain rooms in the Protestant quarter of Belfast.[70] On the other hand, some agnostic union organisers ignorant of local custom found few followers when they scheduled meetings on Sunday. Another reason why it was difficult to organise the women in the Irish linen industry was its depressed state in the late nineteenth century.

In Scotland a branch of the WPPL and a Council for Women's Trades were established in 1887 with the help of Clementina Black and the Glasgow United Trades' Council. In addition, a Glasgow Union of Women Workers was formed which was affiliated with the National Union of Women Workers. Scotland produced two dynamic women trade union leaders— Kate Taylor and Margaret Hardinge Irwin.[71] The League organisers on tour worked tirelessly when the opportunity presented itself—sometimes thirty-six hours straight. A fortnight was spent among the girls involved in fish curing in Aberdeen. On other occasions poor weather, employer intimidation or faulty advance notices left the organisers with an empty house.[72] One important gain made during this period was the admission of women into the Scottish Mill and Factory Workers Association established in 1889. By 1896 in Forfar, Dundee, Brechin, Kirriemuir and Kirkaldy over 9,000 female members were recruited, making the Scottish unions second only to those in cotton textiles in women's membership. Two-thirds of the 2,200 members of the Forfar Factory Workers Union were women. The average earnings of women weavers in the jute and linen industry was 12s., about one-half of the earnings of Lancashire male cotton weavers.[73]

While most of the Scottish unions established during the 1890s proved hardy, some fell by the wayside and others remained in embryo. During the autumn tour of 1895 the League visited Dundee where Rev. Henry Williamson, a Radical Unitarian minister, had in 1885 with the help of the Dundee Trades' Council and Misses Simcox, Black and Whyte helped found the Dundee and District Mill and Factory Workers,[74] but out of 60,000 workers not more than one per cent were unionised. The percentage of members was higher in Alyth where two-thirds of the workers were organised and in Brechin where sixty per cent of the cent of the women were unionised.[75] In Alva the weavers' union led by shrewd and determined men were able to resist a five per cent wage reduction.[76] Lady Dilke hoped eventually to form an amalgamation of textile unions of Northern Ireland, Scotland, Yorkshire and Lancashire, so that the latter two districts would not be retarded by the less organised and lower paid areas,[77] but in the future true stability could only result from international agreements.

League activity was not limited entirely to the textile industry, its organisers in Newcastle founded a union of women paper mill workers in Sunderland. They were aided by Ben Tillett who urged male support and Thomas Burt who supported equal pay for equal work.[78] Male New Unionists seemed more willing to admit women to their unions. The National Union of Gas Workers and General Labourers, established in 1889, opened a women's branch at the India Rubber Works at Silverton with Mrs Aveling as its leading spirit.[79]

In London where women began to replace men as cigar makers, the League in 1890 assisted the Mutual Association of Cigar Makers in forming a London Society of Female Cigar Makers, which in a few years joined the mens' organisation. On the other hand, in Nottingham the Society of Female Cigar Makers, established in 1887, preferred to remain independent of the men's society even though it remained in close touch with it. Mrs Bryant was its Secretary and in 1889 membership rose to 1,200. Other unions admitting women to their ranks during the 1890s were the Amalgamated Society of Tailors, the Amalgamated Union of Clothing Operatives, the Scottish Operative Tailors, the London Society of Compositors, the National Union of Printers Warehousemen and Cutters, various Societies of Pottery Workers, the London Society of Cigar Makers, the British Steel Smelters and Tin and Sheet Millmen, the Chain-makers and Strikers Association, the Sheffield Hand File Cutters, and the Cumberland Miners' Union. Women were admitted to black-coated and general labour unions from the start. Generally London trade unions had so many of their own problems during the 1890s that they refrained from helping women trade unionists, even though George Shipton supported their cause.[80]

On the negative side, male trade unionists in the printing industry took a united stand on the admission of women and at an International Conference of Typographical Societies in 1886 resolved that . . .

> women are not physically capable of performing the duties of a compositor, this Conference recommends their admission to membership of the various typographical unions upon the same conditions as journeymen, provided always the females are paid strictly in accordance with the scale.[81]

Paying the women the rate for the job in effect shut them out of employment and it was not until 1892 that the first woman was employed. In 1894 the Printing and Kindred Trades' Federation, 'anxious to show the members' appreciation of the courage and loyalty with which the women had supported the men in a recent strike', invited the League to co-operate in forming the National Union of Women Bookfolders. Mr G. C. Jones, a men's trade unionist, was appointed Secretary. It flourished and ten years later at its own request joined a men's group.[82]

In spite of the recession of 1892, seven new societies were formed in other industries. Miss Hutchinson helped organise the Northampton Boot and Shoe Operatives, while Miss Marland aided the Swindon Trades' Council to form the Women Workers' Union. As trade contracted after 1893, some of the old reliables fell by the wayside. After ten years existence the East London Tailoresses failed despite the efforts of Mr Schloss as Treasurer.[83] Upholsteresses who dwindled away as a result of a depression in trade and the use of machinery were another casualty.[84] Its leader, Miss Mears, died shortly thereafter.[85]

The years 1896 and 1897 saw a further turnover in League staff. Miss Marland, a former cotton textile worker, ceased work as a provincial organiser and was replaced by Miss Barry, of the East End Branch of the Amalgamated Society of Tailors. Miss Mona Wilson was hired as an additional organiser in 1897 and Miss Gertrude Tuckwell became the new Honorary Secretary.[86] While the number of women trade unionists was increasing during the 1890s, the number of women representatives at the 1895 TUC Annual Conference decreased as the result of the change in its rules to eliminate the duplication of representation caused by trade unions sending members not only from their unions but also from Trades' Councils. The revised rules stipulated that trade unions would have one representative for each

1,000 members, or fraction thereof, while Trades' Council representation was eliminated. In addition any person not working at his trade or a permanent paid official of his union was barred as a representative. The reforms aimed to preserve the TUC as an organisation of workers—not middle-class politicians.[87] Since the WTUL was by its own definition not itself a union, this reduced the number of women delegates. Before the change, as many as nine women representatives attended the TUC Conference, afterwards the number fell to three.[88] After 1895 a typical women's contingent might consist of Mrs Callaghan, President of the Oldham Weavers' Union, or some other woman representative of the textile unions, Miss Sergeant, from the Bristol based National Union of Working Women (until it ceased existence before the turn of the century), and Miss Whyte, of the London Bookbinders. Women in the textile unions usually deferred to men delegates, such as Allen Gee, Ben Turner, John Holmes or Thomas Birtwistle, who were usually careful to look after women's interests as in 1897 when Allan Gee condemned any change in the status of the women's branch of the Factory and Workshop Department.[89] While fewer women attended as delegates, League officers continued to attend as visitors. This increased the importance of the separate Women's Conference (which included men as representatives), held between sessions of the TUC Conference. Lady Dilke usually provided a lavish buffet for those in attendance and in 1896 when no meeting-place was available, it was held in her hotel suite.[90] This seemed ineffective and by 1899 the League complained that the TUC had gone flat and needed reorganisation.[91]

The result of the 1895 TUC rules revision upon women's trade unionism in Scotland was different; a separate Scottish Trades Union Congress was established. It admitted the Scottish Women's Protective and Provident League and the Scottish Council for Women's Trades to the Scottish Trades Union Congress (STUC). Miss Irwin was nominated as Chairman of Parliamentary Committees, but although she had the greatest number of votes in the election to the Committee she deferred to Robert Smillie, Secretary of the Lanarkshire Miners. From 1897 to 1898 Miss Irwin acted as 'Interim Secretary' of the STUC, but refused to be permanent Secretary because she felt it might be prejudicial to the interests of the STUC if the post of Secretary was filled by a woman. Nevertheless, when no other candidate came forward, she accepted the position and served from 1898 to 1901. During the course of the 24 September 1898 meeting of the Parliamentary Committee, she was criticised for omitting reference in the minutes to George Carson's proposal for a campaign for the Eight-Hours Bill and she was censured later by Robert Allan, of the Edinburgh Trades' Council, who blamed the meagre results of a fund-raising campaign on her failure to include reference to the Committee's efforts to promote the Labour Representation Committee. Robert Smillie agreed and in 1902 George Carson, Secretary of the Tinplate Workers, succeeded Miss Irwin as Secretary. Regardless, relations between the STUC and the Scottish Council for Women's Trades (SCWT) remained cordial in spite of Miss Irwin's jaundiced view of strikes and support for conciliation boards and women's suffrage. Miss Irwin turned her energy to a campaign for a government enquiry into housing conditions for itinerant workers engaged in potato gathering, fish curing and fruit picking. By 1911 the Scottish branch of the National Federation of Women Workers (NFWW) became a member of the STUC, since it was felt that it was a more bona fide trade union than the Scottish WPPL or SCWT. Nevertheless in 1912 when the NFWW attempted to oust the SCWT from the STUC and Miss Irwin's organisation received support from the Scottish Miners' Federation, it ceased affiliation.[92]

Women trade unions made advancements during the 1890s in other fields besides organisation. The naming of Eliza Orme, Clara Collet, MA, May Abraham and Margaret Irwin as Lady Assistant Commissioners to the Royal Commission on Labour (1892) paved the way for the appointment of women factory inspectors.[93] On 24 January 1893, F. W. Verney arranged for a deputation[94] to see Mr Asquith, the Home Secretary, to urge the appointment of women inspectors to carry out the provisions of the Factory Acts of 1878 and 1891.[95] The result was the naming of Miss Abraham and Miss Mary Paterson as the first two Women Factory Inspectors in spring 1893. Miss Abraham's beauty often enabled her to win arguments at the Home Office merely by stamping her foot and looking determined.[96] The number of women inspectors gradually increased to five in 1897, twenty-one in 1914, thirty in 1918, until by 1921 there were forty-two women and 195 men inspectors.

The Factory Act of 1891 gave the League a useful tool to improve women's working conditions. It limited the employment of women after childbirth, raised the age for the employment of children and provided for the regulation of dangerous trades.[97] The Chairman of the Dangerous Trades' Committee, H. J. Tennant, was also the husband of May Abraham. From 1890 to 1902 League members, Mona Wilson, Gertrude Tuckwell and the Christian Social Union, tirelessly agitated for prevention of phossy jaw in the match industry and lead poisoning in potteries.[98] The result was the Factory and Workshop Act of 1891, 'Potters' Charter of Health', giving the Home Secretary the power to investigate dangerous trades and set up special rules. Miss Marland, of the League, got the United Ovenmen, Kilnmen and Saggers' Union, and Printers Transferers' Union to organise women's branches at Hanley and Burslem.[99] The male unionists in the pottery industry were a timid lot and Lady Dilke, who usually had to reproach women for not accepting the help of men, warned the men that if they did not seek higher wages they would be displaced by women. How they would make their jobs more secure by requesting higher wages was not mentioned. The union initially composed of 1,300 members declined to 500 in two years.[100]

Overall during the 1890s the number of women in trade unions grew slowly, as is shown in the following table:

	1876*	1886	1896	1904
Textile Unions	19,000	34,500	106,540	111,089
All Other	700	2,400	11,348	15,196
Total	19,700	36,900	117,888	126,285[101]

* Approximate figures.

During the 'Era of Lady Dilke' textile unions accounted for the greatest increase in numbers and after a rapid growth between 1886 and 1896, the period of 1896–1904 slowed down.

In 1900 the League surveyed trade union leaders to discover the reasons for this slow growth. To Miss I. O. Ford, Honorary Secretary of the Leeds Society of Workwomen, one reason was that women trade unionists had to undergo a total change of consciousness—they had to rebel against being submissive as taught by orthodox religion.[102] Margaret Bondfield claimed that the biggest obstacle was the feeling that their occupation was temporary before marriage and stressed personal contact with the dues collector as the best way to maintain branches.

Both male textile leaders, Allan Gee, General Secretary of the General Union of Weavers and Textile Workers, and David Shackleton, Secretary of the Northern Counties Weavers' Association, claimed that women workers were loyal but not active trade unionists. One might add that if they both owed their positions to this fact, Gee honestly admitted that some men did not understand women's grievances and urged that women be trained to run their own organisations in the mills. On the other hand, G. C. Jones, Secretary of the Women's Printing and Kindred Trades Union, was pessimistic, viewing women as not only the weaker sex but as weak trade unionists as well. His view of which women made the best members, differed from most. He saw unmarried women as the best members while married women were the first to blackleg; however, the opposite generalisation was true in the close-knit textile communities. Will Thorne, Secretary of the Gasworkers' and General Labourers' Union, explained women's lack of participation in branch work as due to the household duties and male disapproval of pushy 'go-to-meetings' women. He also saw their 'uncharitableness to each other' as a force that worked against their solidarity.[103]

In view of all the obstacles listed above, the contributions of Lady Dilke to the growth of the women's trade union movement ought not be underestimated. With her motto, 'Don't think of the Empire on which the sun never sets—think of the wage that never rises', she tried to teach men and women trade unionists that it was folly to pit sex against sex. She took a largely London-oriented group and with the help of male textile leaders expanded it into a national organisation. By her strategy of yearly tours and liberal contributions of cash, she built upon and modified the foundations laid by Mrs Paterson. The League ceased to be a propagandist and organisational body relying on the sympathy and subscriptions of middle-class Liberals, and began to move towards a more independent position in closer alliance with the whole trade union movement.[104] As she grew tired and ill, it remained to be seen if the League would be able to find a leader who would be true to the *Women's Trade Union Review* motto, 'Remember that you do not lose that which we have won'.

3

Mary and Margaret 1903-1914

TOGETHER they looked like an eagle and a sparrow—Mary MacArthur was tall and robust while Margaret Bondfield was small but perky. Although Miss MacArthur was seven years younger, Miss Bondfield recognised in her a leader of genius and did everything possible to have others acknowledge her talents. It was truly a fateful meeting that brought these two pioneers of women's trade unionism together. The gathering was chaired by John Turner of the Shop Assistants' Union in a dark and dreary schoolroom in the town of Ayr. Ironically both these champions of the cause of industrial women in urban areas originally came from small rural towns, but both soon gravitated to London. Here in 1903, Miss MacArthur became Secretary of the WTUL after Miss Bondfield recommended her for the post to Lady Dilke. It ushered in an era that deserves to be known as the period of Mary and Margaret.

Margaret Bondfield was born on 17 March 1873, in Somerset.[1] She was the tenth of eleven children and came from a politically active family. Her father had been a Radical during the days of the Anti-Corn Law League, while her mother was an energetic Congregationalist and also active in politics.[2] Margaret attended the Board School and after a year as a pupil teacher, at the age of fourteen, left for Brighton to work as a shop assistant. There she experienced the 'living-in' system first hand, working a seventy-four hours week and living in a dormitory with no privacy. She furthered her education in the evenings at the home of Mrs Hilda Martindale, a Liberal and a women's rights advocate.

In 1894 Miss Bondfield left for London where after a three months search she found employment as a shop assistant and worked sixty-five hours a week. The hours and wages were typical

C

of most shop assistant jobs in the metropolis and she was paid £15 plus living-in (worth £20), and premiums of £5, or roughly £40 a year. In London she visited her brother Frank, a member of the printers' union, and met James MacPherson, Secretary of the National Union of Shop Assistants, Warehousemen and Clerks (in the future referred to as the Shop Assistants). The Shop Assistants were founded in the 1890s and admitted members irrespective of craft or sex as long as they were employed in the industry of distribution. Since many white-collar industries enforced a marriage bar requiring married women to retire upon their marriage, the Shop Assistants established a marriage dowry scheme which refunded part of the members' dues if no benefits had been claimed. The practice was indicative of women's views of both employment and union membership as dead-end or temporary phases of their lives. After joining the union Miss Bondfield was elected to the London District Council in 1896 and a year later to the National Executive at the age of twenty-four. She was largely responsible for abolition of the living-in system by the Shop Hours Act of 1906.

Union activities introduced her to a number of leaders of the labour movement and she became friendly with Amie Hicks and Claire James, both active with the rope makers and box makers unions, and Lillian Gilchrist Thompson, sister of Sidney Gilchrist, the famous metallurgist.[3] At the Ideal Club she met the Webbs, Bernard Shaw, and became a member of the Fabian Society. For a while she was attracted to Hyndman, Quelch and the SDF, but was repelled by its theories of violence. Instead she joined the ILP and became a friend of Margaret Gladstone, soon to be the wife of Ramsay MacDonald.[4] In addition, she joined with Edith Hogg, from 1896 to 1898, in surveying shop assistants' conditions for the Women's Industrial Council. Their report became the basis of a series of articles written by Vaughan Nash in the *Daily Chronicle*. Because of her knowledge of shop assistants' grievances and her clear, resonant voice, she was chosen Assistant Secretary of the Shop Assistants' Union from 1898 to 1908, with a salary of £124 a year.[5] The period was one during which the union enjoyed rapid growth; in 1898 out of an estimated 250,000 shop assistants, 2,897 were unionised; by 1907 the figure increased to 20,218 and peaked at 125,000 in 1919, before declining in the twenties. The Shop Assistants were affiliated to the WTUL and Miss Bondfield served on its General Committee where she became a trusted advisor to Lady Dilke.[6]

One of the reasons for its growth was the support given by the union to the Early Closing Bill and the Seats for Shop Assistants' Bill. The Early Closing Bill became an Act in 1904 and was sponsored by Sir John Lubbock (later Lord Avebury), who had for thirty-one years championed the cause of shop assistants.[7] It involved a form of local option but the Shop Assistants preferred a Bill sponsored by Lord Dilke calling for uniform compulsory closing.[8] Another measure supported by Avebury, the Seats for Shop Assistants' Bill passed the House of Commons but was rejected by the House of Lords, as the result of the efforts of Lord Wemyss, leader of the Liberty and Property Defence League, the doctrinaire opponents of most welfare legislation between 1882 and 1914. In thanking Lord Salisbury for his help in defeating the Bill, Wemyss expressed the hope, 'that the House of Commons, having taken shop girls' seats in hand has thus touched bottom in Social Legislation'.[9] Nonetheless, the efforts to improve the Shop Assistants' lot stimulated interest in union organisation. Between 1900 and 1914 a number of white-collar women's unions were founded—in 1903, the Association of Women's Clerks and Secretaries, in 1901 the Association of Women Clerks in the Post Office, in 1903 the Civil Service Typists' Association, in 1912 the Federation of Women's Clerks and in 1900 the National Union of Women Teachers.[10] These stayed aloof from the WTUL. It was during this period of expansion that in 1902 while on an organising campaign for the Shop Assistants in Scotland with John Turner, the unions organiser, Miss Bondfield met Mary MacArthur.[11]

Mary MacArthur was born in Glasgow in 1880. At Glasgow High School she once won a medal for the best work of the year but was admonished for her lack of sobriety. Here she established and edited a magazine and recorded in her diary the prophecy and hope, 'I must, I will be famous'. After a year in Germany she returned to Ayr and began to work as a bookkeeper for her father, a successful draper and a staunch Conservative.[12] Bored, she moonlighted as a writer for the local newspaper and it was in this capacity that she first met John Turner and Margaret Bondfield. Turner converted Miss MacArthur to the cause of trade unionism by explaining to her how it forced less enlightened employers to pay the same wages as humanitarian employers and, therefore, enabled them to continue to compete with their greedy counterparts. Mary soon exhorted all her father's employees to join the Ayr branch of the Shop Assistants' Union and became its first Chairman.

While Turner converted her to trade unionism it was William C. Anderson, Chairman of the Glasgow Shop Assistants' Union and a future Chairman of the ILP and Labour Party Executive, who converted her to Socialism. He asked her to marry him in November 1903 but she refused, explaining that her work came first.[13] Miss MacArthur eventually became Mrs Anderson in 1911. (Mrs Anderson was almost always called Miss MacArthur during her lifetime and will be referred to as Miss MacArthur throughout this work.) While she probably absorbed some of her husband's political views, it was a two-way process and Miss MacArthur probably dominated the partnership. As Katherine Glasier said, 'If he slowed down and became too moderate she will shove him'.[14] She was a mover and in 1902 became Chairman of the Scottish District Council of the Shop Assistants' Union. Even though her father was a political Conservative, he was liberal when it came to understanding his daughter's trade unionism, but when she espoused the cause of Socialism and began to work for Robert Smillie, Labour candidate for South Ayrshire, a silent gulf appeared between Mary and her parents. The next year, aged twenty-three, she left for London.

The cultural shock of life in London was profound; she never forgot the sight of two wild-eyed young women fighting outside a gin palace.[15] It helped to spur her efforts to improve social conditions. At first Miss MacArthur roomed with Miss Bondfield in a flat above 122 Gower Street, while working as a shop assistant, but her rise was meteoric. In July, Mona Wilson, following her triumph in the arbitration case involving lead poisoning in the pottery industry, resigned as Secretary of the WTUL to become the one woman on the National Health Insurance Committee under Sir Robert Morant. According to Gertrude Tuckwell, Miss Wilson had done a very good job on the legislative phase of the League's work but the organising phase had lagged after May Abraham, who had organised the laundresses, had left the union. The WTUL needed a new Secretary, someone to round up new members and upon Miss Bondfield's recommendation, Lady Dilke named Miss MacArthur to the post. This fair-haired, rosy-cheeked Brunhilde changed the character of the League from a ladylike, semi-philanthropic group of statistical tabulators of facts to a dynamic expanding organisation which in two years would grow from 50,000 to 70,000.[16] As Miss Tuckwell said, 'She acted as if something great was always going to happen and she made an atmosphere in which it usually did'.[17] Miss MacArthur literally sprang into action on the very night of her appointment as Secretary. While attending a debate between Lord Lytton and Lord Avebury on Early Closing Legislation she jumped on a chair, threw her hat in the air and wildly led a group of shop assistants in cheering the proposals made by Lord Lytton.

At this time the League's offices were extremely humble, there was no telephone or typewriter but there was a Legal Advice Department over which Miss Sophie Sanger presided, and a copying press. Miss Sanger loaned her economic textbooks, but Miss MacArthur had neither the time nor inclination for book knowledge. Most of her opinions were absorbed from conversation. Her early speeches contained long quotes from the Webbs' *History of Trade Unionism*; but Beatrice Webb, while admiring her, considered her intellect a trifle low-brow.[18] She kept Will Anderson in a state of awe as she plunged into the intellectual currents of London—vegetarianism, teetotalism, free thought and other Bohemian pursuits.[19] The youthful crudity of phrase and thought with which she denounced the middle classes caused many of the League's middle and upper-class supporters to admire her with a mixture of appreciation and uneasiness.[20] In fact although she was dependent upon their aid she resented upper-class benevolence.[21]

She quickly identified the major obstacle to union organisation : 'Women are badly paid and badly treated because they are not organised and they are not organised because they are badly paid and badly treated.'[22] Trade unionism was the key to breaking this cycle. The task was difficult since young women felt they were working temporarily and did not need to join a union while widows and spinsters were hard to organise because they needed money and could not endure a long strike. While not denying that trade unionism should be valued for its social and educational benefits, Miss MacArthur emphasised its economic side in her organising efforts. She was also careful not to neglect her own financial situation and was well paid for her efforts, receiving a salary of £350 a year by 1914.[23]

Miss MacArthur's organising tactics usually featured passing out handbills with the question : Do you want higher wages and shorter hours? The recipients were also given complimentary tickets with the following message, 'Reserved. No seats reserved after 7.45 pm.' The major grievance of most of the operatives appeared to be the system of fines for errors made during the manufacturing process. Once she had a crowd assembled, Miss MacArthur could put her message across with force and brevity. Her favourite line was to describe to prospective members how a union was like a bundle of sticks, showing how each individual stick could be easily broken but how when bound together they were unbreakable. When she finished her audiences wanted still more, 'Keep on, miss, it's better than t' seaside'.[24] Following one visit to organise a union in Wigan she received a letter telling her that the girls were so enthusiastic that everyone wanted to run for office and began to make speeches à la MacArthur.[25] Whatever the cause, the fact remains that women's participation in governing some trade unions increased. By 1914 Weavers' branches included two women on committees at Blackburn, four at Glossop and 'several' at Oldham. The Weavers sent eight women to the TUC annual conference between 1901 and 1914 in comparison to 125 male delegates. However when in 1902 the Salford and District Power Loom Weavers were founded, composed entirely of women, including women officials, and grew to over a thousand by 1907, the Northern Counties Weavers Amalgamation did its best to drive it out of existence.[26] J. J. Mallon described her main characteristic as breathlessness. She swirled from meeting to meeting, strike to strike, Congress to Congress, shouting instructions to those she left behind in the dust and rattle of her car; however, she realised that this role was but a caricature of her true self and could join others in poking fun at her high pretensions.[27] When it came to militance Miss MacArthur was a pragmatist, she understood that the best psychological moment to form a union existed when some crisis arose which made workers angry enough to strike. Thus, she was not in favour of strikes for strikes' sake, but only of those which had a good chance of success. In Leicester when some women struck because some of their co-workers refused to join the union, she urged them to wait until they became stronger.[28] On other occasions Miss MacArthur used the strike as a tactic to show some employers that the union should be taken seriously.[29]

Under Miss MacArthur the WTUL revived its efforts to recruit industries outside the textile industry, especially the sweated trades. Publicity was a weapon she used with great skill. A case in point was her staging of a demonstration in connection with a strike by the box-makers of the Corruganza Works in Tooting Sommerton in August 1908. Miss MacArthur led a march to Trafalgar Square in the rain where photographers and newspaper writers were treated to speeches made by the girls' leaders. One, affectionately known, not only for her large size but because of forthrightness in talking to the factory manager, as the 'Battersea Bruiser' and dressed in a dingy sealskin jacket and a black hat with a feather in it, described to the crowd in picturesque dialect how she was dismissed. Other girls like 'Poll,' and 'Annie' described how their already low wages were cut. There was little doubt that they had conveyed their message to the spectators assembled because while the skies brightened the crowd rained coins, including half crowns, upon the speaker's stand.[30]

The shower of coins was symbolic of the pressing financial problems faced by the WTUL during this period, although these were eased by increased contributions from the textile unions, a fact symbolised by D. Shackleton's assumption of the post of WTUL Treasurer. Nevertheless shortages could cause anguish. In 1906 during a snowy winter in Dundee, Miss MacArthur wired Gertrude Tuckwell to forward £100 to sustain a prolonged strike of jute workers, but Miss Tuckwell was unable to secure the amount requested. The strike failed and though eventually the Dundee and District Jute and Flax Workers Union was formed, the incident was one of the factors which led to the formation of the National Federation of Women Workers (NFWW).[31] Up to this point the policy of the WTUL was to organise women in the same societies as men but in many women's trades, men's unions did not exist or if they did, they refused to admit women. So in 1906 the WTUL, which was not itself a trade union, decided to form a general labour union for women open to all women belonging to unorganised trades or not admitted to their appropriate union. One major advantage was that by combining a dozen or so unions in a general union, a much larger strike fund could be amassed. If individual workers could be made stronger by unions, small struggling local unions could be strengthened by a national federation.

The NFWW's constitution provided that three members of the WTUL serve as advisory members on its Executive Committee and thus assured a close connection. Miss MacArthur was the first President of the NFWW while remaining Secretary of the WTUL and Miss Louisa Hedges, formerly Secretary of the Dressmakers Union, became its first General Secretary. In 1909 Miss MacArthur became General Secretary of the NFWW and Gertrude Tuckwell replaced her as President.[32] Some friction between Miss MacArthur and Miss Hedges led to a special emergency meeting of the Executive Committee of the WTUL on 23 June 1909 to investigate 'certain reflections' made by Miss Hedges to Miss Sanger about Miss MacArthur. The Committee decided that her allegations were entirely frivolous and that in attempting to collect evidence against a colleague and in discussing the private affairs of the League with outsiders, she had committed a breach of loyalty. The Executive Committee of the NFWW asked Miss Hedges to resign.[33] The nature of the charges was not entered in the minutes and thus it is impossible to ascertain who the outsiders were or what was the substance of the charges.

The NFWW in its first year organised seventeen branches with 2,250 members. It affiliated with the TUC and enabled two additional women to attend the TUC conferences. By 1914 it had 20,000 insured members. The NFWW should not be confused with the National Union of Women Workers in Great Britain and Ireland, founded to federate all the important national women's societies and to encourage and assist the formation of local councils and unions of women. The NUWW grew out of the crusade by Alice Hopkins to help raise the standard of living of women and take care of girls and during the 1880s conferences were held at Barnsley, Aberdeen, Leeds and, in 1891, at Liverpool; however, it was at Nottingham in 1895 that a definite union was formed.[34] By 1910 there were forty-three branches of the NUWW and 160 affiliated societies. In that year an Annual Conference was held and such subjects as education, emigration and immigration, public health, international matters, legislation and national insurance, etc. were discussed.[35] Despite its name the group seems to have done little to organise women into trade unions and was non-political. Neither the WTUL nor the NFWW were affiliated with the NUWW.[36] During World War I the NUWW[37] was active in organising patrols to aid the rescue services and to help in rolling bandages.

Meanwhile Miss MacArthur led the ranks of the WTUL and the newly formed NFWW with such high visibility that as Mary Agnes Hamilton said, 'They were no more than a stage army, but they said that they were the women workers of Great Britain and they made so much noise that they came to be believed'.[38] Every army needs a trumpet and in September 1907 the NFWW initiated a monthly newspaper, *The Woman Worker*. By January 1909, Miss MacArthur, busy with other chores, hired Robert Blatchford of *Clarion* fame as editor and under him the paper exhibited the influence of his individualist, puckish and well rounded personality. He prided himself that the paper was a free house, not a tied house, and indeed a broad spectrum of opinion was found in its pages. Eventually it went through a series of editors ranging from Julia Dawson[39] to Winifred Blatchford, and featured Victor Grayson,[40] Margaret Macmillan, Mrs Bruce Glazier and Mrs Ramsay MacDonald as regular contributors. Its circulation was healthy and reached 32,000 on 7 April 1909. In August 1908, the alliance between Blatchford and MacArthur ruptured when Miss MacArthur criticised Blatchford for not unionising waitresses at a Clarion Café in Blackpool.[41] At this time she also clashed with Ramsay MacDonald on the question of the minimum wage[42] but her independence of mind did not prevent her election to the National Administrative Council of the ILP in 1909.[43]

Space considerations preclude a detailed description of the circumstances surrounding the establishment and fate of all the trade unions associated with the WTUL and NFWW, but an account of those which loomed large in their eyes will serve as examples of the reasons for their success and failure. Shortly after assuming the post of Secretary of the WTUL, Miss MacArthur continued the practice of spring and autumn tours. She succeeded in forming successful unions in Littleborough where 200 women hosiery workers had been threatened with fifteen to fifty per cent wage reductions, in the Midlands among the hosiery and boot and shoe operators, in Dundee where the jute workers were rejuvenated, in Paisley among the thread girls, and in London where the tailoresses and telephonists were organised.[44] The Dundee and District Jute and Flax Workers Union was one of the stronger WTUL unions and by 1910 had 4,000 women among its 5,000 members. On some occasions the unions were founded as the result of invitations from employers such as Sir George White at Leicester;[45] however, this phenomenon diminished as Liberal politicians and their industrialist supporters began to lose the support of the trade union movement to the Labour Party after 1906.

In Leicester the Women's Section of the National Union of Boot and Shoe Operatives was founded in 1904 with 1,213 members. For its first two years its officers were men but in 1906 following a scandal concerning embezzlement, Lizzie Willson became its Secretary. At the time it was hoped that naming a woman officer would quiet the friction between the male and female unionists but such was not the case and Miss Willson condemned male unionists as insensitive to women's questions and something of a sex war developed. Nevertheless in 1910 Miss Willson became the first woman elected to the NUBSO Council and during a dispute over a uniform piecerate attempted to have Margaret Bondfield appointed as arbitrator for the Women's Section without mentioning it to the NUBSO Council which she condemned as incapable of dealing with the needs of its women members. In 1911 she ordered a slow-down to win an argument over a new set of work rules and was enraged when the men who were thrown out of work filed for dispute pay. Miss Willson then formed a breakaway union, the Independent National Union of Women Boot and Shoe Workers, with 446 members, but most other women outside of Leicester remained loyal to the male-dominated union. The breakaway union did survive and had 1,300 members in 1920.[46] This is one of the rare cases of a female break-away union during the period; far more common were amalgamations between the two. It took a combination of a grievance and a strong personality to cause women workers to stand up for their rights and split on sex lines.

With the advent of the 1908–9 recession both the WTUL

and the Women's Labour League turned their attention to finding jobs for unemployed women at the same time as male unions
sought to keep women out of 'their' industries. Women workers
won a signal victory at the 1908 TUC Conference when efforts
by the brass workers to get it to exclude women from the brass
trades were defeated.[47] Other suggestions to find jobs for women
were submitted to John Burns, President of the Local Government Board; these included an unemployed workroom and
country colony, but he viewed this as impractical.[48] A private
start in this direction was made by Mr Fels, a financial angel
of the WTUL and a 'back-to-the-land' enthusiast, who funded
a private experiment and settled ten women on land that he
owned.

The hard times described above also hit the cotton industry
in 1908 but were preceded by three excellent years during which
the cotton unions increased their numbers from 213,000 in 1905
to 275,000 in 1910. In the latter year, of this total, 148,981 were
women, a figure that constituted 67.3 per cent of all women in
trade unions. Part of the reason for this growth was the refusal
of the weavers to accept learners unless they joined the unions
and the renewed use of the old practice of barring a member from
office if his wife and children were not union members. Some
weaving districts claimed up to ninety-five per cent membership.[49] In late 1911 the Weavers riding the crest of a recruiting
campaign which increased their number to 165,000 decided to
attempt to force employers to accept a closed shop in any district
where membership reached eighty-five per cent. A four weeks
lockout in December cost the union £15,000 and a humiliating
defeat. Another outcome of the dispute was that while the
Weavers became more confirmed in their adherence to the
Labour Party, their militancy became more restrained.[50]

The good times between 1903 and 1908 were also marked
by a number of strikes that took place 1906–7 over 'bad work'
or the use of poor quality yarns at Hebden Bridge and over the
low wages for fustian cloth weaving. Although these disputes
drained union funds, some advances were made. The weavers
received a two and a half per cent raise in January 1906, the
balance of a seven and a half per cent raise previously promised
and by 1907 the Brookland's Agreement was modified to give
Oldham workers a 3s. a week raise.

On the industrial side of the ledger the good times also witnessed a period of rationalisation, expansion and increased net
profits. Eleven and a quarter million new spindles were started,
worth £11,000,000. Increased production was made possible
by the use of the new Northrup loom. Formerly the hand-loom
weaver had been able to weave six yards of cloth per day, the
first power loom raised it to thirty yards, the two-loom system
increased it to ninety yards, the four-loom system brought it up
to 180 yards and the Northrup loom consisting of twenty looms
and attended by one weaver raised the output to 1,000 yards
per weaver per day. Profits increased accordingly. The Fine
Cotton Spinners and Doublers' Association earned an average
annual net profit of approximately £300,000 during the three
years, 1905 through 1907.[51] The use of women and rationalisation did not always have a salutory effect on family life. As
some male textile workers became unemployed they were content to live off the earnings of their wife or family.

In the cotton spinning industry the period witnessed an
increase in the number of working wives and widows; according
to James Haslam, writing in the *Englishwoman*, the number was
thirty per cent. The typical situation seems to have been that
women worked until they married, as shown by the census
returns for 1911.[52]

Age	Percentage Employed
15–20	66
20–25	62
25–35	33
35–55	23

Where both husband and wife worked and the family included
young children, the wife got up early and had to pay 5s. a week
to a baby sitter. When pregnant, wives often worked up till a
few days before the birth of the child and many returned to work
after only fourteen to twenty-eight days even though four weeks
were provided by the Factory Act.[53]

In July 1908 with a downturn in the economy the Master
Spinners Federation gave notice of a five per cent pay cut and
eventually 120,000 workers were locked out. During the seven
weeks stoppage employers cleared their stocks, while the workers

lost wages and used up their strike fund. Although the operatives were forced to accept the reduction, opinion on the management side was not unsympathetic to the workers' arguments. As a Lancashire Mayor, himself a master cotton spinner and manufacturer, said :

> I think that after two or three years of unparalleled prosperity resulting in the payment of sometimes enormous dividends . . . to propose now a reduction in the operative wages, whose income for months have been reduced by broken time, and whose cost of living is higher and tending to be higher . . . is cruel, is utterly selfish, is void of consideration for other human beings who, though organised are weak indeed by comparison with the forces of combined capital against them.[54]

As strong as the cotton weavers were in Lancashire, the ring spinners in the Yorkshire cotton industry as late as 1912 were still not organised and neither were the woollen workers. In fact there were only 4,677 women trade unionists in the Woollen and Worsted industry. In 1913 a WTUL campaign to organise them[55] suffered from bad timing, since it was launched during a recession. On the eve of World War I the textile industry remained the bastion of women's trade unionism. From 1904 to 1914 the number of women in trade unions increased from 126,000 to 357,956 and, of the latter total, 253,630 were in textile unions.

While the textile industry contained the largest number of women trade unionists, Miss MacArthur refused to give up on organising women in the sweated trades; however, she also realised that unionisation was only part of the answer to their problems—some other approach or legislation was needed. The plight of workers in the sweated trades received renewed exposure in 1901 when Seebohm Rowntree published his book, *Poverty: A Study of Town Life*, setting forth his famous poverty line. It claimed that 7s. a week was the basic minimum wage required by a single man for food, rent and sundries, and 21s. 8d. for a family of husband, wife and three children. Efforts by the WTUL to organise the sweated 'home-worker' had failed mainly because of the difficulty of organising the 'pocket-money' worker or those who really did not have to work.

Sir Charles Dilke tried as early as 1898 to pass a Wages

Boards Bill to fix minimum wages, modelled on the system existing in Australia since 1895, but was unsuccessful. Finally, late in 1905 Miss MacArthur went to see Mr A. G. Gardiner, editor of the *Daily News*, to plead with him to do something to help the girls whose wages were below 7s. a week and finally disarmed any reservations he had by bursting into tears. Together with James Joseph Mallon, George and Edward Cadbury, she organised the Sweated Industries Exhibition based on the Berlin Exhibition of 1905 of Sweated Industries. They were aided by Miss Sanger and Constance Smith, both members of the Christian Social Union and the International Association for Labour Legislation, a forerunner of the International Labour Organisation,[56] who were well acquainted with labour conditions throughout the world and particularly Germany. Miss Smith and Mona Wilson had earlier staged a leadless glazed potteries exhibition in the campaign that led to their 1902 arbitration victory.

The Exhibition was opened 2 May 1906 by Prince Henry of Battenburg at Queen's Hall and proved more effective than meetings or written propaganda. It continued for six weeks and at one point when attendance flagged Miss Tuckwell got Lady Mary Trefusis, lady-in-waiting to Princess May (later Queen Mary) to show sympathy by visiting the Exhibition. It was the beginning of royal kindness to any project helping women workers.[57] A typical exhibit displayed clothes made by East End seamstresses who got 6d. for blouses that sold in the West End for 30s. The work of artificial flower makers, fur stitchers and pullers, tennis and racket ball makers, box makers, chain workers, was shown with the wages earned by the workers, the cost of the item and the family budgets listed. Over 30,000 people attended the Exhibition. On the day it closed the East End Branch of the Amalgamated Society of Tailors and Tailoresses called an unofficial strike against the middlemen and, together with non-unionists, some 10,000 workers marched through the streets. They won a twelve hours working day with one hour for dinner and a half hour for tea and the abolition of piece work.[58]

Still the problem of out-work remained and a Select Committee of the House of Commons was appointed to enquire into the problem. Miss MacArthur testified and gathered representative workers to give evidence.[59] Humanitarianism could be dangerous—one girl, a lacemaker, who made baby clothes at 1d. a garment, had diphtheria which Miss MacArthur contracted, making her seriously ill for six weeks. Although the Board of Trade's Enquiry into Earnings and Hours in 1906 did not become available until 1909, its figures provide an interesting comparison between workers in sweated and unsweated industries. They read as follows:

	Per Week	
Textiles (Non-sweated)	18s.	8d.
Clothing (Sweated)	13s.	6d.
Metal (Sweated)	12s.	8d.
Printing (Non-sweated)	12s.	2d.
Pottery and Cherical (Sweated)	11s.	10d.
Food and Tobacco (Sweated)	11s.	3d.

The average weekly earnings for adult women were less than half those of men, 10s. 10½d. vs. 25s. 9d., while over one-third of the women in industry earned less than 12s. a week.[60] The enquiry also estimated that a woman needed 15s. a week to maintain herself in decency and that some sections of the clothing industry paid 10s. a week to over 100,000 women while in the metal trades some weekly rates were 2s. 6d.[61]

In the summer of 1906 an Anti-Sweating League was formed with J. J. Mallon, Warden of Toynbee Hall, as its Secretary, and a three days conference of 300 trade union delegates was organised in October by Lord Dilke, G. R. Askwith and Sidney Webb. During the course of the Conference a proposal to establish Wages Boards was denounced as a middle-class dodge by members of the Social Democratic Federation, and they shouted down trade union leaders who tried to reason with them. At this juncture Miss MacArthur came forward and spoke with such compassion and persuasiveness that even the SDF concurred. The President of the TUC, D. J. Shackleton and Arthur Henderson also gave their endorsements.[62]

Within parliament pressure was exerted by Lord Dilke, Ramsay MacDonald and Sydney Buxton. A deputation led by the Archbishop of Canterbury and Sidney Webb, one of the originators of the Trade Boards idea, went to see Prime Minister

Asquith. Unfortunately the intellectual Asquith and the scholarly Webb turned the occasion into an academic debate and the meeting came to a stormy and abrupt close. Afterwards Winston Churchill, President of the Board of Trade, convinced Asquith that the idea had merit and three days later Lord Dilke, Mallon, Miss MacArthur and Clementina Black met with Clara Collett, William Beveridge, G. R. Askwith and Churchill to hammer out a bill. Although Churchill favoured a more inclusive measure, Mallon supported a less radical bill in the hope that it would have a greater chance of passage. The Trade Boards Act of 1909 became law in the face of the absence of 200 Liberal MPs. It provided for Boards composed of employers, employees and impartial persons who were to fix minimum wages for four of the most sweated trades—light chain-making, machine-made lace and net finishing, paper-box and cardboard-box making and ready-made and wholesale bespoke tailoring.[63] Power was given to the Minister to extend its coverage to other industries where exceptionally low wages prevailed. The system was essentially one of forced collective bargaining in trades where trade unionism was unable to make itself effective. The Act was a triumph for workers below the poverty line in the four industries and while it was not a minimum wage it served the same purpose for them.[64] Even though its compulsory features came under attack in future years, Churchill would remain one of Miss MacArthur's favourite politicians, a man who could get things done.

Passage of the Trade Boards Act was one thing—enforcement was another. The NFWW had made attempts to organise the women of the Black Country. An early attempt to combine the women with the Midland Trades Federation had failed because the women, as out-workers (meaning that they worked outside the factory or in the home) were difficult to unionise and equally difficult to bring under government regulation. Their hours, wages and working conditions were similar to those of the sweated clothing workers of the East End. The particular target selected was the chainmakers of Cradley Heath, Staffordshire, an expanding industry up to 1914. The factory workers were well organised in the Chainmakers' and Strikers Association and had relatively high wages, a fact that enabled the inefficient out-workers to struggle along and survive but only by accepting low wages. Most of the out-workers were wives or daughters of men in the factories but some were widows and earned as little as 4s. to 5s. weekly.

Between 1906 and 1909 Charles Sitch helped organise and served as Secretary of the Hand-hammered Chain Branch of the NFWW and together with Miss MacArthur he was instrumental in including the workers under the Trade Boards Act of 1909. The Board fixed a 2½d. per hour minimum wage and raised time and piece rates 150 per cent in 1910. This raised wages to roughly 10s. a week.[65] Thirty employers outside of the Employers Manufacturing Association decided to fight a delaying action and succeeded in getting 1,000 workers to contract out of the Act for a period of six months as was allowed by the Act. Prior to the Act going into effect they accumulated a large backlog of chain to be sold at the low rates to give the public the impression that the Trade Boards were responsible for the resultant unemployment when demand fell. In the autumn of 1910, the NFWW got the Employers Manufacturing Association to pay Trade Board rates if those who had contracted out could be forced to comply. To accomplish this, they would have to be organised and repudiate their contracts. Sitch, J. E. Berry and Julia Varley utilised torchlight parades, banners, bands to raise a strike fund; within a few months contributions totalling over £3,000 poured in from railwaymen, miners, power-loom weavers, engineers, bishops and aristocrats (like Lady Beauchamp who contributed £200). By the tenth week most of the middlemen agreed to support the organised employers and the struggle was brought to a successful conclusion.[66] The agitation raised £2,700 in excess of the needed funds and £1,000 of the windfall was used to found a trade union institute for the chainmakers, while £150 was given to the Anti-Sweating League, £500 to the WTUL for organisation, £300 for the NFWW and £500 for future strike emergencies. From the chain industry of Cradley Heath the NFWW seemed to have forged a link with financial security, but this was shortlived.[67] Personnel changes also caused instability. In 1910 Miss Main, then NFWW's Secretary, resigned and the post was temporarily filled by Miss Mollison. Eventually Mrs Lowin, who had been fired when she led a strike at the Idris Soda Factory and who had been an organiser of the carpet weavers at Kidderminster, became Secretary.[68]

The Cradley Heath agitation and success had an effect similar to the Match Girls strike of 1889 and sparked militancy throughout the Midlands.[69] A similar campaign was launched by the NFWW to force compliance with the Trade Boards Act among the Nottingham lacemakers and in Manchester, Liverpool, Leek, Glasgow and Perth, centres of the box trade.[70] In Ireland, Jim Connolly agitated to obtain Trade Boards among the ropeworkers of Belfast and in 1913 an Amending Act added four new trades: shirt making, wrought hollow-ware and tin box making, food preserving and sugar confectionery, and linen and cotton hand embroidery. By 1913 thirteen boards were in operation, while the linen embroidery and laundry Trade Boards, after being delayed by World War I, became operational in 1919.[71]

Following the passage of the Trade Boards Act the next legislation affecting women's trade unions was Lloyd George's Health Insurance Act of 1911. The Labour Party wanted a non-contributory bill but had to choose between a contributory bill or none at all. The rate of contribution set was 4d. by the employee, 3d. by the employer and 2d. by the state. Women whose daily wage did not exceed 1s. 6d. were exempted from contributions. This change resulted from Miss MacArthur's efforts to get Lloyd George to amend his original Bill; but the incident left ill feeling between the two, further aggravated by events on the home front during World War I. Eventually Marion Phillips and the Labour Party succeeded in getting workers earning less than 1s. 6d. per day exempted and sickness benefit for girls under twenty-one raised to 5s. per week. Protest against the Act led to a giant meeting of Mistresses and Servants, organised by Lady Desart at the Albert Hall, to get domestic servants excluded from the Bill, but their effort failed.[72]

Women's claims under the National Health Insurance Act turned out to be far heavier than bargained for because it was actuarily unsound. Critics of the Act quickly blamed its failure on women who had been encouraged by its provisions to malinger. In response Miss MacArthur launched a press campaign that forced an official enquiry. She said:

The Act shows that people who are underfed, badly housed and overworked are seldom in a state of physical efficiency and it has expressed in terms of pounds, shillings and pence the truth that where an industry pays starvation wages, it does, in literal, sober fact levy a tax upon the community.[73]

Although many of Lloyd George's enemies paid him tribute, Miss MacArthur did not and claimed the Act was not good enough and required a system of maternity care and a state preventive medical service. Miss MacArthur would soon be better able to empathise with working mothers. In September 1911 she married William Anderson and in 1913 her first baby, a boy, was born dead, but in July 1915 she gave birth to a daughter, Nancy.[74]

The shortcomings of the Act were remedied by the Amending Act of 1913. This covered maternity benefits and also included illegitimate children in its provisions. Miss MacArthur and Miss Bondfield were instrumental in obtaining these additions. The benefit was made the property of the mother and called for a state preventive medical service. The National Health Insurance Act required all workers earning less than £160 a year to join an approved society for payment of insurance benefits. These provisions required the NFWW to expand its staff to thirty and move its offices to 34 Mecklenburgh Square. Dr Marion Phillips was hired temporarily as Secretary at £130 a year,[75] but resigned to devote her services full time to the Women's Labour League and her place was taken by A. Susan Lawrence.[76]

The Act gave the NFWW an opportunity to recruit members who in order to qualify for coverage had to join an approved insurance society, but it also presented a challenge, for some women found it difficult to spare the 1½d. a week and pay union dues. Some therefore dropped out of the trade union and insured with an approved society not affiliated to a trade union. To solve the problem the NFWW formed an insurance section and affiliated this section to the General Federation of Trade Unions, an affiliation of 113 unions. This gave the fund greater stability. In order to make women loyal to trade unionism rather than a private insurance firm, a provision was made where any woman in an unorganised trade was eligible to join the insurance section of the NFWW and could join it without joining the Trade Union section.[77] While the NFWW handled the insurance matters of some women trade unionists, the WTUL, through its legal advice department, handled complaints of violations of the Workmen's Compensation, Truck and Factory and Workshops Acts. The cases were investigated and then called to the attention of the proper government department.

During the recession of 1908 unemployment reached its highest level since 1886 but by 1910 the number of unemployed declined, while the number of strikes in industry increased. Some explain this as the result of a fall in real wages, others by the impact of the press and the motor car in awakening in the working classes a feeling of resentment, while others accounted for it by the general spirit of the times—featuring protests by the Irish, women's suffrage groups and General Elections over the Budget and House of Lords Questions. The advent of Syndicalism, if not a cause of some of the unrest, was at least another sign of the disillusionment of the working classes with political action. In 1909 and 1910 strikes occurred in the coal mines and in the summer of 1911 they took place on the railways, tramways and docks. These were especially severe in Liverpool, Glasgow and Cardiff. There was even a strike by the contestants in a beauty show at Folkestone. All the gun-makers of St James' and Pall Mall had sold out their supply of revolvers by 17 August.[78] It was a hot summer in London and it seemed particularly so in Bermondsey where in some sections one stand-pipe and water-closet served twenty-five houses.[79] Here a combination of neighbouring industrial unrest on the docks, the propaganda of the suffragettes and temperatures in the high eighties resulted in a spontaneous epidemic of strikes in Bermondsey, Stepney and Rotherhithe. The heat was a particular stimulus to strikes in the canning industry. At Plaistowe's Jam Factory the previous year there had been a strike and a seventy-member union was formed in July 1910.[80]

The Bermondsey strikes started 9 August 1911 in the food making industry, confectionery works, jam and biscuit factories and pickles factories. The workers were unorganised, had no unions, no strike pay and no savings. Their wages ranged from 7s. 6d. to 9s. a week for women and 3s. for girls. Two hundred girls and fifty men struck at Lipton's headquarters and another 1,000 came out at Maconochies Jam Factory in Millwall over the introduction of young girls into adult women's work.[81] In twenty-four hours 14,000 workers were on strike in what the

Daily Chronicle labelled a 'Labour War'. The strike caused a run on food stores, attacks on food wagons. Solidarity on the part of the strikers was achieved with the use of hat pins on the recalcitrants. During the strike, in spite of the heat, many of the girls wore their Sunday best with fur boas and looked healthy according to the *Daily Chronicle*,[82] or unhealthy if one accepts the account in the *Daily News*. Miss MacArthur, Herbert Burrows, Alfred Salter, Marion Phillips, Mrs Lowin and Ben Tillett all rallied to the cause and issued an appeal to bring food to the Labour Institute at Fort Road. Miss MacArthur was driven to a state of hysteria by the heat and fatigue,[83] but within a week 4,000 women, eighty per cent married with children, were organised in unions. The strikers' husbands worked at casual labour and so the women were considered the principal wage earners; therefore, a strike fund of £486 was raised since outdoor relief was refused the strikers. One by one, settlements were reached and increases of from 1s. to 4s. a week were won at Lipton's, E. T. Pink, Peak, Frean and Company.[84]

In the year before World War I, Miss MacArthur continued to champion the cause of women in sweated industries. Eight hundred pounds were raised at a Conference on Sweated Industries held by the Duchess of Marlborough, enabling the NFWW to hire twelve special organisers. The National Anti-Sweating League also guaranteed an annual sum to organise women in industries affected by the Trade Boards Act. To this end, in March 1913, 700 Net Workers of Kilbirnie successfully struck for an increase in wages and trade union recognition. At Millwall, Deptford, Bermondsey and Coventry unions were organised to assure compliance with the Trade Boards Acts minimum, sometimes ensuring compliance a month or so before the Act went into effect. Robert Phillimore of the LCC gave both his personal direction and financial help to the strikers at Deptford.[85]

While the Kilbirnie net-weavers' strike was in progress and settlement seemed far off, Miss M'Lean, NFWW organiser, asked the Parliamentary Committee of the Scottish TUC for help. As a result, Messrs Gavin and Carson succeeded in making terms with one employer giving the women a pay raise which forced the other employers to make similar settlements. The Parliamentary Committee later criticised the NFWW for waiting so long to call for aid and in August 1914 when a strike occurred

at Kilsyth the women appealed to the Parliamentary Committee
not the NFWW; however, the Parliamentary Committee merely
advised them to return to work, showing little recognition of the
special forms of attention unorganised women required and with
which the NFWW and WPPL were so well acquainted.[86]

In Ireland Mary Galway continued the struggle to organise
and hold together the women in the Textiles Operatives Society.
In 1911 she staged a counter demonstration to a successful strike
by a group founded by James Connolly which eventually became
known as the Irish Textile Workers' Union. Miss Galway had
been accused of recruiting the better-paid Protestant workers in
the 'making-up' section, leaving the other girls unorganised. Miss
Galway asked the Belfast Trades Council to disaffiliate the
ITWU complaining that Connolly should not compete with her
in organising the women in the TOS. In response Connolly
argued that his group had won better conditions than Miss
Galway and that 18,000 workers were still outside the fold. Miss
Galway continued to oppose the Connolly group which in 1912
was led by James Larkin and his sister Delia at the Irish Trade
Union Congress (by 1913 it was known as the Irish Women
Workers' Union). She accused Connolly of using tactics which
gave rise to sectarian and police bigotry among genuine trade
unionists of Belfast.

Other problems also abounded. Most Belfast women seemed
to lack dedication and only social activities and dances held the
unions together. Union organisers had their work cut out for
them and earned more prestige than salary. Nelly Gordon left
a 17s. 9d.-a-week job in the mills to take a post paying 7s. 7d.
as a union organiser. Another problem that caused greater
divisions than unity was Connolly's desire to urge 'one big
union'. It was Jim Larkin who finally decided that women would
benefit from their own separate union shortly after his sister
Delia arrived from Liverpool. The Irish Women Workers' Union
(IWWU) possessed over the next twenty years a number of
excellent organisers including Helen Chenevix, Louie Bennett,
Marie Johnson, Nelly Gordon, Winnie Carney and Helena
Molony—the last of these would be second-in-command to
Countess Markiewicz in the soup kitchens and stores in Liberty
Hall in 1913. Irish nationalism proved divisive and shortly
thereafter Delia Larkin disagreed with their emphasis on Repub-

lican Socialism and resigned from the union and returned to Liverpool.[87]

During the early years of the twentieth century as the WTUL and NFWW began to make progress for women economically, efforts were also being made to add to women's political power so that they could better achieve their industrial goals. Late in 1901, as the result of the Taff Vale decision, the Manchester Women's Trades Union Council launched an effort to get working-class women to support the cause of women's suffrage. The Council was founded in 1894 to organise women into trade unions and was independent of the WTUL. It was composed of a Federation of Women Workers and also contained a number of small unions, including fancy box makers, bookbinders, tailor-esses, india-rubber makers, shirt makers, upholsteresses, and leather makers. Some of its early supporters included Mrs A. T. Lyttelton, C. P. Scott, editor of the *Manchester Guardian*, and Sir William Mather, another pillar of Lancashire Liberalism, the wealthy philanthropic owner of an engineering works.[88] The Honorary Secretary of the Manchester Women's Trades Union Council was Eva Gore Booth, the daughter of an Irish baronet, and sister of Countess Markiewicz, the first woman elected to the House of Commons, but who as an Irish Nationalist refused to take her seat.

Two further examples of women's trade union interest in suffrage were in 1902 when the cotton unions in Lancashire, where women outnumbered men 96,000 to 69,000, after David Shackleton's election at Clitheroe subscribed £900 a year to the Labour Representation Committee, in effect paying his salary, and in 1901 and 1902 when a petition signed by 67,000 textile women of Lancashire, Cheshire and Yorkshire, supporting women's suffrage, was presented to the House of Commons. Though greeted with indifference, it had the support of a number of women textile leaders such as Miss Reddish, who was also a member of the Bolton School Board, Mrs Ellis of Bradford, Mrs Wimbolt of Stockport, Miss Agnes Close of Leeds, and Miss Silcock, President of the Weavers' Union in Wigan.[89] The movement also involved Esther Roper, Secretary of the Lancashire and Cheshire Women's Suffrage Society, and Miss Christabel Pankhurst. At this time Miss Pankhurst, while speaking to the Oldham Trades Council on the subject of women's suffrage, met the former Clarionette, Annie Kenney, of the Oldham Card and Blowing Room Operatives, who was to become the most notable working-class suffragette.[90]

In October 1903, in an effort to enliven and enlist working-class women in the Votes for Women campaign, Mrs Emmeline Pankhurst, a member of the ILP, launched the Women's Social and Political Union. While eschewing political party affiliation, it sought to win the support of the Labour movement and Labour Party. In 1904 a split took place in the Manchester Women's Trade Union Council when the Pankhursts caused six of its fourteen branch unions to withdraw to form a new organisation, the Manchester Women's Trades and Labour Council which aimed at direct political representation for women workers in parliament. By 1910 the Pankhursts' organisation had over 3,000 members in ten branches and the original body, 2,600.[91]

Another significant event in 1904 was the founding of the People's Suffrage Federation (which later became the Adult Suffrage Society) with Sir Charles Dilke as its President. It stood for adult suffrage (or universal male and female suffrage without property requirements) and took issue with other women's suffrage groups willing to accept a more limited enfranchisement for both men and women. Margaret Bondfield was its President from 1906 to 1909, and one of its members, Keighley Snowden, summarised its philosophy as follows, 'we are for socialism and socialism without adult suffrage is impossible'. Relations between the WSPU and the Adult Suffrage Society were cool.[92]

In October 1905, Christabel Pankhurst and Annie Kenney were arrested following a speech made by Sir Edward Grey, at Manchester Free Trade Hall, an incident signalling the start of a campaign of civil disobedience. Their actions won the support of Keir Hardie, but Margaret Macmillan and others in the Adult Suffrage Society later condemned their militancy.[93] Later, in less spectacular fashion the MWTLC formed in January 1906 the Women's Textile Committee to support the bid for a seat in Parliament from Wigan by Thorley Smith as a 'woman's suffrage candidate'. After the failure of this effort, the policy of WSPU and the MWTLC concentrated on the defeat of all Liberal candidates, regardless of their personal views on women's suffrage, because of Campbell-Bannerman's refusal to pledge his party to support the cause. It assumed a position of neutrality toward Labour and Conservative candidates. The purpose of this tactic was to pressure the party in power to accomplish reform or force it from office and was derived by Mrs Pankhurst from the time her husband had been defeated by Irish Nationalist voters even though he supported Home Rule. In 1910 Christabel Pankhurst launched a special campaign against John Burns and the Liberals who were accused of opposing women's suffrage. It was claimed that Socialist and Liberal MPs had ignored the plight of unemployed women and that women's suffrage was necessary to be able to exert pressure on them.[94] These tactics and the evolution of the WSPU into a single-issue organisation (winning votes for women) cooled relations between it and the Labour movement. Matters were not improved by Christabel Pankhurst's decision to abandon utilising women from the East End in the WSPU because it alienated women who were opposed to the Labour Party.

While these developments were taking place, the WTUL in 1907, following a division of opinion at the Second Annual Women's Labour League Conference,[95] announced that although it supported adult suffrage it was assuming a position of neutrality between the warring factions of the suffrage movement. The League required financial aid from male and female contributors and it was deemed best not to risk offending anyone on this non-economic issue, for instance in 1904 the Derbyshire Miners refused to send a subscription to the WTUL because they thought it supported women's suffrage. In 1913 the policy bore fruit when the Miners' Federation contributed £50 in response to a special appeal.[96]

Miss MacArthur's stand was practical, but also her heart was devoted to the economic side of the women's question and mixing trade union organisation and women's suffrage could hinder the former as had the arguments over protective legislation during the 1880s. Further evidence of her neutrality was demonstrated when she refused L. Sitch's request to use NFWW members, who were chainmakers, in a suffrage demonstration—although chainmakers were used, they were not NFWW members.[97] Still it is interesting to contemplate the effect that closer co-operation between the WSPU and the WTUL would have had both politically and economically.

Maintaining neutrality was not an easy thing. From 1907 to 1910 the Labour Party Annual Conference supported adult suffrage rather than the partial enfranchisement of women. In 1911 the Second Conciliation Bill which would have granted suffrage to a limited number of propertied women was opposed by Arthur Henderson of the Adult Suffrage Society. At the Labour Party Annual Conference of 1912, Ben Turner supported Henderson and called upon the delegates to reject the half loaf of manhood suffrage. This view was opposed by Robert Smillie, a miners' leader, who explained that while his union favoured both men and women getting the vote at the age of twenty-one, they felt it made more sense to accept universal manhood suffrage even if women's suffrage was not included. In spite of her neutrality, Mary MacArthur then reminded Smillie of her opposition to limited women's suffrage based on property and asked him to change his position; however, her plea failed and adult suffrage was then reaffirmed by a vote of 919,000 to 686,000 votes—six hundred thousand of those votes coming from miners.[98]

The path to women's suffrage was strewn with land mines. Politicians of all political parties were loth to make any changes that would place their parties at a disadvantage. In the hurly-burly of the political arena it is small wonder that various groups—unenfranchised males, middle-class women and working-class women—all tried to use one another to attain their goals. Among working-class women, Annie Kenny, clothed in clogs and shawl, might have become an effective bridge between women workers and the other two groups, but she willingly allowed her role to deteriorate into that of a sycophant of Christabel and Mrs Pankhurst. Sylvia Pankhurst split with her mother and sister to find fulfilment as an organiser of some small unions in the East End.[99] Even though the WSPU would steal the headlines with its theatrics, Margaret Bondfield, Mrs Despard, Theresa Billington-Grieg, and the Adult Suffrage Society, continued to strive for universal adult suffrage.[100] It is interesting to note that the United Textile Factory Workers Association took no action to support women's suffrage during 1910–1914 and that the Bolton Spinners were one of a minority of four against women's suffrage at the 1913 TUC Annual Conference.[101]

Events took an unexpected turn during World War I when Mrs Pankhurst and her daughter, Christabel, turned their energies from militant suffrage agitation to fervent patriotism. In gratitude Lloyd George manoeuvred through Parliament a women's suffrage act in 1918. The nation's difficulties turned out to be the suffragettes' opportunity. Mary MacArthur and Margaret Bondfield supported the bill even though it failed to fully satisfy them; they were realists and took what they could get. The Act is often viewed as one which rewarded working women for their participation in the war effort, but if this were so, by granting only household suffrage to women over the age of thirty, it discriminated against single women, most often young workers who had made an equal contribution. World War I would see an increase in the numbers of women trade unionists. To understand why the role of the group of women under thirty was not more fully appreciated by Lloyd George and the Coalition Government requires closer examination of the relations between Lloyd George and the NFWW and the WTUL during the war.

4

The Era of Molly the Munitions Maker
World War I

ON Sunday 2 August, Mary MacArthur and her husband took part in the huge demonstration held in Trafalgar Square to protest against the possibility of war. She felt the nation was being pushed into war by party and vested interests and viewed it as a threat to the continued growth of the WTUL and NFWW.[1] Though Labour Party leaders (Hardie, Henderson, MacDonald) had denounced the war, the invasion of Belgium and the beginnings of hostilities caused most of these to change their opinion and support the war effort but R. MacDonald, Will Anderson and some other ILP members continued to criticise the war.[2] To protect working-class interests during hostilities the War Emergency Workers' National Committee (generally known as the Workers' National Committee) was formed on 6 August. Mary MacArthur and Margaret Bondfield, representing the WTUL and Women's Co-operative Guild respectively, were among its women members along with Dr Marion Phillips (Women's Labour League) and Susan Lawrence, of the LCC. By 24 August, support for the war had progressed to the point that the TUC and the Labour Party declared an industrial truce with capital for the duration. They promised an effort to terminate existing trade disputes and in the future to attempt to reach an amicable settlement before resorting to a strike.

Oddly enough one of the first effects of the war on women in industry was to raise the number of unemployed women workers to 190,000—mostly in cotton and luxury trades. This resulted from the partial cessation of foreign orders and a reduction of avoidable expenditure at home. These figures are misleading since on the eve of the war the textile industries were already in a recession and the Weavers' Amalgamation had

88,551 (men and women) total unemployed.[3] As late as February 1915, 39,000 women were still unemployed.

On 10 August, to ameliorate some of the problems caused by the war for women, the government created the Queen Mary's Needlework Guild, an unpaid volunteer group to collect, repair and make garments for those in need.[4] The Workers' National Committee and the WTUL protested against this development as a threat to the unemployed women in the garment trade. In response, ten days later the government created the Queen Mary's Work for Women Fund, a string of workshops which by the 23 January 1915 provided jobs for approximately 9,000 formerly unemployed workers.[5]

It must be remembered that during the early months of the war Miss MacArthur was recovering from the shock of stillbirth and was pregnant again. Her first child, Nancy, would be born in July 1915. Despite her condition she accepted Queen Mary's request to serve as Honorary Secretary to aid Lady Margaret Crewe, Chairman of the Fund. Women employed in the workshops were paid 3d. an hour with a maximum of 10s. a week for a forty-hours week, but the hourly rate was less than the minimum set by the Clothing Trade Board. In October members of the East London Federation of the Suffragettes (later the Worker's Socialist Federation) led by Sylvia Pankhurst engaged in an angry confrontation with Mary MacArthur at the Offices of the Central Committee for Women's Employment. Branding the programme as Queen Mary's Sweat-Shops they demanded a minimum wage of a pound a week. Miss MacArthur defended the scheme as fair since the average national wage of women was only 7s. 6d. Eventually after a considerable increase in the cost of living, a ten per cent increase was granted women in the workshops in April 1915, although by that time many of these had been phased out as women found more lucrative employment in industry. In retrospect, given the exigencies of the war and the failure of earlier attempts to have the government establish such programmes, the scheme was a landmark in improving the conditions of those affected by economic downturns. Throughout the war Miss MacArthur's position was generally somewhere between the hypercritical Sylvia Pankhurst and the dogmatic patriotism of Christabel and Mrs Pankhurst.

While Sylvia Pankhurst excoriated the Queen Mary's Workshops, Miss MacArthur looked upon the occasion as an opportunity for future change and influence. She told her WTUL colleagues, 'The Queen does grasp the whole situation from a trade union point of view. I positively lectured her on the inequality of the classes and the injustice of it.' Of Miss MacArthur's role, Lady Crewe remarked, 'her personality was so dominating that as she herself deprecatingly said, she felt she must have the main control of any work for which she was partially responsible, but those who worked with her had no cause for regret and gladly conceded her the leader's place'.[6]

From July 1914 to July 1918 the number of women employed increased by 1,345,000. Of this number ninety-nine per cent were employed in new occupations or as substitutes for men. The estimated number of females directly replacing (or 'diluting' the number of) males in January 1918 was 704,000. Here was a golden opportunity to increase the number of women trade unionists, and their number increased from 357,956 (253,630 in textiles) in 1914 to 1,086,000 (423,000 in textiles) in 1918.[7] The first expansion of women's employment came as the result of the spread of the munitions trade in the spring and summer of 1915. A second growth came after the first Conscription Act at the end of 1916. Married women, the wives of soldiers and widows motivated by patriotism, were most affected since a large number of single women were already employed. Of the new workers, one-quarter left domestic service and one-third deserted the household for industry.

If World War II women war-workers in the United States were known as Rosie the Riveter, the era of World War I for British women war-workers probably should be known as that of 'Molly the Munitions Maker'. The women war-workers came from all classes but on some occasions class consciousness could lead to ugly incidents. Middle-class women were regarded by others less fortunate as spies of management and had their tools hidden or walls chalked with disparaging messages.[8] In Belfast where the textile mills went on slack time, voluntary workers with university degrees and motor cars were the object of particular animosity.[9] Women went into a number of other industries besides munitions. They planed, moulded, mortised and dovetailed in sawmills; drove trucks in flour and oil and cake mills; made upholstery and tyre tubes; bottled beer and manufactured furniture; worked in cement factories and foundries and tanneries, in jute mills and wool mills; broke limestone and loaded bricks in steel works and worked as riveters in ship-building yards. They could be found in car factories, in quarry-ing and surface mining and brickmaking. They worked as posters and carriage cleaners on the railways; in power stations and gas works and on sewage farms; as policewomen and park attend-ants and street and chimney sweepers. Only underground mining, stevedoring and steel and iron smelting were still all male.[10]

Nevertheless, it was in the munitions industry that the employ-ment of women attracted the most attention and where dilution caused the most problems. By the end of the war between 600,000 and 750,000 women were employed in the munitions industry. A large percentage of these were in the engineering industry where before 1914 approximately 170,000 women were employed with less than 20,000 of these in machine or general engineering shops. By 1918 there were 594,000 women employed in the engineering industry and 170,000 in machine shops.[11] Before the war began, the government-run Woolwich Arsenal employed 14,000 men and no women but by 1916 half of its 100,000 workers were women.[12] By 1917 the government ran four munitions factories, owned more than a hundred others and controlled wages and conditions in more than four thousand others.

From the very outset of the war the Federated Society of Iron Founders viewed the employment of women as a threat to future job security. Its executive congratulated its men for resisting an attempt to employ women as core-makers and in not allowing patriotic sentiment to outweigh sound judgment and commonsense in protection of their trade interests.[13] Such solidarity was absent in the engineering industry and one of the first disputes took place after the introduction of women, at about half the men's rates of wages without first consulting the trade unions, at the Vickers Works at Crayford. The situation was resolved by the Crayford Agreement in November 1914, denying women employment in place of *skilled men*, while allowing their use to operate automatic machines and repetitive work.

In December 1914 the Engineering Employers Federation proposed a national agreement to the five major engineering unions providing that trade unions should relax their rules while employers paid standard rates of wages until the war ended, when pre-war conditions would be re-established. It suggested utilising women on operations employing *skilled men*, but which could be performed by semi-skilled or female labour. Wages would be those usually paid in the district for the *operation performed*. After the end of the war women substitutes were to be the first let go; however, no reference was made to women who replaced *semi-skilled* or *unskilled* men.[14] These would be paid 2½d. per hour, a rate ½d. lower than the Queen Mary's Workshops! When the talks deadlocked, the request made by the Engineering Employers Federation for government action to outlaw strikes and lockouts, suspend restrictive practices and set up munitions tribunals, was rejected as neither practicable nor necessary.[15]

As a result, the situation festered and in February culminated in a strike on the Clyde, protesting against the use of unskilled men in skilled jobs. The trouble on the Clyde actually dated from June 1914 when the Glasgow District Committee of the ASE began negotiations to raise their wages to parity with engineers in other parts of Britain. When these dragged on the shop stewards, originally merely collectors of dues, led the workers in refusing overtime on all war contracts. The ASE executive recommended acceptance of a ¾d. an hour increase but the men rejected this by a vote of 8,927 to 829.[16] It was out of this strike that the syndicalist-influenced Shop Stewards Movement evolved and spread to Sheffield, London and other engineering centres. The Shop Stewards Movement developed on the Clyde mainly because of the strong militant socialist tradition there, over-crowded housing conditions and high rents exacerbated by wartime conditions and the fact that shop stewards were closer to the rank and file than union officials in efforts to resist employer and government efforts to end restrictive practices.

In late February 1915, to cope with a shell shortage and mounting unrest—the number of strikes had been rising since August—Lloyd George, then Chancellor of the Exchequer, called together leaders of the Employers' Federation and thirty-three trade unions (including the ASE but not the NFWW) involved in making war materials. Out of the discussions came the Shells and Fuses Agreement of 4 March 1915 which implemented most of the proposals made in December 1914 by the Engineer-

2. Emma Paterson

1. Membership card, 1833

3. Strike committee, 1875

4. Lady Dilke

5. Gertrude Tuckwell

7. May Abraham

6. Bryant and May strike, 1888

8. Margaret Bondfield and her parliamentary secretary

9. Mary Macarthur addressing strikers

10. Demonstration by members of the National Federation of Women Workers

1. Tailors' strike, 1912

12. Strike at Milwall, 1914

13. Woman munitions worker,
   World War I

14. Woman munitions worker,
   World War II

15. Women trade unionists' pressure group, 1924

6. National Women's Advisory Committee, 1950–51

17. Festival of Women, Wembley 1957

18. TUC Centenary parade, 1968

ing Employers Federation. The ASE obviously did not feel threatened by such limited application of dilution.

In an effort to extend the Shells and Fuses Agreement to all of the Munitions industry, a meeting was held at the Treasury culminating in the Treasury Agreement of 11 March 1915. The voluntary agreement provided for the substitution of arbitration for stoppages of work and the relaxation of trade union restrictions. After first rejecting the Agreement, the ASE signed it on 25 March. One clause of the Agreement of special interest to women workers provided that :

> The relaxation of existing demarcation restrictions or admission of semi-skilled or female labour shall not affect adversely the rates customarily paid for the job. In cases where men who ordinarily do the work are adversely affected thereby, the necessary readjustments shall be made so that they can maintain their previous earnings.

On 25 March Miss Sylvia Pankhurst wrote to Lloyd George asking for an exact interpretation of the words, 'shall not affect adversely the rates customarily paid for the job'. Lloyd George replied that the words guaranteed, 'that women undertaking the work of men would get the same piece rates as men were receiving before the date of the Agreement. That, of course, means that if the women turn out the same quantity of work as men employed on the job they will receive exactly the same pay.' This meant, in effect, men's piece rates but not time rates.[17] Unfortunately in munitions women worked for time rates and soon men's piece rates practically disappeared. As a matter of fact most of the large armament firms evaded piece rates payments by adopting the premium hours system. This guaranteed the worker a fixed time rate at a basic rate, but paid a bonus if the job was finished in less time, above and beyond the basic rate, equivalent to one-half or some other fixed proportion of the time so saved. In the case of women employed on men's work, the usual number of hours were worked, but the time rate was reduced by one-third or one-half; therefore, women might equal or even excel men in output and still only receive about two-thirds or one-half of men's wages. In spite of the fact that some industrial experts claimed that women were superior to men on piece work and on the assembly line because they were better

D

able to cope with the monotony of fast repetitive jobs,[18] their ability did not convince employers that women should be paid as much as men. Instead employers retorted that 'women's wages should have been paid to men'.[19]

To rectify the problems still facing women in March 1915, the Workers' National Committee proposed that : (1) all women should join an appropriate trade union, (2) women doing the same work as men should receive equal pay for equal work, not just equal piece rates, (3) men whose places were taken would get them back after the war, (4) the women displaced after the war should be guaranteed employment and (5) women representatives should be appointed on the newly constituted Labour Advisory Committee and on Courts of Arbitration.[20] To muster more muscle to achieve these goals the WTUL and NFWW launched a vigorous campaign in April featuring the motto, 'Don't Black-leg Your Man in Flanders'.[21]

Recruitment itself could present problems. Although the ASE had opened membership to unskilled male labourers since 1912, a motion to allow women into their ranks was defeated in 1915 because of the fear of the precedent it would set after the war. At first the ASE and the Workers' Union, a general workers' union not affiliated with the TUC, tried to make an agreement over recruiting activities and work jurisdiction, but negotiations broke down by June 1915. The ASE then advised its members to urge women to join the NFWW rather than the Workers' Union and established committees with the NFWW to fix wage rates. By summer 1916 a negotiating agreement was also made between the ASE and the National Union of General Workers.[22]

With this new united front, the ASE and NFWW sent a deputation to the Minister of Munitions calling for a pound a week wage for all women in engineering and ship building.[23] Dr Addison, Assistant to Lloyd George, gave them a favourable reply but explained that he could only enforce wage rates in national establishments.[24] Private firms resisted the demand, claiming that the cost of new and expensive machinery made higher wages impossible and that women were traditionally paid less than men. Maybe so, but to pay women less than a pound a week for vital war work was a national disgrace, for while the newspapers handed out lavish compliments to women workers, their wages were little above those at Cradley Heath.

The NFWW had a good claim to organise women munitions workers, having championed the cause of women fuse makers and cartridge fillers who had been paid sweated wages of $2\frac{1}{2}$d. or $2\frac{3}{4}$d. per hour before the war. To bring them into the fold the NFWW expanded its staff to one hundred persons, including forty outside organisers.[25] Miss Isabel Sloan was shifted from the WTUL to the NFWW to aid Miss Bondfield, its Organising Secretary.[26] Later in June 1917 Miss Sloan moved to a more influential position as Assistant Commissioner to Sir George Askwith, Chief Industrial Commissioner of the Board of Trade.[27] In order to improve the quality of organisers they were required to take a labour examination and a fund was established to provide two years of college education. The NFWW's rapid expansion during the war also required a restructuring of its organisation and District Divisions were established at Bristol, Coventry, Newcastle, etc., to facilitate geographical togetherness as compensation for the isolation dissimilar unions faced in a large heterogeneous general union. A key policy change was the decision to allow branch funds to be used to support workers during lockouts.[28] During this period the WTUL operated on a paltry income of £700 a year and its increased activity left it with a £233 deficit.[29]

NFWW recruiting efforts faced competition from the Workers' Union. It had 5,000 female members before the war and increased that number to 80,000 by 1918, a quarter of its membership, thanks to the endeavours of twenty organisers led by Julia Varley, its chief women's organiser.[30] This figure was larger than the 76,000 women in the NFWW or the 60,000 in the National Union of General Workers.[31] In spite of all these efforts two-thirds of women munitions makers still remained unorganised. While women were welcomed into general unions, only one woman was a member of the Executive Committee of any other single important general labour union, but the number of delegates at the 1918 TUC meeting increased to twenty-eight.[32]

As these recruiting efforts were taking place, Lloyd George faced the continuing dilemma of increasing munitions production, especially shells, while keeping down the cost of the war which had evolved into a war of endurance on the home front as well as on the battle front. Complicating matters was the fact that high worker morale on the home front was best sustained by maintaining their standard of living which in turn increased the cost of the war. Clearly the free market was inefficient but compulsion smacked of socialism. By the summer of 1915 the Treasury Agreement was clearly a failure, mainly because it was voluntary and did not regulate profits. The shell shortage continued through the spring and summer of 1915 and was a factor in bringing down the Asquith government. Finally Lloyd George opted for a limited form of compulsion—the result was the Munitions of War Act passed on 2 July 1915. It prohibited strikes and lockouts and substituted arbitration on the theory that during wartime employers, workers and the nation could ill-afford to have industrial war at home at the same time as the nation was fighting a world war. Restrictive practices were to be abandoned for the duration and in return profits from war industries were to be limited to one-fifth in excess of the pre-war rate. Strikes would only be permitted if after a dispute was referred to the Board of Trade for arbitration, no ruling was given after a certain amount of time. The government made a pledge 'to use its influence' to secure the restoration of previous conditions in every case after the war. The provision that caused the greatest difficulty was the so-called 'leaving certificate', which in the name of producing a stable labour force prohibited workers freedom to improve their wages by changing jobs.

Shortly after passage of the Act, a strike by the South Wales Miners in July 1915 forced Lloyd George to back down on its enforcement. By September discontent over the leaving certificate culminated in the passage of a resolution made by Miss Bondfield at a Labour Party Conference at Bristol demanding its abolition and giving workers a voice in the discipline of 'controlled' establishments through their shop stewards.[33] These signs of unrest led to the appointment of the Central Munitions Labour Supply Committee with A. Henderson as Chairman and Miss MacArthur as one of the members. In September and October it issued two Circulars, L_2 and L_3, which fixed women's time rates at a pound a week if engaged on men's work other than fully skilled and prescribed the same piece rates and premium bonus rates. By 5 November 1915 the ASE agreed to co-operate in introducing dilution as long as employers observed the conditions in these Circulars. A weakness in the Circulars was that while they were mandatory in National Factories, they were only a recommendation to sub-contractors and even the Admiralty refused to pay women the specified pound a week. Some good did come from the regulations, for in November they were used as guide lines in a pact concluded between the Workers' Union and the Midland Engineering Employers' Federation;[34] it called for 16s. a week time rate for a fifty-three hours week. Although the ASE and NFWW criticised the pact it soon became the practice of munitions tribunals to grant leaving certificates to all applicants whose wage fell below that standard.

Meanwhile, in October the Clyde Workers' Committee formed out of the Labour Withholding Committee which had led a strike in February and reasserted itself on the question of dilution. One of the points of contention was the interpretation of the L_2 Circular as related to whether women doing an easier part of a skilled man's job should be paid the full district rate. The Government's Clyde Dilution Commission ruled that a woman's starting rate should be a pound and that after the fourth week the rate should be raised until the men's full rate was reached by the end of the thirteenth week.[35] The ASE accepted this solution because they did not want women under-cutting their pay scale, but the employers rejected it. Few of the 13,000 women got more than a pound a week while men received 50s. or 55s. With most employers still ignoring the pound a week minimum the ASE and NFWW called a Conference to exert pressure upon the government for an obligatory Act. Continued unrest on the east coast and on the Clyde forced the government to pass the Munitions of War Amendment Act in November 1915 which became effective in January 1916. It gave the Minister of Munitions the power to (1) fix wages and hours for women and (2) set up Special Arbitration Tribunals to regulate other conditions of women's labour.[36] New safeguards were also included against imprisonment under the Act. One of the Munitions Arbitration Tribunals formed in February included Madeline Symons and Susan Lawrence of the WTUL. In eighteen months it made 150 awards and raised rates from $2\frac{3}{4}$d. to 3d., $3\frac{1}{2}$d. to 4d. and $4\frac{1}{2}$d. to 5d. an hour.

Gradually both working conditions improved and the pound minimum was achieved when wages went up from 15s. to 23s. and the premium bonus to at least 10s. Or was it? Not in real wages, for inflation had lessened its value. Food prices had risen sixty-five per cent by 1916, eighty-five per cent by 1917 and one hundred and twenty per cent by 1918. This meant that real wages were less than in some of the sweated trades under the Trade Board Acts before the war.

In July 1916 the Ministry of Munitions issued Order 447 consolidating the Tribunals for those women employed on work not recognised as men's work before the war. It fixed a 4½d. minimum for time work and 4d. an hour for piece work but only in mechanical engineering where workers were organised and not in the weakly organised electrical engineering industry. This was still too low to meet the increased cost of living and did not remove the grievance over leaving certificates. Finally on 24 February 1917, Order 49 put the decision of the Clyde and Tyne Dilution Commissioners into effect, covering women employed on time rates customarily done by fully *skilled* men, but this only applied to the munitions portion of the engineering industry.[37] Also neither Circular L_2 nor Order 447 was applied by the Minister of Munitions to a single Irish firm, where wages had in some cases been only half of those in England.[38] To help organising efforts in Ireland, the NFWW granted £1,000 to its Dublin branch for a club house.[39] Eventually a strong NFWW organisation was formed there by Christine Maguire and in 1917 the Statutory Wages Order was extended to Ireland at the National Shell Factory, Dublin.[40]

Improvements for women workers were secured only by continued pressure. Government officials, like Dr Addison, Minister of Munitions, at times failed to gauge the intensity of women trade unionists. In October 1916 he complained that their only real grievance was the absence of grievance : women never earned as much pay and the complaints came not from the women but from the NFWW leadership. That this was wishful thinking on his part is shown by the resolution passed in 1916 at the NFWW's Biennial Convention asking for (1) protection for women other than those under L_2, (2) weekly state grants for mothers two months before and three months after birth of children, (3) regrading of income tax, (4) regulation of food prices, (5) nationalisation of land, railways, canals, mines and (6) unemployment payments to all workers at trade union rates or maintenance till such work was found. Miss MacArthur correctly observed that concessions from the government were obtained only as the result of NFWW pressure.[41] Dilution might provide workers to produce munitions but thanks to Miss MacArthur they would not be produced on the cheap.

To further the aims of women in industry, the Standing Joint Committee of Womens' Industrial Organisations (in the future referred to as the Standing Joint Committee) was formed late in 1916. It was composed of the WTUL, the NFWW, the Women's Co-operative Guild and the Women's Labour League, with Miss MacArthur its first Chairman. Both the Labour Party and Government recognised this body as the main voice for women in industry.

In January 1917, in a letter to *The Times*, Miss MacArthur continued her efforts to achieve implementation of government promises, complaining of the excessively long periods of arbitration (sometimes nine months) and the fact that awards were not retroactive.[42] This forced the government, in April 1917, to issue new orders covering ninety per cent of women in controlled establishments, raising rates 1d. an hour and increasing substituted women's wages from 20s. to 24s. for a forty-eight hours week with a bonus of 11s. for cost of living.[43] Leaving certificates were abolished in 1917 when the NFWW and men's trade unions told government they could no longer answer for the discipline of their members as long as they were in force. More improvements were made by the new Munitions Minister, Winston Churchill, who replaced Dr Addison on 17 July 1917. Churchill abolished a new unofficial blacklist of undesirables and in November reorganised the Ministry of Munitions by adding a Men's and Women's Trade Union Advisory Commission with representatives from the NFWW, Workers' Union and National Union of General Workers.[44]

As the final year of the war began Miss MacArthur continued efforts to increase the low wages of some munitions workers and complained that the 4½d. an hour wage established by the statutory orders for other than substituted women was low and not enforced.[45] It was officially estimated that at least 100,000 women munitions workers were still not covered by statutory orders. The Women's Trade Union Advisory Commission persuaded the Ministry of Munitions to refer requests for higher wages to a Special Tribunal held 16 August 1918. NFWW witnesses protested that the present minimum for a forty-eight hours week was 28s. and that to fulfil Lloyd George's promise (allowing for inflation) a 'double' pound should be paid. Also since women had been denied equal pay since March 1917, they were paid 15s. to 25s. less a week than men, and resented acting as black-legs—doing men's work for less money. Eventually a 5s. advance was won, effective in September.[46] This made a net wage advance of approximately fifty per cent (after adjustment for inflation) since the beginning of the war.

Besides the munitions industry, another which expanded and employed women trade unionists was the aircraft industry. They worked mainly in wood-working, but also machined canvas, worked metal, painted, varnished and doped. The proportion of women increased from under fifteen to over thirty per cent or by 35,000 of whom 23,000 replaced men. The demands of the war resulted in subdividing and simplifying processes with the provision of jigs. Skilled woodworkers protested against these speed-up and piecework systems. By August 1916 a National Committee was formed to raise wages and in September they staged a strike or 'collective turning in of leaving certificates'. The result was the issuance on 2 October 1916 of Order 621, approximating the terms in Circular L_2 and raising wages,[47] but the Employers' Federation refused to accept the provisions and the government declined to enforce it. Employer resistance in March 1917 led the WTUL to complain that girls in aircraft factories were being fired if they joined unions.[48] These incidents led in February 1918 to unions declaring their intention to strike within nine days unless the government enforced the agreement. Churchill threatened the men with imprisonment but eventually[49] switched positions and ordered the employers to implement the agreement.

In July 1918 a strike occurred in London at Waring and Gillow (or the Alliance Aeroplane Company) after a shop steward was dismissed, and the company refused recognition to the Shops Committee. Churchill met with the workers represented by the National Aircraft Committee including two members of the NFWW on 9 July and after a stalemate Churchill invoked his powers under the Munitions Act to take over the factory. Even though the Shops Committee was recognised and the shop steward reinstated, a subsequent enquiry resulted in his dismissal being upheld.[50] In the aircraft industry, as in munitions, it took the combined efforts of men and women to secure enforcement of government regulations.

In addition to efforts to secure satisfactory wages, women's trade unions also had to contend with the relaxation of the pre-war Factory Acts. These had limited hours to ten and a half a day in most factories and had forbidden night and Sunday work. During the early years of the war, the urgent need for munitions for a conflict whose requirements exceeded early estimates, and the shortage of trained workers, resulted in women working two twelve-hour shifts (instead of the three eight-hour shifts favoured by government inspectors). Some women worked up to seventy-eight hours a week. The NFWW complained that women workers appeared worn white and declared 'it was no use killing girls to save men's lives, you must keep girls efficient if you want to keep the balance of things right'.[51] To investigate the effect that these working conditions had upon the work force a Health of Munitions Workers' Committee was established 17 September 1915. It urged a return to pre-war hours, restriction of overtime, abandonment as soon as possible of night shifts and discouraged Sunday work. It said that a fifty-hour week yielded as much output as a sixty-hour week and that no one should work for longer than four hours without a break.[52]

In September 1916 the Factory Department of the Home Office, based on the Committee's recommendations, issued a general order limiting hours to sixty a week, prohibiting girls under sixteen from working at night and reducing Sunday work after April 1917.[53] These recommendations began to improve conditions according to the *Report of the Chief Inspector of Factories and Workshops for 1917*.[54]

Problems surrounding dilution and the organisation of women outside the munitions, engineering, woodworking (aircraft) and chemical industries followed a similar pattern but seemed less acute because their products were less important to the war effort. Nevertheless, problems did arise in textiles, an industry in a depression on the eve of the war. Here the proportion of women as a whole increased from fifty-eight per cent to sixty-seven per cent even though the absolute number did not increase and as of January 1918, 60,000 women substituted for men. By mid-1916 a labour shortage occurred because of increased male enlistments and the loss of workers to munitions works. Dilution also took place in textile dyeing and bleaching, where in the well-organised Yorkshire and Lancashire districts women were employed for the first time outside the warehouse. It was common for three or four women to take the place of two men, so that generally speaking their labour was uneconomical and provided an excuse for low wages. The most bitter protests against women workers came from male trade unionists with a long history of female labour. In mule spinning, in the spring of 1915, the men requested the use of Belgian boys instead of women and complained that it was better to close the mills than to go back to the days when women worked in spinning rooms.[55] The Yorkshire Cotton Operative Association tried to disaffiliate from the WTUL at this time but were talked out of it.[56] The Cotton Spinners' Amalgamation decided to follow the Bolton example and admit them as piecers but not as minders or jointminders. Piecers were usually paid by male spinners at usually 7s. a week, later 14s. a week.

In the wool industry the proportion of women to men increased from fifty-six per cent to 62.5 per cent with approximately 10,900 women substituted. Bradford men wool combers complained that the competition from women doomed them to almost perpetual night work.[57] Although the textile trades produced materials used in the war and might have been included under the provision of the Munitions Acts they were not.

In the transport industry (excluding municipal tramways) from July 1914 to July 1918 the number of women workers increased by 80,000. On the tramways over 20,000 were employed, mostly as conductors. Management and trade unions disagreed over their effectiveness. The management objected to their unreliability and inefficiency while the trade unions explained that this resulted from long hours, often fifty-four hours a week.[58] Women conductors were paid men's wages; however, friction developed in London when women were denied a 5s. advance granted men in July 1918. Mrs Fountain, whose leadership of the strike earned her the WTUL Gold Badge as the year's most exemplary union leader, called for equal pay for equal work for women.[59] At first the union ignored their pleas but in August when the companies discharged some of the women conductors, the men struck to support them. Public opinion was in sympathy with the women and the Committee on Production granted them a 5s. raise using the precedent of a similar award to munitions workers. The incident led to the appointment of the War Cabinet Committee on Women and Industry.

Inflation caused hardships for workers whose wages were not under government control and the NFWW called for a minimum wage system in the sweated trades, many still not regulated by Trade Boards. In July 1918 the WTUL appointed an organiser whose sole duty for three months was to establish unions in the laundry industry.[60] Many women were still earning 1¼d. or 2d. an hour although food prices had increased 120 per cent above pre-war level. In the clothing trade 13,000 women replaced men. The United Garment Workers increased membership by 30,000 and of these 20,000 were women. Much of the credit for this feat was due to the work of Miss Anne Loughlin. The increase in membership was partly due to a favourable arbitration award made in October 1917 granting a bonus of 1½d. to male members and 1d. to women. This was the first time the union ever secured a general increase in wages by organised action throughout the whole of the industry. A second similar award was won in July 1918.[61]

In industries outside the munitions trades the relaxation of work rules was generally accomplished by private agreements or arbitration. Women trade unionists were practically unanimous in calling for equal pay with men on time rates and piece rates, while employers trotted out the same old arguments—(1) men's wages were intended for the needs of a family bread-winner, not single women and (2) they would cause men to refuse work at women's rates. Outside the munitions industry, the government did little to support workers' claims. In November 1915 when the Minister of Munitions advised private employers to observe at least 'equal payment by results', Mr Herbert Samuel, then Post-Master General, said, 'It may be plausible but is quite unsound. A better phrase is equal standard of comfort for people doing equal work. If you pay a single woman the same wage as you pay a family man, you are giving her a much higher standard of comfort than you are giving him'.[62] This of course was true but what of the divorced woman or widow with a family. Were these women paid by the same criteria? Were single men superior to single women? Were schemes that paid for the work done not more just than the introduction of other criteria ?

One of the major labour developments during the war was the emergence of a strong syndicalist movement, especially in the engineering industry. Since women, along with unskilled men, were a serious factor in dilution it was inevitable that syndicalism would have an impact on the women's trade union movement. Syndicalists on the Clyde aimed at the replacement of craft exclusiveness by industrial organisation and so dilution did not seem to pose the danger that it did to the skilled craftsmen of the ASE Executive. Early in the war the syndicalist leader, David Kirkwood, achieved 100 per cent unionisation of the women at the Parkhead Forge Works of Sir William Beardmore in Glasgow. In 1916 when a request for a pay raise for the women was stalled before the newly-created Arbitration Tribunal, Miss MacArthur and Kirkwood threatened a strike and the request was quickly conceded.[63]

Kirkwood and Tom Clark were favourites with the NFWW, perhaps because Kirkwood was also an ILP member,[64] and when Kirkwood and other shop stewards were deported by the government in the spring of 1916, the Biennial Convention of the NFWW demanded their immediate release. They had good reason to regret the loss of Kirkwood, for shortly afterwards the 'most fully organised and vigorous body of women shell workers in the district rapidly disintegrated'.[65] This incident shows why both the account in the *Woman Worker*, that claimed several branches of the NFWW were literally made by ASE men, and the opposite views of the *Women's Industrial News*, that ASE actions to organise women had no pressure behind them and secured only negligible results, had elements of truth in them.[66] The ASE Executive paid lip service to the agreement with the NFWW while shop stewards earnestly tried their best to organise women. The acceptance of women also varied from place to place. In Sheffield the number of members in the NFWW grew from 350 before the war to 5,000 by 1918 and Mrs Wilkinson, of the NFWW, was elected to the Trades Council Executive in 1918 and later was appointed its first woman president.[67] If the NFWW was accepted in some regions by male trade unionists, events on the Clyde, in November 1917, revealed an instance of NFWW independence. The reconstructed CWC called for a strike following the firing of four girls at Beardmore's East Hope Street factory. The NFWW formally disowned the strike, while the Glasgow ASE took up the women's cause, but by then the women were reinstated and in December work was resumed.[68] In the long run, women should have harboured no illusions about the attitude of men towards their presence in the engineering industry. J. T. Murphy, a leader of the Sheffield shop stewards, said women were 'tolerated with amused contempt as passengers for the war'.[69]

That was in the long run, over the short haul the NFWW in October 1918 passed a resolution officially recognising the Shop Stewards Movement as the real and direct representatives of the rank and file. Miss MacArthur reported that model rules for implementing this resolution would be distributed. Nothing seemed to come of this resolution, perhaps because Miss MacArthur had second thoughts. For instance, at the same meeting when some members called for a more militant stand on unkept Government promises she implored them to :

> Leave this matter in the hands of the Executive. It has been said that we have been trying to provoke our members to stop work; our Executive has had a difficult job during the last six months to prevent strikes. Do not allow the Press or the Ministry of Munitions to provoke you into a strike, but I ask you to have confidence in your Executive and in your officials and to remember that we are acting with other unions.[70]

In any event, it is difficult to imagine Miss MacArthur, the architect and autocrat of the NFWW, converting it into a syndicalist type organisation with a corporate style leadership.

The rise of the syndicalist movement during the war in the vital munitions industry forced the government to experiment with new methods of conciliation. In October 1916 a Committee on Relations between Employers and Employed, under the chairmanship of J. H. Whitley, Speaker of the House of Commons, was appointed to investigate the current state of industrial relations and recommend future improvements. To cope with the demands of the Shop Stewards Movement it was proposed that employers and employed in each industry be brought together on a national, district and works basis by voluntary Joint Industrial Councils. These would discuss problems of management, wages, productivity and working conditions and stress voluntary negotiations and not compulsory arbitration. A Standing Arbitration Council was recommended for disputes where the parties could refer any particularly difficult cases, but strikes and lockouts were not to be prohibited.[71]

The Whitley Industrial Councils were envisioned as a method of promoting effective co-operation between employers and employees as a guarantee against class war. Unorganised trades seized the idea gladly, but the Triple Alliance of miners, transport workers and railway men stood aloof. Miss MacArthur considered them promising and worth a try even if the proposal was not a labour idea. She advocated there be two parliaments—one in which the workers sat as workers and another in which they sat as citizens and consumers. She expressed reservations about the fact that the state did not have a representative on the Councils and feared they would become closed corporations to the detriment of other industries and the consumer at large. The WTUL later fired off a protest when some Councils began to support tariff reform.[72] She also feared the possible rise of an anti-political movement that would challenge the normal political channels through which labour had traditionally expressed itself. This was typified by the power of the Triple Alliance and Engineers who while committed to political action at that time could, if they chose, utilise direct industrial action to bring the nation to its knees.

To avert this Miss MacArthur hoped for something more inclusive on the lines of the Industrial Conference summoned by Lloyd George on 27 February 1918. This consisted of thirty-one representatives of employer organisations and thirty-one trade union representatives, with Sir Thomas Munro as Acting Chairman and C. S. Hurst, Minister of Labour, as Secretary. At its first meeting Lloyd George urged establishment of a permanent National Industrial Council. The Conference did recommend that it be recognised as the official consultative authority to the government on industrial relations. It proposed that a permanent industrial council consisting of 200 members elected by employers associations and 200 by trade union organisations be established, with the Minister of Labour as permanent chairman. A minority labour report of the Conference went further and prescribed substitution of a 'democratic system of public ownership and production for use with an increasing element of control by organising workers themselves for the existing capitalist organisation of industry'. This view came not from the syndicalist-minded section of labour nor the Triple Alliance or engineers, who remained outside the conference, but the more moderate section.[73]

While Miss MacArthur had high hopes for this new vision of society, by August 1917 vested interests both in trade unions and the Federation of British Industries criticised local works committees as dangerous. The FBI saw them as a threat to employer prerogatives and felt they should be entirely voluntary. As a result the Whitley Councils movement failed to blossom, even though Industrial Councils were established in the pottery, building, silk, furniture, match, rubber, chemical, paint, baking, leather, hosiery and vehicle building trades.

One result of the Whitley recommendations was the proposal that there be two classes of industry—those with Industrial Councils and those with Trade Boards. The latter would hasten collective bargaining in trades where workers' organisations were too weak. There was special need to aid those workers in sweated industries still outside the Trade Board Act of 1909. The NFWW naturally supported the Ministry of Labour's Trade Board (Amendment) Act of 1918. Although the War Cabinet Committee on Women in Industry recommended a guaranteed minimum wage, the Trade Boards were a substitute. The Boards could be established by the Minister issuing a draft Order, allowing forty days for objections and then if Parliament did not reject the Order, the Board became operative. They could fix minimum mandatory time and overtime rates, but only recommend piece rates. By 1920 twenty-three new Boards were established with seventy per cent of their workers women. The industries included sound like a roll call of NFWW affiliated unions—jute and flax, laundries, milk distribution, tobacco manufacturing, grocery and provision trade, toy manufacturing, button making, and cotton and general waste reclamation.[74]

If trade union executives during the war were troubled by 'advanced' shop stewards on one side, they also had to contend with another group which seemed to encroach upon their prerogative—the welfare worker. These were government workers provided by the Ministry of Munitions as part of the special provisions for mess-rooms, first aid centres, canteens and rest rooms for women workers.[75] The *Women's Trade Union Review* regarded them as benevolent despots whose aim was 'to get more out of us', in contrast to factory inspectors who were appreciated for their interest in the workers' true welfare—ensuring proper safety provisions and preventing illegal overtime and shortened meal hours. Part of the animosity stemmed from class conflicts. Although both women factory inspectors and welfare workers were generally drawn from the middle classes, the inspectors often had formerly been affiliated with the trade union movement while welfare workers were more the war-volunteer, patriot type. If employers often looked at inspectors as government intruders, trade unionists and their leaders displayed similar feelings towards welfare workers.

Women workers especially resented their stress on the vulgarity of high heels and open-neck blouses.[76] Both for safety reasons and to avoid distractions, Miss Lilian Barker, Lady Superintendent at the Woolwich Arsenal, required women to wear khaki-coloured overalls belted at the waist with a hair-confining cap, and cosmetics were forbidden.[77] Elsewhere the wearing of curling pins and the tendency to glad-eye male workers were also discouraged. Some objections to welfare workers bordered on the irrational or hypocritical. Trade union leaders complained of the dangers of long hours but at the same time carped about welfare workers being dictatorial in sending workers home with 104-degree fevers and providing entertainments for workers in industry. The root of the conflict was a demarcation dispute since the welfare workers were responsible to the management, whereas trade union leaders felt they should be independent and free to make recommendations to the Home Office.[78]

At the close of the war there were 1,086,000 women in thirty-six exclusive female trade unions and 347 mixed unions, and during the war the number of women trade unionists increased by sixty per cent in comparison with forty-five per cent for men. The reasons for this growth were their increase in wages, desire for equal pay, the example of male co-workers, increased initiative and responsibility caused by the absence of their menfolk. Public and government recognition of the value of women's labour and of the importance of trade unionism also had the effect of weakening employer opposition to women's trade unionism. On the negative side, two-thirds of the munitions workers resisted trade union recruiting efforts either because of their hostility to trade unionism or because they realised that they were only working for the duration.[79] The industries undergoing the greatest increase can be grasped from the following table:

Female Members of Trade Unions[80]			
		Percentage of all Trade Unionists	Percentage of all Female Workers
	1914	1918		
Miners	140	10,000	1.0	8.3
Textiles				
Cotton	210,272	260,000	64.6	74.3
Wool	7,695	53,000	57.6	30.5
Tailoring	11,353	88,000	78.0	54.0
Boot and Shoe	10,915	28,000	30.8	41.2
Printing	8,285	39,000	27.5	27.3
Pottery	1,804	20,000	60.6	59.0
Distributive Unions	18,357	62,000	41.9	7.6
Food and Tobacco	3,317	7,000	15.8	28.9
General Labour Unions (Includes Munitions	23,534	216,000	19.6	——
Total including other unions not listed above	357,956	1,086,000	17.0	19.9

By June 1918 the impact of the cessation of the war in Russia was felt on British industry, and reduced demands for munitions led to layoffs for 50,000 women workers. Miss MacArthur urged the Ministry of Reconstruction to work out a plan for the demobilisation of the three million civilian workers in war industries. On 19 November, 6,000 women from the Woolwich Arsenal and other factories set out for Westminster led by their shop stewards and carrying signs proclaiming 'Shall Peace Bring Us Starvation?' Some women only had 7s. unemployment pay to fall back on. Miss MacArthur and her staff intercepted, explaining that demonstrations were not permitted at Westminster. She then led them to Whitehall to meet with Winston Churchill's Deputy, Sir Thomas Munro, to whom they presented demands for retroactive unemployment pay at the rate of a pound a week and a one month holiday with pay for those laid off. Government action was swift and the Wages Temporary Regulation Act became law on 21 November. It granted all of the above requests and in addition provided that wages could not be lowered below the present standard without agreement with the trade union or by arbitration with the local Munitions Tribunal.[81]

In order to meet the requirements of the Munitions Acts which committed the government to the restoration of trade union customs after the war, the Restoration of Pre-War Practices Bill was introduced and eventually became law in August 1919. Employers were quick to co-operate with skilled workers in expelling women from their jobs so that production during the post-war boom was not interrupted.

Miss MacArthur's efforts on behalf of women workers during the war made her a natural choice as a woman candidate by the Labour Party. In the summer of 1918, even before the Armistice, she became the first woman to be adopted as a parliamentary candidate at Stourbridge in Worcestershire. It was a district which included a number of chainmakers whose cause she supported. Although her campaign was well financed with over £700 in contributions from NFWW and WTUL[82] branches, she had to contend not only with the authorised candidates but also with Mrs Pankhurst and representatives of the Woman's Party. They branded her a Bolshevist, a traitor, a pro-German and one who had held up the supply of munitions.[83] Her past association with conscientious objectors and shop stewards did not help her cause[84] and the election was won by J. W. Wilson (Liberal) who polled 8,920 votes, to Miss MacArthur's (Labour) 7,587, while Victor Fisher (Coalition) polled 6,690. At least she could take consolation in having beat out Lloyd George's candidate. Lloyd George later had his revenge by advising Queen Mary that Miss MacArthur not be included on the first post-war Honours List, because she and her husband had been far too radical;[85] although Julia Varley, of the more co-operative Workers' Union, did receive an OBE. More disappointments were in store for her in 1918. In June, her close friend, Susan

Lawrence had narrowly defeated her in the election for membership on the Labour Party Executive Committee.[86] An even more numbing blow was to follow, when Will Anderson died in February 1919 as the result of the 'flu epidemic.

Three economic crises would cause women's past services to be forgotten almost as rapidly as Tommy Atkin's. These were the adjustment of the economy to absorb five million returning service men, the summer of 1919 when inflation caused the economy 'to go mad' and the depression of 1921. As early as July 1918 the press and public became less complimentary of women workers, criticising their fondness for gramophones, smoking and pretty clothes. The view of the *Daily Graphic* was probably typical when it wrote :

> The idea that because the State called for women to help the nation, the State must continue to employ them is too absurd for sensible women to entertain. As a matter of grace, notice should be at least a fortnight and if possible a month. As for young women in domestic service, they at least should have no difficulty in finding vacancies.[87]

In retrospect, the war did not raise many new problems or solve many old ones for women's trade unionism. In an atmosphere of full employment and patriotic co-operation, many attitudes were temporarily altered—male workmen allowed women to fill old and new jobs and in some cases helped organise them in unions. This feeling of gratitude for the contribution made by women workers to the war effort remained in the politicians' minds long enough for them to grant women the vote and pass both the Trade Boards Act and the Wages Temporary Regulation Act in 1918. As P. Abrams argues, social groups benefit from war to the degree in which they participate.[88] The fact that women were essential to the war effort gave them tremendous bargaining power and even entry into the arena of policy making. They were able to take advantage of the situation because of their trade union organisation and the persistence and negotiating skill of Miss MacArthur of the NFWW, and William T. Kelly, leader of the Workers' Union. Their faith in the government as an agency to redress grievances (even though it encountered delays and required pressure) was fulfilled time and time again. Even government regulations obnoxious to trade unions such as the oppressive leaving certificate were abolished and late in 1918 Miss Squires, a WTUL organiser, was appointed Director of Welfare by Churchill.[89] Getting the government to legislate equal pay for equal work was another matter— even in munitions the women's cost of living bonus was 11s. against 16s. 6d. for men.

Women's trade unions took advantage of the war as an opportunity for accelerated growth. The failure of the NFWW to grow even larger, in spite of the assistance it received from the ASE, was probably due to ASE jealousy and the strict neutrality displayed by the NFWW towards the war effort. The WTUL was even cool to supporting the War Savings Committee.[90] More patriotic women workers probably joined the Workers' Union whose officials gave the war effort more enthusiastic support.[91] Too much should not be made of the changes in attitudes during the war. Class and sex conflict was not shelved even for the duration and it re-emerged after the Armistice. In the majority of industries and the TUC, women were still regarded as threats by male trade unionists. The experiences of women war workers, however, did have two long-range effects on women's trade unionism. They shattered the myth that women could not do skilled work, and the organisational training received proved valuable to some who became leaders in women's trade unionism after the war. During the 1920s both the NFWW and the General Workers' Union, after their amalgamations with the National Union of General Workers and the Transport and General Workers' Union, respectively, would have to make painful adjustments both psychologically and structurally which will be described in the next chapter.

5

Amalgamation, Depression, and Membership Problems 1918-1931

In the field of trade unionism events prior to and immediately following the Armistice seemed to augur a return to the atmosphere of the 1911–14 industrial crisis. In August 1918 a police strike in London coincided with a strike of its transport workers demanding equal pay for women. Three days after the Armistice, the Labour Party withdrew from the Coalition government and the domestic labour situation worsened. In January-February 1919 the Clydeside erupted in the famous forty-hour strike led by the Clyde Workers' Committee. Authorities fearing a political rising made liberal use of troops to maintain order and the 'Battle of George Square' followed, but the strike ended in a fortnight and national officers of the unions concerned disciplined local officials who had supported the movement.[1]

Gradually 'normal' conditions returned aided by a boom, which lasted until the summer of 1920. This boom, fuelled by the pent-up demand for goods that had been in short supply because of the production of war materials, was marked by higher wages in most industries, but also by inflation. Further labour conflict and a possible general strike caused by the miners' wage demands in 1919 were cleverly avoided by Lloyd George who referred the matter to a Royal Commission. Though trouble spots remained in a number of other industries, the worst of the possible conflagrations seemed under control.

Following the Armistice a reaction to wartime compulsory legislation developed and decontrol became the new watchword. After the Wages (Temporary Regulation) Act expired on 21 November 1919, an Industrial Courts Act was passed giving parties the option, rather than compelling them, to bring disputes before a permanent arbitration tribunal. The WTUL viewed this as a disaster for women since without compulsory arbitration industrial disputes became the old unequal conflicts.[2]

As war veterans were assimilated by industry, women were displaced and by autumn 1918 the era of 'Molly the Munitions Maker' was over and 750,000 women (mostly in the munitions industry) were let go. By 1919 the number employed in engineering fell to 200,000. Many women were happy to quit the strain of 'men's work' and return to their families; however, others who found it necessary to work preferred to stay at their new jobs rather than return to domestic service or sweated industries. It was estimated that 650,000 women were unemployed in early 1919 of whom only 500,000 were receiving unemployment benefit. This was true because those who refused domestic service were refused their benefits. Over 6,000 women were listed as unemployed at the Woolwich Exchange. The NFWW sent a deputation led by Madeline Symons and Dorothy Jewson to the Minister of Labour to protest against the practice and request the government to take action to use the former munitions works for constructing housing or manufacturing housing accessories, but since the government did not want to compete with private industry their pleas went unanswered.[3]

Though the number of women trade unionists declined in the months immediately following the war, within a year of the Armistice, as the private sector recovered, the general labour unions recovered most of their losses. The years 1919–21 were marked by increases in membership especially among the General Union of Textile Workers who reported a 32,000 member increase between 1919 and 1921 and the National Union of Tailors and Garment Workers which reached a peak of 102,000 in 1919,[4] but from 1921 to 1936 the numbers of both male and female trade unionists decreased. When an economic slump began in 1921, the NUTGW lost 9,000 men and 48,000 women[5] and the total number of women trade unionists did not begin to increase until 1936–39 as the following figures show.

	Men	Women
1918	5,324,000	1,209,000
1920	7,066,000	1,342,000
1921	5,628,000	1,005,000
1925	4,671,000	835,000
1933	3,661,000	731,000
1936	4,495,000	800,000
1939	5,288,000	1,010,000

(Figures indicate the total numbers of workers in trade unions which differ from the numbers affiliated to the TUC.[6])

Following the war both men's and women's trade unions embarked on a period of amalgamation. On 10 August 1920 a Women's National Advisory Committee was formed composed of the Dock, Wharf, Riverside and General Workers' Union, the National Amalgamated Union of Labour, the National Union of General Workers and the Workers Union. These unions comprised a total of 125,000 women trade unionists. Miss Julia Varley was elected Chairman of the Committee.[7] While these events were taking place the NFWW and the National Union of General Workers (originally the National Union of Gas Workers and General Labourers) met between July 1919 and 1921 to discuss amalgamation. At this time the NFWW was led by its President, Mrs Lauder, and its Treasurer (since 1909), Miss Craig. Its financial condition was strong with assets of £31,000 and it contained a number of vigorous districts, especially Redditch, Birmingham, Edinburgh, Edmonton and Coventry. Miss MacArthur had never intended to build a permanent independent trade union organisation for women and she supported amalgamation to avoid sectional strikes and overlapping between organisations. So the NFWW (80,000 members in December 1919) became a District of the NUGW (40,000 members in December 1919). It kept its own Executive Council and became the Woman's Department of the NUGW.[8] By 1921 eighty-seven (or forty per cent) of the 209 unions affiliated to the TUC included women. The Women's National Advisory Committee described earlier soon went out of existence and three general unions emerged which catered to women workers—the Transport and General Workers Union, the Workers' Union and the National Union of General Workers (after 1924 renamed the National Union of General and Municipal Workers or NUGMW). Eventually the TGWU and WU amalgamated in 1929.[9]

The NUGMW had from its beginning admitted women to membership and it now allowed two women members on the General Committee of the Union, one an official and the other a member of the rank and file. In addition to having District status in the NUGMW, provision was also made for a special department with extra organisers and officers to cater to women not only in the women's district but to women in mixed unions. Miss MacArthur[10] was to have become the first Chief Woman Officer of the NUGMW but died of cancer in January 1921. Margaret Bondfield was named instead and continued in that post until she retired in 1938. Between 1919 and 1923 she was aided by Miss Susan Lawrence (1871–1947), Miss MacArthur's chief assistant. Miss Lawrence served the NUGW as Secretary of the Legal Advice Bureau and represented it on five Trade Boards, the Committee on Relations between Employers and Employed and the Civil War Workers' Committee. She was the daughter of a Vice-Chancellor, and had been a Conservative until she was forty. Severely tailored, monocled, Eton-cropped and a chain smoker, she was the first woman elected to the LCC. Miss Lawrence's experience with the LCC Charwomen converted her to socialism and in 1923 she became the first woman to be returned to parliament by a London borough, East Ham.

As Mrs Drake pointed out in her *Women in Trade Unions*, becoming part of a mixed union had a number of disadvantages: (1) the low scale of contribution and consequently a lower rate of benefit placed women in the role of second-class 'on the cheap' members, (2) the minor part played by women in management led to apathy among female rank and file, (3) a subordinate position for women organisers, (4) inferior status, since women had lower wages, were comparatively younger and had a tradition of social and economic dependence upon men. All of these meant that their needs were relegated to a lower priority than those of male members. To overcome these disadvantages three remedies were usually attempted: (1) the all-woman branch, seldom a success when formed from members of a mixed union because of conflicts that emerged between men and women members, (2) the reservation of places for women on committees of management, and (3) the women's advisory council. The latter provided a training ground for inexperienced women workers in organising and committee. It was hoped that the women on the council would exercise an influence on affairs of the union out of proportion to their number, as had been true in the Shop Assistants' Union. On the other hand advisory councils could become merely instruments to mollify criticism by rank and file women and deceive women leaders with a sense of pseudo-participation. Another drawback of mixed unions was the tendency for men to monopolise organising efforts, with the result that mainly males were recruited. For instance in 1921 six large mixed unions with a female membership of between 10,000 to 175,000 had no women organisers at all; five large unions had one; while two, besides the NFWW, had sixteen or more.[11] Women's resentment was two-fold: (1) the feeling existed that only women organisers could organise women, and (2) the matter was regarded as a legitimate bread and butter issue, since women trade unionists could claim a right to the job of organiser in a mixed union.

Meanwhile the WTUL became part of a revamped TUC whose new constitution, revised in 1920, came into effect in 1921. Affiliated unions were divided into seventeen trade groups and each was allotted representation on a General Council composed of thirty-two members in rough proportion to the total membership of the unions that composed it. In this transformation of the Parliamentary Committee of the TUC into the General Council of the TUC a special Women Workers' Group was created. This assured that at least two women would be members of the TUC General Council. Unlike the other seventeen groups, the WWG was not a trade group but its representatives were drawn from mixed unions with a large proportion of women members. Thus the WWG had functions similar to the WTUL Council since it was responsible for co-ordinating efforts to organise women and promoting common action on matters relating to women. Miss Irene M. Cowell was named its first Secretary. Candidates for the General Council were nominated from each trade group but elected by the whole membership of the TUC.

The early twenties were marked by a number of other attempts at amalgamations by unions which included women. They were not always consummated. The National Union of Printing, Bookbinding, Machine Ruling and Paper Workers, the largest union in the industry, with half its members women, and composed of the relatively less skilled workers in the trade, failed in its attempts to amalgamate with the National Society of Operative Printers and Assistants (NATSOPA). The former union required that at least six of its twenty-four member National Executive be women.

The textile trades remained fragmented despite the many

amalgamations within it. The total number of insured workers in the industry in 1925 was 1,343,000 of whom (61 per cent) 816,000 were women. Forty-seven per cent of all workers or 626,000 were organised of whom 348,000 (56 per cent) were women. In the cotton industry (64 per cent) 370,000 of 580,000 workers were organised in 1925. The structure of the cotton unions was complex with local unions in each craft and the chief crafts federated in craft 'amalgamations'. Thus cotton 'amalgamations' were a type of organisation between a federation of the ordinary type and a complete amalgamation. For example in Preston there were the following craft unions : Preston and District Carders and Spinning Overlookers' Association, Preston Card and Blowing Room and Spinners' Association, Preston Provincial Association of Operative Cotton Spinners, Preston Beamers, Twisters and Drawers and Preston and District Power Loom Weavers, etc. Each of these crafts had unions in other centres such as the Amalgamated Weavers Association, the Amalgamated Association of Beamers, Twisters and Drawers, etc. The Amalgamated Weavers Association for instance included thirty-seven district unions of weavers. While each local body had administrative autonomy and arranged for their own benefits and contributions, trade negotiations were carried on by the Amalgamation. The Amalgamation was governed by a Council elected by district association committees in proportion to their membership. A further federation of the 'amalgamations' was the Northern Counties Textile Trades Federation which consisted of the Weavers, Loom Overlookers', Textile Warehousemen's, Tape Sizers', Warp Dressers', and Mill Enginemen and Firemens' Amalgamations. The majority of cotton unions were also affiliated to the United Textile Factory Workers' Association which concerned itself mainly with political and social problems that affected the cotton operatives.

In the woollen industry of 255,000 insured workers in 1925 there were 92,000 trade unionists in twenty-eight organisations. The major union was the National Union of Textile Workers formed in 1922 with the aim of including all workers in all the textile trades with the exception of the cotton industry. It included workers in the bleaching, dyeing and finishing, carpet, silk, jute trades as well as most of the woollen and worsted industry. In addition 36,000 of the 131,000 workers in the linen and jute trades were organised in twenty-three unions. The largest of these was the Dundee and District Jute and Flax Workers with 14,000 members.

In the clothing industry there were about twenty unions which admitted women. Two of the largest were the Amalgamated Society of Tailors and Tailoresses and Kindred Workers formed in 1866 with a membership in 1925 of 8,800 men and 6,200 women. It had separate sections and rates for men and women and tried unsuccessfully as late as 1925 to amalgamate with the Tailors and Garment Workers Trade Union which had itself been formed as the result of an amalgamation of the United Garment Workers' Trade Union and the Scottish Operative Tailors and Tailoresses' Association. It contained 13,000 men and 37,000 women. In an industry closely related to the clothing trade there were ten unions catering for boot and shoe workers. The largest, founded in 1874, was the National Union of Boot and Shoe Operatives which in 1926 had 57,000 men and 24,000 women and which granted special rates for women and youths.

Amalgamations during the twenties also saw the creation in 1921 of the National Union of Distributive and Allied Workers formed by the combination of the Amalgamated Union of Co-operative and Commercial Employees, the Allied Workers and the National Warehouse and General Workers' Union. In 1923 it absorbed the Scottish Slaughtermens' and Allied Workers' Union, the Amalgamated Fur Workers Union, and the London Hairdressers' Union, and soon after it absorbed the Irish Linen Lappers and Warehouse Workers' Union. It included workers in food and drink, clothing and footwear, drugs and fine chemicals, soap, candles, oil, fats, tobacco, gas and mantle trades. Membership included 66,000 men and 30,000 women in 1926 when attempts to amalgamate with the National Amalgamated Union of Shop Assistants, Warehousemen, and Clerks failed. The latter union, founded in 1891, had a membership of 24,000 men and 12,000 women. Though a majority of the votes cast favoured the merger, the amalgamation had to be deferred because fifty per cent of the membership failed to vote. Women in the Shop Assistants Union scored an important victory when one of their number Miss Mabel Talbot was elected president of the union.

Other unions, containing women, which tried to amalgamate

during the twenties were the Association of Women Clerks and Secretaries (2,000) and the National Union of Clerks and Administrative Workers (6,300). The former had been created in 1903, while the latter was born in 1890 but merger attempts in 1926 failed. Women comprised varying proportions of other unions in the glass, pottery, chemical, food, drink, tobacco and brushmaking industries which also underwent amalgamation during this period. The Amalgamated Union of Operative Bakers, Confectioners and Allied Workers founded in 1861 counted 500 women and 12,000 men. The National Society of Brushmakers, the product of an amalgamation in 1917, counted 3,200 members, one third of whom were women, while the National Cigar Makers and Tobacco Workers' Union, 2,500 strong, was the product of an amalgamation in 1920.[12]

In the midst of these amalgamations (and before some of them), the economic climate worsened. Between December 1920 and January 1922 the number of workers in receipt of unemployment benefit increased from 1,090,000 to 1,948,000. Prices began to fall as did wages, especially those keyed to the cost of living or selling price of the product, and by 1923 the cost of living and wage rates stood in the same relationship to one another as they did in 1914. Part of the problem resulted from changes already becoming evident in the international economy before World War I and which continued after it—especially the development of foreign industries that rivalled those in Britain. An unfavourable change in foreign exchange values and currencies also had an unfavourable effect on Britain, so dependent on international trade.

The slump's effect on women's wages was mixed for their wages were governed by four mechanisms: (1) Trade Boards, (2) Joint Industrial Councils set up as the result of the Whitley Report, (3) trade union agreements, and (4) unorganised bargaining. Between 1918 and 1920 over sixty Trade Boards were established covering three million workers but between 1920 and 1925 as a result of the slump of 1921 the number of workers covered fell by fifty per cent—generally employers withdrew from participation in Trade Boards (the Grocery Trade Board established in 1919 broke down because of employer objections) or workers left following decisions to lower hourly wage rates (the Clothing Trade Board in 1921).[13] In other industries where Boards con-

tinued in existence, stalwart leadership could at least lessen wage
cuts as was the case with the Leicester District of the National
Union of Boot and Shoe Operatives. The operatives led by Miss
Mary Bell Richards (who in 1915 had become the first woman
on the union's Executive Council) negotiated smaller wage cuts
than those that took place nationally between March 1920 and
1922.[14] Major unions which favoured Trade Boards were the
NUGW, the Shop Assistants' and the National Union of Distribution and Allied Workers.

In 1923 Parliament appointed the Cave Committee to
examine the purposes of the Trade Boards and recommended that
only the Boards for sweated industries be continued. Miss
Bondfield disapproved of these recommendations because they
would leave workers unprotected during a period of severe unemployment. While critical of Trade Boards for fixing general
wage rates with reference to the lowest grade of ordinary workers,
she complained that there were too many obstacles placed in
the way of establishing new Boards. Nevertheless the Trade Board
Act of 1923 included most of the Cave Committee's recommendations. The effectiveness of Trade Boards depended upon
the economic climate and the policy of the government in power.
In 1923 with unemployment still at 11.7 per cent they continued
to work to the advantage of the workers when cuts agreed to by
the Trade Boards were at first postponed and then later reduced
to 2s. above that of unorganised firms. In 1925 when the economy
temporarily improved a bit, unions actually got Trade Boards
to raise rates in eight industries, but from 1926 to 1938 improvements for women covered by Trade Boards were few and they
thus came under trade union criticism.[15]

Another method of wage regulation was the Whitley Councils
but their impact was mixed because women's trade unions were
unable to organise sufficiently to maintain rates throughout an
industry. This was true in the Optical Instrument Industry,
Needle and Fishing Tackle Trade and among Match Workers.[16]

In industries where wages were regulated by trade union collective bargaining such as engineering, in which women were
active during the war, and the textile industry, long the main
bastion of women's trade unionism, wages came under pressure
from the slump. In January 1921 the Birmingham and Wolver-
hampton engineering employers cut the basic rates for women

from 43s. 6d. to 35s. 9d. In July 1921 the Engineering Employers' Federation reduced wages paid the Amalgamated Engineering Union by 6s. a week on time rates and fifteen per cent on piece rates and withdrew the twelve and a half per cent and seven and a half per cent bonuses awarded in 1917 and 1918.[17] Its demand for reassertion of the employers 'managerial functions' in determining overtime succeeded after a thirteen-week lockout in 1921. The AEU which barred women from membership was unable to successfully resist because 91,773 of its members were unemployed.[18]

The 1921 slump also hit the textile industry, especially cotton, with exceptional severity and it remained a sick industry throughout the twenties and thirties as both the industry and trade union membership went into a slow continuous decline. One of the causes was Japanese competition which increased from 1913 while British exports declined as indicated below:

	British Cotton Cloth Exports (Millions of Linear Yards)	Japanese Cotton Cloth Exports (Millions of Square Yards)
1913	7,075	235
1918	3,699	1,006
1923	4,329	812
1929	3,765	1,791
1932	2,303	2,032
1938	1,448	2,181[19]

For a time the Wages (Temporary Regulation) Act renewed by the Industrial Courts Act of 1919 prevented wages from falling, and seemingly good trade in May 1920 actually resulted in a one-year pact providing a seventy per cent advance on the standard piece rate or 25.57 per cent on actual wages of the time—the highest point ever reached! The slump changed all that.[20] In early 1921 the Federation of Master Cotton Spinners at Manchester was forced to reduce hours to thirty-five per week and close the mills completely from 18 March to 30 March, laying off 500,000 workers. Employment Exchange payments and Union and Cotton Control payments helped but the first six months of 1921 were the worst in recollection. For a time union strength held and the Ramsbottom Weavers' Association reported that the majority of the members remained loyal and paid their contribution.[21] Things changed after 7 May when the Employers' Federation gave a month's notice of a ninety-five per cent reduction in the piece rate to cope with foreign competition. The operatives offered to accept a forty per cent reduction which they claimed would lower wages below the 1914 standard of living. The two sides finally agreed to a sixty per cent reduction on standard piece rate immediately, with a further ten per cent cut to take effect in six months. The pact was accepted by a ballot of the operatives with a 27,000 vote majority.[22]

By January 1922, 36,000 women in the textile industries were unemployed and even more put on short time. The total for all industries at that time was 370,000 out of a total of 3,209,000 women covered by the Unemployed Insurance Acts. This included eighteen per cent of the 15,000 women making nuts and bolts, eighteen per cent in potteries, fourteen per cent in hollow ware, 19,000 in the distributive trades, 11,000 in tailoring, 12,000 in flax, linen and hemp, 17,000 in manufacturing of food and drink and 16,000 in hotel, college and club service.[23]

To ease the unemployment problem the Women Workers' Group made a series of recommendations in early 1921 to the TUC General Council. These included the extension of homecraft and homemakers' training schemes for industrial women.[24] In March a National Conference of Unemployed Women was held, composed of 234 unemployed women delegates from trade unions affiliated to the TUC. The long list illustrated how widespread women's trade unionism had become. It included women clerks and secretaries from government offices and commercial employment, actresses, boot and shoe operatives, tailoresses, restaurant and canteen workers, charwomen and cleaners, engineering workers, cable and rope workers, packers, cartridge workers, tin-box workers, blouse makers, weavers, machinists, shop assistants, chain makers, pottery workers, lace makers and domestic servants. The Conference's call for 'work or training' for women became a rallying cry during the years of unemployment. They reminded the government that women did not benefit from the £5,500,000 allotted by parliament to relieve unemployment up to March 1922.

Unemployed women workers were aided by two programmes: the Homecraft and the Homemakers. Between May 1921 and 1924, 9,828 women were trained under the Homecraft scheme to become domestics; while during the same period 1,560 women received a pound a week maintenance for a thirteen-weeks course in domestic work until they were ready to resume work in their regular occupation. The programme cost the government approximately £190,000.[25] At the same time the WWG criticised the government for using the slump as an excuse to force women into domestic service—consequently lowering its status.

If parliament seemed to place a low priority on alleviating women's unemployment, it reflected the still general feeling that a woman's place was in the home or at least at the end of the unemployment queue. That this attitude was reinforced by the slump is evidenced by the call of the National Conference of Women Workers to end the discharge of skilled women clerks in the health, housing and employment services and the substitution of untrained ex-servicemen. The conference also condemned the view that unemployment could be remedied by further reduction in wages, especially those of the lowest paid workers. It urged the government to take immediate steps to bring about the stabilisation of foreign exchange, the extension of credits and the re-establishment of world trade.[26] This was no small order and called for sacrifices from other nations and from workers and capitalists quite beyond the government's capabilities. The conference finally charged industry with the duty of maintaining unemployed workers and the inclusion of all workers employed as domestics and in agriculture under unemployment insurance plans.

Following the Conference a deputation led by Miss Varley visited Dr Macnamara, the Liberal Minister of Labour, and in April a letter was sent calling for an increase in the inadequate Unemployment Benefit of 12s. a week. Faced with an increase in unemployment payments from £500,000 in 1913–14 to £53,000,000 in 1921–22, the government pleaded fiscal insolvency, explaining that the rate had been reduced from 16s. to 12s. only because the £22,500,000 accumulated before the war in the Unemployment Fund had been exhausted by the beginning of July 1921.

Throughout 1922 the WWG made continued efforts to heighten public awareness of the plight of unemployed women. Questions were addressed to Ministers in the House of Commons, articles were published in the *Daily Herald* and the Labour Press and press releases were sent to the general press. It also encouraged unemployed women to join the National Un-employed Society.[27] In 1923 Miss Varley and Miss Bondfield renewed their attempt to persuade Sir Montague Barlow, the Conservative Minister of Labour, to find a means of absorbing unemployed women into branches of work other than domestic service and to provide training in other branches of industry, but since women were already drawing unemployment benefit in all trades it was decided not to train them in fields where they were already redundant. When the problem was later passed on to the new Labour government a similar reply was made with the now familiar explanation that no funds were available, fore-shadowing the crisis of 1931. There seemed no solution except make-work schemes.

One measure to help those affected by the slump came in March 1923 when the Emergency Unemployment Insurance Act was extended so that workers could receive benefit for as long as forty-four weeks. It required a maximum contribution of 6d. for male workers and 4d. for female. With the Labour Government in power in 1924 an Amending Act increased the amount of benefits but tacked on to it the condition that workers be denied payments if they were 'not genuinely seeking work'. It was particularly obnoxious to have skilled women workers denied benefits if they did not accept forced labour as domestics. The continued deficits incurred by the fund led to the appoint-ment in 1925 of the Blanesburgh Committee to deal with the problem. The requests of the TUC General Council for higher benefits and abolition of the 'not genuinely seeking work' clause were rejected, but the Committee did advocate eventual replace-ment of the tripartite equal payments clause (one-third employer, one-third employee and one-third government) by an increased government share. Nevertheless, both the NUGMW and the Shop Assistants' Union castigated Miss Bondfield for having signed the report and they reminded her that 'Early service does not justify later anti-working class action'.[28]

One method by which unemployment could have been reduced

E

was to shorten the work day and in 1919 the ILO meeting at Washington condemned the two-shift system used during World War I, but the British government refused to enact its recommendations. As a substitute the Employment of Women, Young Persons and Children Act was passed which allowed the two-shift system with the consent of workers and Factory Inspectorate. In 1927 the TUC Women's Conference called for a cut in hours of work for women from ten to nine per day and also an end to the two shift system.[29] Reduction of hours was one way to spread work, and another was to reduce the influx of younger workers. The dilemma of how to accomplish this was never solved.

Equal pay for women remained an issue during the twenties even though some women including Mrs Webb declared it too ambiguous to enforce. Nevertheless in 1922 the TUC leadership called upon unions to make every possible effort to remove variances in remuneration on the ground of sex since they menaced the standard of living of all workers. Some women leaders suspected that the motive might have been to raise women's wages to those paid men with the hope that an employer would then prefer the male. For this reason some women leaders were not eager to press the issue during the slump. Amongst the rank and file, male and female, there was opposition to the movement even though the distributive unions and National Union of Boot and Shoe Operatives and National Union of Teachers were committed to the policy. It was not until 1935 that the AEU passed a resolution in favour of equal pay five years before they decided to admit women into the union.

While all three political parties supported equal pay, once in office they failed to implement the principle, pleading economy during the slump. Generally employers opposed equal pay, while even some trade unions like the NUGMW paid organisers and central office staff at a lower rate. In 1922 co-operatives paid women sixty per cent of men's wages. The issue was not strictly men versus women, it appears that there was a crucial division between (1) white-collar women with self confidence especially the emancipated civil servant and (2) blue-blouse union members plagued with insecurity over low wages, unemployment, unpleasant work and lack of training and education.

In 1923 the TUC surveyed each of the UCWW by means of

a questionnaire posing two questions : (1) Whether the union's wage agreement involved equal pay, and (2) whether the proportion of women to men was increasing because women were paid at a lower rate. The results showed that in most industries, with the exception of the Lancashire weaving industry, women got lower rates. Replies to the second question revealed that the ratio of women to men had decreased and thus the fear that women were replacing men in industry was groundless. There were four exceptions, the most notable being the clothing industry where the ratio of women increased especially after the adoption of the Hoffman pressing machine. This must have been consoling to the male wing of the TUC, or was it ? A closer look at the situation shows a statistical fallacy—those sampled were only trade unionists. If non-trade union women were included the *total number of women in the work force* (not the number of insured workers) was 2,170,000 in 1914, 2,729,000 in 1918 and 2,796,000 in 1923. The increase in the number of women occurred mainly in the light engineering industry. Thus the decrease in the number of women trade unionists went contrary to their increase in the overall work force. Nevertheless though the numbers of women employed increased between 1911 and 1931 the percentage in relation to the number of men did not. In 1891, 31.0 per cent of the work force was female, in 1911 it fell to 29.6, in 1931 it rose to 29.8 and in 1951 was 31.8 per cent. Thus the percentage was remarkably stable.[30]

As the number of female members in general unions began to decline from 191,000 in 1918 to 43,000 in 1923, or by seventy-eight per cent, some women trade union leaders began to have second thoughts on the terms of amalgamation. These resentments were exacerbated when the NUGMW abolished the separate Women's District and integrated its branches and organisers into its regular geographical districts. Each of these provided women with representation but they were under the control of the geographical district secretaries. Later women organisers were forbidden to come up to London to attend meetings of the Women's Committee, which became an advisory committee of lay members, and the proportion of women's representation on other committees was cut. Thus rendered a figurehead, Miss Bondfield threatened to resign but was dissuaded by being given 'complete control of all national women's questions'.

This meant she was in charge of propaganda and educational work among women, negotiated for women workers nationally, sat on Trade Boards, collected statistics on women and administered women's provident schemes.

The leadership role of women in the NUGMW was further diminished when the National Women's Committee was abolished as was the provision for a women's representative on the General Council.[31] Women's influence locally declined further during the twenties and thirties as women officers died or resigned and no successors were appointed and men replaced them. Male district secretaries explained that most women preferred to be looked after by men, who could handle them more easily than could women. Some women like Mrs Platt didn't think so and together with eighty other women shop stewards in the Northern District of the NUGMW held annual meetings on questions concerning women.[32] Throughout these changes Miss Bondfield hung on to the post of Chief Women's Officer of the NUGMW and ironically in September 1923 she was elected the first woman Chairman of the TUC General Council.

Miss Bondfield, like most other male and female trade union leaders, was plagued by an identity problem of divided loyalties. Women trade union leaders were sometimes forced to wear four hats: (1) as leader of their union or of the women's section of them, (2) perhaps as members of the WWG, (3) possibly as representatives on the TUC General Council and (4) as members of the Labour Party. Each woman leader would have to decide which of the four hats was her favourite. Although Miss Bondfield was used to playing second fiddle to others in authority, as she had with Mary MacArthur, accepting the position of 'complete control of all national women's questions' was small recompense for allowing the role of women in the NUGMW to be neutralised but there was little else she could do. Both the demand for women workers and the number of women trade unionists were in decline and it would have been foolish and difficult for her to have started a breakaway union and gone back to the days of the NFWW. As it was (though according to her autobiography she had decided to devote more time to trade unionism than politics when she declined to stand for the National Administrative Council of the ILP) she had kept her options open and had stood for parliament at Northampton unsuccessfully in 1920 and

1922. Perhaps her election to parliament in November 1923, when Stanley Baldwin went to the country with a proposal for tariff reform, enabled her ego and conscience to be able to accept the defeat she had suffered as a women's trade union leader.[33] Ironically this prevented her from taking up her post as Chairman of the TUC General Council and in 1924 she resigned from the General Council to accept Ramsay MacDonald's invitation to become Parliamentary Secretary to Thomas Shaw, Minister of Labour during the first Labour government. She was given special responsibility for dealing with women's unemployment.[34]

Miss Bondfield's place on the TUC General Council was taken by Mary Quaile from 1923 to 1926. Miss Quaile had been a catering worker in her youth and came to the women's trade union movement by way of the Women's Trade Union Council, a body established in Manchester in 1896. An outstanding speaker, she became its Organising Secretary in 1911 and in 1919 was appointed National Women's Organiser of the Dock, Wharf, Riverside Workers' Union (later T&GWU). Ernest Bevin was its men's organiser.[35] Also at this time Julia Varley was elected Chairman of the WWG and Mary Carlin (1874–1939) took Mary Quaile's post in the T&GWU. Miss Carlin began her active trade union career through a strike of model makers in Gloucester and became an Organiser in the Dockers' Union in 1916 when she helped unionise tobacco, chocolate and laundry workers in Bristol. In 1919 she became a member of the Laundry Trade Board and later served for nine years as a member of the National Executive of the Labour Party.[36] Thus female leadership positions were now held by women from outside NFWW and WTUL circles. An era had come to an end but the new leaders faced some of the same old problems—especially the problem of recruiting new members.

In May 1924 the TUC General Council, alarmed that women's membership in unions affiliated to the TUC since 1921 had decreased by nearly 400,000 and now stood at approximately 500,000, took steps to arrest the trend. A year earlier, the energetic Fred Bramley became Secretary of the TUC and suggested the establishment of a regular conference of representatives of the trade unions catering for women workers, to help spur recruitment. The WTUL and its predecessors had always, until it was absorbed by the TUC held a Conference of delegates interested in the organisation of women during the same week as the TUC Conference; however, after its amalgamation with the TUC, the practice ceased and was replaced by a public demonstration to which women were invited. At the Hull Congress in 1924 the WWG urged the TUC General Council to revert to the original format and it was decided to call a Women's Conference in Leicester, on 20 March 1925, to develop ways to improve recruitment and solve problems facing women in the trade union movement.[37] Though the use of conferences lapsed between 1928 and 1930, they were revived in 1931 and have been held annually since then. It virtually became a women's conference although at first there was a large proportion of male delegates. Although Margaret Bondfield attended the Leicester meeting, her time was increasingly occupied by Labour Party matters rather than affairs of the women's trade union movement, and leadership of the conference fell to Julia Varley (1881–1952).

Miss Varley was a veteran trade unionist but by 1925 seemed worn out by her earlier efforts. During her youth she had joined Ben Turner's Textile Workers in her home town of Bradford and from 1893 to 1899 she served as Secretary of the local Weaver's Union. Physically she bore a female resemblance to Ernest Bevin—a husky, rugged, grandmother-like appearance with a mouth in need of upper dentures and a broad nose adorned with steel glasses. In 1909 she helped unionise the chainmakers of Cradley Heath by organising parades featuring women between the ages of sixty and ninety wearing chains around their necks with signs reading 'Britain's Disgrace, 1d. An Hour' and later she served two stints in jail for suffragette activities.[38] Miss Varley became a full time officer of the Workers' Union in 1912 in time to play an active role in organising women workers during World War I and with the end of the war she became chief woman organiser of the Transport and General Workers' Union. In 1926 she was elected to the TUC General Council and served for the next twelve years but failed to display much of her former leadership potential due to the chronic ailments of old age.[39]

As a result, the Leicester meeting was dominated by Fred Bramley who expressed disappointment at the small turnout— twenty-two unions and a total of thirty-nine representatives.

These included four men, ten married women and twenty-five single women. A detailed examination of the Conference is important for assessing the problems faced by women's trade unions during the twenties when membership was contracting under pressure from the slump.

Miss Quaile, of the important T&GWU, called upon the strong trade unions (male-dominated) to come to the aid of the weak and blamed past Executive Councils and union officials for not having made special efforts to organise women.[40] Several constructive suggestions for increasing membership were made by Miss Edith Howse (Union of Post Office Workers and later Mayor of Wembley) who urged greater emphasis on the use of education classes, the cinema and social activities, since women could not attend meetings because of household duties, while others urged special meetings devoted only to questions concerning women.

Ben Turner, exhibiting some gallows humour, offered the women the consolation that because of the slump the problem of recruitment was not exclusive to them, two-thirds of the men in textiles being also unorganised. He reported that what success they had came from personal contact rather than canvassing at the mill gate, although in some districts mass meetings had proved valuable. No one method proved a panacea.[41] Miss Carlin called for greater use of female organisers because male organisers only made inane jokes and failed to tout the benefits of unionism. She further objected to the excessive use of union funds for political organisation while little help was given to trade union organisation, particularly the women's section. These complaints that Trade Councils had become so involved in politics that they were neglecting union work must have been accurate for similar complaints were made at the Scottish TUC.[42] The truth must have hurt, for when Miss Howse urged that something be done to force the General Council to take action at once she was censured by Bramley, who urged limiting discussion to general principles rather than making unfair attacks on the General Council.

As a result of these discussions the Conference recommended that Trade Councils form women's sub-committees and that area conferences be convened. These would be composed of trade unions, women's sections of Labour Parties, Women's Guilds,

Co-operative Societies, Trade Councils and Adult Schools. It further recommended that during Congress week a National Women's Conference be held to elect four women to act in a consultative capacity with the WWG and that where a delegate had not been appointed to the Congress a woman should still be sent. To spur achievement a medal should be presented to a rank and file member. It also recommended appointment to the General Council staff of a Chief Woman Officer to act as Secretary of the WWG. Despite these structural recommendations actual participation at the TUC Annual Conference by women remained fairly constant from the twenties through the thirties—in 1925 there were eighteen women of 727 delegates, representing some 4,000,000 men and 300,000 women while in 1936 women numbered twelve of 603 delegates, representing some 3,000,000 men and 400,000 women.[43] The Conference did result in the TUC launching a drive in 1926 to recruit women, with the Manchester and Salford District as its initial target. Margaret Bondfield, MP, Mary Quaile and Walter Citrine, new TUC Secretary, spoke and 270 delegates attended. The campaign was then extended to Bristol where 340 delegates participated, Leicester where 170 delegates were present and Leeds where 150 delegates attended with the local Trades and Labour Councils in charge of arrangements. Participation of male trade unionists at these conferences was sparse—often only five per cent. Men seemed to feel that as long as they were in unions women did not matter—an attitude shared by many women who seemed content for men to join the ranks of trade unions while they were satisfied with any possible benefits. Following the Leicester meeting on 17 April, fifteen thousand leaflets were circulated at factory gates and by house-to-house distribution in selected areas. But these efforts soon came to a standstill, even before the first Annual Women's Conference could be held, by the occurrence of the General Strike. While the General Strike was an epic-making event for male trade unionists, its impact on women was to overshadow the TUC's drive to aid the growth of women's trade unionism. The financial and psychological blow that it dealt to trade unionism in general made its effects on recruiting efforts even more deleterious. The miners' cause acted as a magnet for energy and funds, and as women supported their struggle it resulted in relegating women's needs to their usual low priority once again. With the exception of women in the printing industry, they remained for the most part on the fringe of the strike since few women were called out on strike. Probably the most active was the Paper Worker's Union in which one half of its 70,000 members were women.[44] While women leaders like Margaret Bondfield and Julia Varley were members of the TUC General Council which was sympathetic to the miners in their struggle against longer hours and lower wages, and which called the semi 'general strike',[45] they themselves seemed lukewarm to the idea of sympathy strikes.[46] Although most unions were not required by the TUC General Council to participate, many chose to exhibit more than moral support. The United Textile Factory Workers made a grant of £30,000 to the TUC and various miners federations.[47]

When the strike was called off, many of the women printers were bewildered and indignant. They seemed to feel that either trade unionism or their leaders were in some way lacking.[48] The National Union of Tailors and Garment Workers, which contributed £7,000 to the cause, reflected on the dilemma facing many unions caused by the debacle of the General Strike.

> If the union continued the policy of aggressive militancy, each new failure would lead to further disappointments among the rank and file and fresh crops of resignations. This would eat into its financial reserves in order to achieve nothing but a reduction in annual income. On the other hand, a policy of conciliation and conservatism, at a time when money wages were being reduced year by year, would equally lead to a loss of membership as the impression grew among the rank and file that the union was doing nothing to protect their interests.[49]

It was in this atmosphere that the First Annual Women's Conference was held at Bournemouth, 7 September 1926, with Miss Bondfield (Chairman of the WWG) presiding and Miss Mary Quaile, Messrs A. Conley, J. Leslie, J. W. Ogden and Ben Turner members of the WWG Committee of the General Council on the platform. Following the passage of the 1927 Trade Union Act which prohibited members of public service unions joining the TUC some of the most militant and articulate women trade unionists were absent but there were others to fill the gap.

The preponderance of men as members of the WWG prompted the fiery little Ellen Wilkinson MP (Distributive and Allied Workers) to lodge four protests : (1) about how the Conference was called, (2) about the delegates authorised by the TUC General Council to speak, (3) about the nature of the resolutions to be placed before the Conference and (4) that only one woman was appointed to speak from the platform. Miss A. Horan (NUGMW) complained sarcastically that the agenda 'savoured of a happy evening for the poor', while Miss Howse criticised the sex ratio of the meeting (comprising forty-eight women and thirty-six men) as unrepresentative and merely playing at trade unionism. She advocated a body without men and recommended that the money spent to bring people there would have been better used doing organising work in the country.

Miss Bondfield adroitly handled Miss Howse's criticism by explaining that the conference agenda was an experiment and that while she had hoped that the unions would have sent all women they did not do so. She advised those who were not pleased to take up the matter with their own unions and also to forward their own suggestions for the next conference agenda.

On more substantive matters Miss Ruby D. Q. Part (one of the Workers' Union's first and youngest wartime organisers from Bristol) censured the General Council's policy supporting the extension of Trade Boards to other than sweated industries as one of weakness and urged that in the future wages and conditions ought to be arranged without any government assistance from Trade Boards. Her union had 33,000 members and not two per cent were covered by Trade Board regulations. Mr W. McConnell (NUGMW and a member of a Trade Board) confirmed that a union which once enrolled 1,000 women dwindled away to nothing after the establishment of Trade Boards. He also condemned the practice of some mixed unions which, by holding meetings in rooms that could only be reached through the bar of a public house, discouraged women's membership. On the positive side it was urged that the sports side of the movement be developed, a method which employers and churches exploited so well, especially since the younger generation seemed indifferent to old-style propaganda and appeals.[50]

Most trade unions were obviously unmoved at the call for a

larger proportion of women delegates as shown by the fact that thirty-one women and forty-eight male delegates attended the Second Annual Women's Trade Union Conference in Edinburgh in 1927. Most of its attention was devoted to denunciations of bodies of women who in the name of equality demanded the repeal of protective legislation for women which did not apply equally to men. One of these bodies was obviously the Open Door Council, a modern version of the Freedom of Labour Defence League, which throughout the period of 1897 to 1920 had pursued similar objectives.[51] A difference was that the FLDL was founded during a period when the attention of most middle-class women was increasingly occupied by the suffrage question and few were interested in defending the 'liberty' of women workers threatened by 'oppressive' legislation. After middle-class women won the vote in 1918 and attained university education, their attention turned to economic problems especially when they were forced to compete for jobs in the adverse economic climate following World War I, and the liberated woman of the twenties renewed her efforts to broaden employment opportunities for women. Thus in 1926, also perhaps inspired by the agitation surrounding the General Strike, the Open Door Council was born. Its purpose was 'to secure that a woman shall be free to work and protected as a worker on the same terms as a man and that legislation and regulations dealing with conditions and hours, payment, entry and training, shall be based upon the nature of the work and not on the sex of the work . . . irrespective of marriage and childbirth'. Among the legislation it opposed was : (1) the prohibition of the employment of women underground in mines, (2) prohibition of night work for women, (3) repeal of the legislation prohibiting employers from employing a woman for four weeks after childbirth, (4) opposition to legislation prohibiting women from employment in industries involving the lifting of heavy weights, cleaning machinery, and that used white lead. It claimed that legislation like the Factory Acts had caused employers to be less willing to employ women and drove women into the least skilled and worst paid jobs. In fact as industries during the thirties introduced the three-shift system which involved night work, some women were displaced in the clothing and textile industry.

The WWG in reply claimed that these arguments were refuted

by information in a Home Office publication, *Report on Factors Which Have Operated in the Past and Those Which Are Operating Now to Determine the Distribution of Women in Industry.* It showed that in spite of welfare legislation the percentage of women in both textile and non-textile factories increased steadily, in textiles from sixty-one per cent in 1890 to sixty-four per cent in 1928 and in newer industries from sixteen per cent in 1890, to twenty-seven per cent in 1928. The Report maintained that restrictions on women's hours in textiles did not displace women but instead served to accommodate men's hours to those of women. Wage rates in textiles were also not a factor in increasing the proportion of women since women weavers were paid the same wage rates as men. A similar increase took place in the clothing industry where the proportion of women to men increased by eight per cent between 1890 and 1928.

The Report held that the major principle determining the divisions of labour between men and women was that heavy work and highly skilled processes were allocated to men and lighter work and unskilled processes to women. It cited as an example the baking industry. In the home, baking was the woman's preserve, but in commercial baking, because the mixing and moulding were heavy work, men remained bakers. In new industries such as artificial silk, tobacco, photography, gramophone, electrical fittings and wireless, the key factor was that hot, heavy, dirty work or work requiring long training was performed by men while light repetitive work, 'immediately remunerative' and not requiring a long course of training, was done by women. The conclusion was that women were employed on unskilled processes not because of legislative restrictions but because of their own attitudes, attitudes which envisioned only a short period in industry and in turn caused managers to be unwilling to train them for skilled occupations.[52] Technology would, in the future, open more jobs to unskilled workers, a fact which male trade unionists well realised.

For the most part the Open Door Council appealed to middle-class women. The protective legislation it opposed, described earlier, was generally not as oppressive to working-class women as their middle-class sisters believed. It was preposterous to expect the TUC to turn back the clock in the name of some sort of ideological consistency. However, there was a place for

the ODC, which counted a number of impressive leaders—
Rebecca West, Mrs Pethick-Lawrence, Vera Brittain, Miss
Shacklock, Chrystal Macmillan, Mary Pickford MP, Elizabeth
Abbott, Miss Rathbone MP and Lady Astor MP. Its championing of equal pay for equal work, opposition to the cliché that a
woman's place is in the home, its championing of the right of
married women to engage in paid work and the redress of
inequities in Unemployment and Health Insurance Legislation
were articles of faith which few women could find obnoxious.
Also when the ILO Conference in December 1933 called for the
abolition of all legal distinctions based on sex it appeared that
laws prohibiting night work for women had become anomalies
and that the WWG was out of step with the modern world or
hypocritical from the standpoint of males who objected to permanent relegation to the night shift.

The Open Door Council sent a number of speakers to speak
to Labour, Liberal and Conservative groups. Though it encountered opposition, the threats upon the economic, social and
political liberty of women during the Depression resulted in a
more positive response. The Married Women's Anomalies Act
of 1931 which collected unemployment contributions from
married women but cut off unemployment payments to them
after a few weeks could even inspire working women such as
Mrs Cooper of Nelson, Lancashire, to support the ODC. Mass
meetings held 14 November 1933 and 12 March 1934, in
London, to support Equal Pay and protest against Local
Authorities and Universities dismissing married women drew
large enthusiastic crowds.[53]

While the TUC had to contend with a resurgence of right-
wing feminism in the Open Door Council, it also had to face a
threat by the Communist Party to steal its women members. In
1927, Beth Turner blamed male trade union officials for the fact
that only one-sixth of the nation's working women were in
unions. She accused them of attempting to drive women out of
industry or consign them to certain occupations which were the
worst paid, and of still opposing the principle of equal pay for
equal work.[54] Communists also tried to make the most of alleged
TUC perfidy during the General Strike.

One of the results of the General Strike and eventual defeat
of the miners was passage of the Trade Disputes and Trade

Union Act of 1927. It prohibited women in unions connected with public services from affiliating with the TUC. Another result was a period of industrial truce and moderation on the part of both employers and unions—direct action was shelved. Many union treasuries had seen their strike war chests emptied and teetered on insolvency. The Workers' Union, the third largest general union, was ready for amalgamation with Ernest Bevin's Transport and General Workers' Union after an expenditure of £58,000 in dispute and out-of-work benefit.[55]

Out of this period came the Mond-Turner talks, 1928–29, between employers and trade unions. Sir Alfred Mond was the chairman of Imperial Chemical Industries and Ben Turner, in 1928, was the chairman of the TUC General Council. The purpose of the talks, which evoked echoes of the corporate state experiments in Italy and Whitley Councils (in fact Mond and Turner had tried unsuccessfully in autumn 1919 to hold similar talks amid the optimism accorded the Joint Industrials Council Movement), was to reconcile differences between the two groups. As a result, the number of strikes, the number of workers directly involved in strikes and the number of working days lost due to strikes during 1927 and 1928 were the lowest of any year during the 1920s.[56] Julia Varley echoed TUC policy when she said the time was ripe for employers and employees to get together,[57] but capital and labour were too polarised for compromise and nothing came of the Mond-Turner talks: its proposal for a National Joint Industrial Council was rejected by the Federation of British Industries and the Council of National Confederation of Employers' Organisations.[58]

The talks did have one result, the coining of a new pejorative 'Mondism' by A. J. Cook, the miners' leader, and the communists who had been building up the National Minority movement as an alternative to the TUC. Some communists within the labour movement like Sam Elsbury, the London organiser of NUTGW, attacked the TUC's support of the Mond-Turner talks. Elsbury was also Chairman of the Bethnal Green Trades Council, one of four communist London trades councils expelled by the TUC, and had broken the union's rule that prohibited running for parliament as a communist candidate in opposition to the Labour Party candidate.

Early in 1928 a dispute occurred at the new Edmondton plant

of Rego Clothiers, Ltd when one girl refused to join the union at a time when negotiations were taking place on a national level for a closed shop. Elsbury acting in collusion with the communist party decided to use the opportunity to embarrass Andrew Conley, General Secretary of the NUTGW and a Mond-Turner supporter. He succeeded in getting the impressionable girls, mostly fifteen to twenty-one years old, to strike contrary to union rules and without the sanction of the Union's Executive Board. Rego Clothiers was thus faced on 8 October with an unofficial strike led by Elsbury but unsupported by the Union. Other grievances were raised such as the cost of lunch money and transportation for the workers from their old neighbourhoods,[59] and a fifteen per cent reduction in earnings caused by the introduction of more modern machinery. The London Trades Councils collected £4,000 to support the hundreds of enthusiastic young girls who sang catchy songs as they marched to Trafalgar Square behind the National Unemployed Workers' Movement band carrying banners with their strike slogan 'Stick It'.[60] The T&GWU refused to transport goods to Rego stores. After ten days Rego Clothiers secured writs against Elsbury and other officials under the new Trades Disputes Act of 1927 for unlawful picketing. A Conference on 20 December of all parties concerned, held under the auspices of Justice Maugham, resulted in the abandonment both of the strike and of legal proceedings. On Christmas Eve, Elsbury and Anne Loughlin, the Union's General Organiser, led a parade of the girls back to work.[61]

Later after the Christmas spirit evaporated, the NUTGW leadership dismissed Elsbury for attempting to discredit and disrupt the leadership of the Union, and in March 1929 Elsbury formed a breakaway union called the United Clothing Workers' Union. The 1927 TUC Conference had already laid down the law against breakaway trade unions and the April issue of its magazine *Industrial Review* condemned Elsbury's 'wrecking organisation' as in line with the communist conspiracy to . . . 'wreck the trade unions in the United States, Germany, France and other countries'.[62] The strike was given good coverage in the Soviet trade union organ *Trud*, published in Moscow, which blessed the breakaway and claimed that the old leaders—traitors and cowards—were being replaced by revolutionists.[63] It was a lesson obviously not lost on Ernest Bevin in later years.

In May 1929 the Labour Party triumphed in the election by pledging to end unemployment. For the first time it emerged as the largest parliamentary party and for the second time MacDonald became Prime Minister. In autumn 1929 the world economy collapsed and the British economy came tumbling after. The figures speak louder than words:

	Per Cent Unemployed
1929	10.4
1930	16.1
1931	21.3
1932	22.1
1933	19.9[64]

The numbers of unemployed mounted—one million in June 1929, 1.5 million in January 1930 and 2.5 million in December 1930. There were great differences in unemployment figures geographically: London and the south-east 9.3 per cent, Scotland 20.5 per cent and Wales 30.9 per cent, and there were variances between industries ranging from 62 per cent in shipbuilding to 5.9 per cent in tramways and omnibus services.[65]

In the second MacDonald government, Margaret Bondfield was named Minister of Labour—the first woman to become a Cabinet Member. Miss Bondfield was given the impossible job of improving the rates and conditions of unemployment insurance and at the same time putting the unemployment fund on a more secure basis as well as doing something about unemployment. For all her failings, and these have been lucidly characterised by Skidelsky as humourlessness, priggishness and a voice that emitted a harsh cascade of sound,[66] she did attempt to use her post for the benefit of women workers. One of the first things done by Miss Bondfield was an attempt to establish Trade Boards for the service trades like catering. An investigation launched in October 1929 verified the existence of low wages, long hours and a lack of organisation in the industry. In August 1930 she issued a Draft Special Order to bring these matters under the control of the Trade Boards Acts. The employers resisted and obtained from the High Court rules *nisi* to prohibit her action. The High Court ruled against Miss Bondfield in February 1931. She in turn appealed successfully to the Court of Appeal in March but the employers appealed to the House of Lords where the case stood unheard when the Labour Government fell. Miss Bondfield's successor did not choose to continue her efforts.[67]

Unfortunately for her reputation among historians addicted to Keynesian economics, she approached labour matters related to women with an attitude of fiscal orthodoxy (mainly drawn from her own experience with union out-of-work grants). She saw little alternative to keeping the fund solvent by increasing a person's weekly contribution to the unemployment fund from 5d. to 7d. for women so that the exhausted fund could be made self supporting while benefits remained 17s. for men and 15s. for women. On the plus side, Miss Bondfield later was successful in removing the 'not genuinely seeking work' clause to the delight of back bench and trade union opinion. It was during December 1930, after the Holman Gregory Commission was established, that a rift appeared between Miss Bondfield and the TUC General Council. Perhaps rebelling at her years of playing yes-woman to the TUC and NUGMW male establishment she rejected the suggestions of Arthur Hayday that the TUC General Council help her write the Unemployment Insurance No. 2 Bill in November 1929, although she did later agree to the formation of a joint Consultative Committee.

Perhaps the action that caused her sisters in the trade union movement the most anguish was her effort to reduce the cost of unemployment payments by the Anomalies (Unemployment Insurance) Bill of 1931. It applied to intermittent, short-time and seasonal workers and married women. The Bill provided that unless a married woman had since marriage paid a certain minimum number of contributions she would be disqualified from benefits no matter how many contributions she had paid before marriage unless she could prove that she was normally employed, would seek work and could reasonably hope to obtain work in the district. This led critics of the Bill to claim that if a woman did not marry but cohabited with a man she would get benefit; while if she married she was penalised and so encouraged to live in sin. Needless to say this was not Miss Bondfield's intention and the Act known as the 1931 Unemployment Insurance Act No. 3 won Miss Bondfield, a spinster, few friends among married trade union women or among those who felt married women had the right to work.[68]

In August 1931 Miss Bondfield sided with MacDonald in favour of government economies and cuts in unemployment benefits, but she defected from the National government when this was formed by MacDonald and it was as a Labour Party member that she was defeated at Wallsend in the general election that followed and again in 1935. Miss Bondfield became a triple loser when she later ran for election to the TUC General Council but also lost.[69] For women trade unionists the twenties in Britain were not 'roaring'. Amalgamation was followed by the Depression of 1921 which in turn caused membership contraction and a loss of identity. Its leaders, Miss Bondfield and Miss Varley were unable to cope with the problems.

6

Recovery and Expansion
1931-1939

AT first, the thirties presented women trade unionists with a
repeat of problems they faced during the twenties: a decrease
in membership, adjustment to membership in mixed unions and
the Depression—now a world-wide phenomenon. The textile
industry, one of the bastions of women's trade unionism, whose
problems and contraction immediately following World War I
were briefly discussed earlier, continued to be hard hit. The
lower wages and more modern machinery of the Japanese cotton
industry presented British mill owners with dark prospects for the
future. They were for the most part still divided into many small
units, although a few big corporations had been created with
the support of banks. In 1930 forty-two per cent of the looms
and thirty per cent of the mule and ring spindles had been made
before 1900. Some rationalisation had taken place before 1914
and immediately following the war but its effect was to leave
both the mill owners and banks saddled with investment in an
industry whose future was bleak, given the Japanese challenge.
Operatives were faced with four choices: (1) accept a lower
standard of living; (2) go on the dole; (3) find new jobs in other
industries; (4) wage a desperate struggle to maintain wages and
preserve jobs through union efforts. Unemployment by 1932
in Lancashire was thirty-eight per cent and opportunities for
advancement from the job of big and little piecer to spinner
became remote. To keep the mills going some employers called
upon their workers to invest in shares of the mill or contribute
'gifts' of 6d. per loom.

In January 1931 the employers of Burnley attempted to get
weavers to work six looms instead of four and thus lower over-
heads without the expense of plant modernisation but through
a one-third reduction of the work force. A lockout occurred and

soon spread to all of Lancashire, but was curtailed by the Weavers' Amalgamation. However in February 1932 the employers renewed their attempt to introduce the six-loom system, demanded a wage cut of fourteen per cent and renounced their agreements with the unions. While the Northern Counties Textile Trades Federation voted to strike by four to one they also called for continued negotiations. The veteran cotton leader, Tom Shaw, was pessimistic, 'Nothing but disaster could come of a protracted stoppage. No amount of trade union action under present conditions can get more than it is humanly possible to give.'[1] However by August the strike spread to the rest of Lancashire and 150,000 workers were out. The Public Assistance Committees refused outdoor relief and instead offered tickets to the workhouse. As the struggle became prolonged Ernest Bevin called upon the TUC to give £500,000 to support the strike but for the year (1932, one must remember) only £58,000 was raised. In October the operatives' leaders faced the inevitable and signed the 'Midlands Agreement'. The six-loom system was instituted at a wage rate of 41s. versus the old rate of 36s. for operating four looms—a mere 5s. extra for a fifty per cent increase in work.

The situation deteriorated further by 1934 when a large number of firms broke the Agreement and forced workers to accept lower wage rates rendering the power of trade enforcement of agreements meaningless.[2] As a way out of the predicament the TUC and the Labour Party exerted pressure that resulted in the passage of the Cotton Manufacturing (Temporary Provisions) Act of 1934. It made any new wage list negotiated by the employers controlling the majority of looms and the Amalgamation legally binding in certain geographic areas, mainly Lancashire, and portions of Yorkshire, Derbyshire and Cheshire.

By 1935 average earnings for all workers fell to approximately 31s. 6d. a week versus 33s. 6d. before the Midlands Agreement, but thousands of other underemployed weavers only earned a wage of 15s. to 25s. a week. A brief boom in 1936 led to an unsuccessful attempt to restore the cuts made in 1932 and by the late thirties the industry faced the anomaly of widespread unemployment and a labour shortage, as youth rejected the blind alley jobs of the textile mill with their low wages for more lucrative employment in the armament industry. Meanwhile other underemployed operatives waited for a return of the good old days. The impact of the events after 1932 on trade unionism was disastrous as membership in the textile unions fell from 282,000 in 1931 to 182,000 in 1939.[3]

As a result of the worsened economic conditions between 1929 and 1934 some observers made women the scapegoats for unemployment. Actually statistics show that the number of insured women employed increased by fifteen per cent while the number of men rose by only 8.7 per cent between 1923 and 1929. During the Depression from 1929 to 1932 the number of males employed fell by 868,450 or 11 per cent while the number of females declined by only 96,690 or 3.1 per cent. Thus in this chosen period between 1923 and 1933 the number of females employed increased by 16.7 per cent while the number of males increased by 0.5 per cent. Male antagonisms seemed justified. What was worse it seemed that the heavy industries traditionally employing men appeared doomed to a perpetual slump, while the newer industries where women could function on equal terms with men had a brighter future. Men viewed women workers, even their own daughters, as threats just as serious as technological unemployment caused by new machinery. Laws passed in Germany discriminating against women workers served as a warning and caused the ACUCWW to urge the TUC to institute a campaign in defence of married women's right to work.

One solution to ease the friction between men and women was to create greater trade union solidarity by bringing more of them into trade unions. The figures for July 1933 show that organisers had their work cut out for them—only one out of seven women workers was in a union.

	Women Affiliated to TUC	Women Organisable
Distributive	58,000	756,450
Textiles (excluding cotton)	43,417	440,700
Clothing	48,202	359,660
Cotton	149,064	320,170
Food, Drink and Tobacco	2,371	235,230
Printing and Bookbinding	29,296	97,500
Boot and Shoe	24,917	55,780[4]

To increase the number of trade union women the TUC General Council, upon the advice of the WWG and Trade Councils Joint Consultative Committee, established the National Women's Advisory Committee of the TUC (hereafter WAC). It was composed of five members elected annually by delegates to the ACUCWW. During the thirties a large percentage of the members of the WAC were men. The powers of both the WAC and ACUCWW were purely advisory to the WWG which was composed of a large percentage of men and also women who were loyal to the policies of the General Council which retained ultimate power.[5]

The First Annual Conference of Representatives of UCWW recommended that at least one woman speaker address all May Day Demonstrations to appeal to unorganised women and urged conducting a campaign among domestic workers. It suggested the formation of broad-based local Central Women's Organising Committees to send the most suitable persons to talk to non-unionists in their own homes or elsewhere.[6] These efforts occurred before the summer crisis over the 1931 Budget had resulted in a National government. In October 1931 the National government won an overwhelming victory at the polls over the issues of socialism, the Budget and the Depression. The election had an effect on recruiting tactics. Afterward Miss F. H. Singer (Association of Women Clerks and Secretaries) advised publishing a newspaper in the style of a fashion magazine with solid truths about Trade Unionism but very few facts and figures; 'It should feature a serial to attract attention but soft pedal Socialism until we have got them into unions. If you rely on preaching Socialism first—well, think of the last General Election.'[7] The incident is revealing in showing the varying degrees of militancy among members of the ACUCWW.

Between 1931 and 1933 while Julia Varley was Chairman of the WAC, Vincent Tewson acted as Secretary. In 1933 Miss Varley, who was nearly blind, retired and the status of the WAC was raised by the appointment of Miss Nancy Adam as full-time woman officer to work on matters affecting the welfare and organisation of women. A petite brunette, with an alluring Scottish brogue, she had served as an organiser for the NFWW from 1912–14 along the Clydeside—recruiting members in paper bag, pickle, jam and chocolate factories. Miss Adam became a

Branch Secretary, 1914–16, and a full-time organiser for Scotland, 1917–21. From 1921–23 she attended Ruskin College, Oxford on a scholarship and from 1924–32 was Vice-President of the London Central Industrial Union of Clerks. Shortly before coming to the TUC Miss Adam was with the National Union of Mineworkers as Secretary to A. J. Cook. Although relations between the WAC and the male-dominated General Council were outwardly tranquil, when she retired after nineteen years of service Miss Adam confided to her successor, while gazing at a large picture of Miss MacArthur, that it had been a mistake to surrender the independence of the WTUL for in doing so Miss MacArthur had unintentionally smothered the independent voice of women in industry.[8]

Area conferences held just before Miss Adam's appointment were not encouraging. Too often Trade Council efforts were frustrated by the indifference of local Trade Union officials. Some organisers refused to serve on local women's organising committees because they were not prepared to divulge their methods of organising.[9] One wonders if they had anything to divulge. The task of securing recruiting aid from local Trade Councils was doubly awkward in light of the fact that the General Council did not allow them representation within the TUC and that it was not until 1934 that they were allowed to send representatives to the ACUCWW. In addition, although a number of these local conferences were established and meetings held during the thirties, it is difficult to document their positive achievements, and reports of foot-dragging from male trade unionists and jurisdictional jealousy from national trade union headquarters make it likely that their achievements were transitory.

Miss Adam concluded that the major reason for lagging female membership in unions was the young woman who regarded her job as temporary, pending marriage, since of the 3,500,000 women and girls in industry 2,000,000 were single. She admonished parents who were good trade unionists for not forcing their daughters as well as sons into unions. With this in mind a letter campaign was launched in early 1934 directed at parents who were trade unionists or members of the Labour Party.[10]

Another obstacle to recruiting efforts was welfare plans seen by Miss Adam as a snare that made girl workers content with low wages, even though she claimed many of the provisions connected with these schemes resulted from trade union efforts.[11] New techniques were clearly necessary in an age when 'kicks' were got from watching and participating in sports, viewing cinema stars in bedroom scenes, gangster films, newspaper sweepstakes, 'hot' jazz and the wireless. Trade unionism to some became as 'dull' as religion and earnest recruiting agents were seen as 'bores' or mere collecting agents for subscriptions. Good roads and bus networks also made organised outings seem less an adventure as a method of attracting members.

In the winter of 1932–33 the TUC launched, with great fanfare by the *Daily Herald*, a new campaign to recruit at least 100,000 women industrial workers in Greater London—one of the few areas that witnessed industrial growth during the twenties and thirties.[12] A few months after it started, Walter Citrine, TUC General Secretary at the Third Annual Conference of Representatives of UCWW held 27 January 1933, signalled a change in the sexist approach to recruiting. The old argument no longer had any force—that women must be organised because when their rates of pay undercut the men's this constituted a threat to the latter. It was to be abandoned and replaced by a policy attracting women by appealing to *their* self-interest—increasing their wages. This approach recognised that women were increasingly being employed on processes upon which men had never been employed and that different tactics had to be used as economic conditions changed. A realist, Citrine understood that historically depressed periods were not the most fertile periods for sowing the seeds of trade unionism and that it was much more difficult to organise an effective defence against reductions during a depression than to demand increases during a prosperous time. The ACUCWW passed a resolution recommending equal pay for equal work and resolved to survey the number of women in light industries and the rate of their wages; however, no action upon either of these resolutions was taken by the TUC General Council. Finally the conference requested the Ministry of Labour to use more modern and reliable indices in the compilation of the Cost of Living Figures and protested against the way the figures were being exploited by Employers' Organisations.[13] This was predicated upon the fact that while between 1918 and 1939 real wages did increase fifteen per cent, the statistics provided little consolation to the unemployed living on the dole or to those who found their money wages cut while productivity was rising.

Happily the years 1933–34 signalled that the lowest depths of the Depression had been reached and witnessed a slight decrease in the numbers of unemployed. There was even an increase of 5,000 in overall female union membership affiliated to the TUC. This brought the total to 416,700 out of a total of 3,530,000 women, while another 200,000 were in civil service and teaching unions unaffiliated to the TUC.[14] But government economy measures caused the 1934 ACUCWW to launch a protest against the means test in the Unemployment Bill. It also defended the role of Trade Boards as an effective brake on efforts by some employers to lower wages. Miss Anne Godwin (Association of Women Clerks and Secretaries) disputed the claim made by MacDonald, among others, that the minimum fixed by the Boards tended to become the maximum. She called attention to the clothing trade where time rates paid adults were from sixty-one to sixty-five per cent above the Trade Board rates and cited other instances where the rates fixed were higher than some trade unions were able to secure. Thus while not a substitute for trade unionism in some cases they proved very useful. For example in the engineering industry wage rates for women were 24s. a week with some firms paying less than the 25s.-41s. a week fixed by Trade Board Rates for some women.[15]

The continued low state of wages was also discussed at the ACUCWW Conference in 1935. Cases were cited of women working in electro-plating factories in the Midlands for wages as low as 10s. for 55 hours. Some women of thirty, fully experienced at the capstan lathe, worked $51\frac{1}{2}$ hours for 14s. 6d.; $23\frac{1}{3}$ hours for 6s. 3d.; and $37\frac{1}{2}$ hours for 9s. 7d. In Outer London and the Home Counties some children of sixteen years worked shifts from eight a.m. to eight p.m. In the Black Country, though the T&GWU spent thousands of pounds on organisation efforts in an attempt to raise wages and shorten hours, the Depression in the nut and bolt trade caused the results to be disappointing.[16]

The presence of such shocking conditions and the inability to remedy the situation was seized upon by the women's editor of the *Daily Worker* as a good example of TUC ineffectualness. She criticised the TUC for its lack of organisation and tardiness in trying to organise women, particularly in the Midlands. Its efforts were compared unfavourably with the successful communist efforts at a West Bromwich washer manufacturer, Hope's Metal Window Factory at Smethwick, the Mullard Radio Factory in London, Unigar Factory and the Joseph Lucas (Birmingham) Motor Accessories Plant in 1932. In Birmingham the Bedaux system and management intimidation of unionists had led to a successful organising drive. The Bedaux system was a form of scientific management involving payment by results, incentive systems and time and motion study introduced in Britain in 1926 by the chairman of an American concern, Charles E. Bedaux. Methods that increased productivity through reduction of the work force could hardly expect an enthusiastic reception during a depression.[17] Later when the Communist Party tried to change its policy of rivalry vis-à-vis the TUC, the members of the latter proved to have a long memory and at the TUC Conference in 1938 issued the famous Black Circular advising unions to exclude communists from posts of responsibility.

Nevertheless TUC organisers on other occasions were capable of resisting the Bedaux system at least for a time. In the early thirties the Leicester Amalgamated Hosiery Union led by Mrs Susan Bird and Miss Elizabeth Bambury conducted a strike against Messrs Wolsey Ltd of Leicester on this issue. As a result Miss Bambury was awarded the Gold Badge of the Congress in 1936. But later the union, after a conference between Miss Moore, a union organiser, and the employers, agreed to accept the system to the chagrin of some of its members. Failures of this sort made such an indelible impression on some women in these industries that they adamantly refused all future efforts at unionisation.[18]

From 1933 to 1936 an uneven economic recovery took place in Britain. Oddly enough in London, the south-east and south-west (three of the four prosperous regions), the unemployment rate in 1937 was actually higher than in 1929, while only in the midlands and north-eastern areas was unemployment lower in 1937 than 1929. Later, between June 1937 and June 1938, another slight slump occurred before an upturn in June 1939. The economic improvements were accompanied by a growth in the number of women affiliated to the TUC—an increase between 1935 and 1936 of 33,000. From 1937 to 1938 another

77,472 were enrolled—a total equal to the entire membership of the NFWW in 1918. The increase was accomplished by the hard work of a fifty-three member women's organising committee. Part of the increase occurred when the largest employer of women in Scotland was unionised by NUDAW with the support of the Edinburgh Trades Council. In 1936 the TUC General Council also began a 'Back to Unions' campaign distributing *A Monthly Newsletter on the Organization of Women*, leaflets, posters and providing speakers to Trade Councils. A number of articles promoting trade unionism among women were also carried by *Reynolds' News, Daily Herald, Star* and *Radio Pictorial.*[19]

Before the upturn, one of the steps taken by the TUC to cope with the nagging unemployment problem was to concentrate support behind the government's School Age Bill in order to prevent adult labour being displaced by juveniles, but the postponement of the Bill's operation until September 1939 and the clause granting exemptions for beneficial employment and home duties diminished its impact.[20]

The 1937 TUC Conference took place after the beginning of rearmament in Britain. Unfortunately only four of the 208 delegates were women, the lowest number in years and demonstrating the value of the separate Conference of Unions Catering for Women Workers.[21] The possibility of war and its consequences caused trade unionists to consider the lessons of World War I. For the most part the need to produce war materials dampened opposition to the Bedaux system. Dick Beech (Chemical Workers' Union) urged that all profits from armaments be paid into the National Exchequer and that trade union hours, rates of wages and conditions be observed throughout the entire armaments industry. Representative worker committees should be elected in every factory with power to see that the conditions were observed.[22] Anne Loughlin called upon women to support male workers by insisting upon prior guarantees from the government in the event of any kind of dilution.[23] Clearly the experience of World War I had not been forgotten and would help prevent some of the conflicts during World War II.

Even so, as early as 1936, as women were absorbed into new trades and war work where there was not 'an established male rate' progress was made in raising wage rates.[24] However in the period before World War II two old problems re-emerged, equal pay and speed-up in the new plants. That equal pay was still far off was demonstrated at the 1938 NUGMW Congress when a motion made favouring equal pay was defeated ninety-eight to fifty. Even Charles Dukes, Secretary of the NUGMW, under whose tutelage membership increased from 269,357 in 1934 to 467,318 in 1939 and included 43,321 women, opposed women officers. He claimed they had 'an entirely different job' and were not suited to rough and tumble work:

> If you say here that a woman carrying full domestic respons-ibilities is as free to do her job as a man is to do it, I won't object, because you had better look the facts straight in the face; it is one thing in the Congress to exalt sentiment, and another thing on an Executive Body. Face up to realities![25]

As for equal pay in industry during the late thirties, women's average wages were approximately fifty per cent of men's. In some industries, Metals, Engineering, Food, Drink and Tobacco, women earned less than half of male salaries.

	Shillings Per Week					
	1924		1933		1935	
Industry	Men	Women	Men	Women	Men	Women
Engineering	51.1	26.3	50.4	26.8	55.0	28.0
Textiles	51.0	28.6	48.0	26.9	49.2	27.5
Clothing, Boots and Shoe	54.8	26.9	53.6	26.9	54.3	27.8
Food, Drink and Tobacco	58.0	27.9	57.5	28.0	56.6	26.6[26]

Two unions that paid equal rate for the job were the National Union of Distributive and Allied Workers (NUDAW) and the Shop Assistants. NUDAW also charged the same union dues for male and female members. Of its total membership thirty per cent or 54,000 were women in 1939, while there wcre 39,000 women in the Shop Assistants. NUDAW was really a general union including cashiers, clerks, dairy workers, meat packers, shop employees, laundry workers and members of the Co-operative movement. The two unions would merge in 1947 to form the

Union of Shop Distributive and Allied Workers (USDAW) with 374,000 members, half of whom were women.

By autumn 1938 there were some 60,000 women in engineering, 26,000 in cycles and aircraft, 76,000 in electric cables and 95,000 in other metals. For the two major classes of women workers wages averaged between 26s. and 30s. a week and had been increased only 2s. versus 10s. for men since 1918. The NUGMW led negotiations that secured an increase to 32s.[27] As new plants were built they often incorporated conveyor belts or assembly lines. These were condemned by Alice Horan (NUGMW) as soul destroying, forcing piece work pace for time wages and developing blind alley employment,[28] and were blamed for the ill health of many women.[29]

Because many of the jobs were in the engineering and electrical industries, a special organising drive was launched in 1937 in those fields. Different tactics in different regions had mixed results. The Plymouth and Luton Trade Councils were able to make gains through special meetings, social events and personal contacts.[30] The Manchester area campaigned consistently throughout the year with special success among young workers, some of whom aspired to hold office before they were twenty-one. However in Coventry efforts failed because of a shortage of organisers. The same year a drive by the Shop Assistants Union brought about agreements with twenty-eight large multiple grocery firms covering 17,000 assistants, while wages were increased by £124,000 per year which proved that with one hundred per cent organisation better conditions could be secured.[31]

While improved wages were one object of organisation, improved hours were also important. Shorter hours were made possible by the rationalisation of production facilities. The adoption of a forty-hour week in New Zealand and France contributed to the pressure for change. The Factories Act of 1937 prescribed as normal a forty-eight-hour work week for women and young persons, instead of the former fifty-five and a half hour week in the textile and sixty-hour week in non-textile factories. Overtime was limited to a hundred hours in the year to be worked only in a prescribed number of weeks in the year. No more than six hours of overtime were allowed in any single week and women and young persons could not work after one o'clock on

Saturday. While these hours exceeded the fifty hours a year limit favoured by the TUC, it was a great improvement over previous Factory Acts permitting 624 hours of overtime a year to be worked in factories outside the textile industry, and 390 hours overtime in textile factories. Seventy thousand young persons not covered under this Act were covered under the Young Persons (Employment) Act, 1938. It regulated the hours of employment at forty-eight hours a week with a weekly half-holiday or whole day off each week for workers over sixteen years old. Overtime was strictly limited and was prohibited altogether for those under sixteen. As of 31 December 1939, hours were to be reduced to forty-four hours per week. The shades of Nassau Senior must have taken satisfaction when woollen and cotton textile employers claimed that their industries could not continue unless children worked a forty-eight hours week. In 1938 the Holiday with Pay Act gave Trade Boards the power to provide a week's vacation for industries under their control.[32]

Attempts at upgrading the status of domestic workers to a profession had been made since the end of World War I. Yet in the depths of the Depression if an unemployed woman was offered a job in domestic service and refused it, she lost the right to unemployment benefit. This, coupled with the fact of their isolation, since domestics did not work in groups, made them difficult to organise. Nevertheless in 1934 a Domestic Workers' Guild was launched at Hampstead by the local trade council which sponsored a social club to maintain interest.[33] Eventually a National Union of Domestic Workers was formed in 1937 and made the responsibility of the TUC Women's Department. It contained 1,500 members out of 1,500,000 domestics. Its charter fixed hours at ninety-six per fortnight but left the actual arrangement of hours to the contracting parties. Wages for resident adult workers were set at 15s. per week in the provinces and 18s. per week in the Greater London area, while for non-resident workers adult minimum wages were 32s. per week in the provinces and 35s. per week in the Greater London area. Provision was also made for an annual holiday of not less than fourteen days of pay while in the case of resident workers board wages were to be paid. The union and its organiser Mrs Beatrice Bezzant soon were busy performing a variety of services for its members dealing with cases of dismissal without notice, broken contracts, wrongful withholding of wages and slander by employers.[34]

Other services provided by trade unions for women were negotiations for pensions and counselling workers in connection with workmen's compensation claims. Millions of pounds were recovered every year in this way. One of many examples was the case of a County Council laundry girl whose arm was amputated above the elbow as the result of its becoming tangled in the mechanism of a washing machine.[35] The girl won a settlement of £1,750 rather than workmen's compensation. The Union provided the service of a solicitor and expert medical opinion without charge. Pressure was also exerted for a wide variety of measures throughout the period from 1918 to 1939 to improve maternity, child care and health services. In addition a series of Trade Union Schools for women workers were held on weekends in conjunction with various Trade Councils to train future leaders. Finally the TUC provided the facilities of the low cost Mary MacArthur Holiday Home for women trade unionists and wives of trade unionists.

In 1939 the attempt was made to increase the pensions for both single men and women but was hampered by the fact that women could retire at fifty-five while men retired at sixty-five. Mr C. Speak (Amalgamated Weavers), representing some 70,000 women, favoured retirement of spinsters at the age of fifty-five with the argument that women made unemployed by the decline in the cotton industry had nothing left after exhausting their Unemployment Benefits but Public Assistance. However, Miss Horan, also from Lancashire, cautioned that employers might then employ pensioners at a lower rate of wages. Most women in clerical work were certainly not worn out at fifty-five and though the work of Lancashire women was more strenuous, she knew they were still full of life and would continue to want to work instead of accepting a ridiculously low pension figure of 10s. Miss Florence Hancock (Advisory Committee) said that in spite of the scheme's popularity in Lancashire she opposed early pensions for spinsters because the policy she represented had always been for equality of pay and opportunity and it would be hypocritical to argue otherwise. Besides if the workers did augment their pensions it would work to the disadvantage of other employees and to the advantage of the employer.[36] This debate is interesting because it reveals not only divisions between men and women but also three divisions in women's unionism : (1) between white collar and blue blouse attitudes, (2) between married women and spinsters and (3) between women in 'sick' industries and healthy industries.

By 1939 women's trade union membership had made good the losses it suffered after 1921 and stood at 1,010,000. Its fortunes were chiefly affected by the behaviour of the economy, international trade and transformations of the internal structure (technological change and amalgamation). The following chart indicates the growth in some of the key sectors of industry where women's trade unionism was developed :

	1918	1933	1939
Distributive	62,000	58,000	54,119
Textiles	163,000	43,417	45,897
Clothing	88,000	48,202	78,604
Cotton	260,000	149,064	109,000
Food, Drink and Tobacco	7,000	2,371	5,284
Printing and Bookbinding	54,000	29,296	39,191
Boot and Shoe	28,000	24,917	34,095
General and Municipal Workers	216,000		43,321[37]

But in order to take advantage of the right conditions good leadership was needed. If women's leadership at the top in the TUC received less than enthusiastic support from the TUC male establishment, leadership had to be demonstrated at other echelons. Anne Loughlin, of the National Union of Tailors and Garment Workers, personified these efforts. Five foot tall, lean and athletic-looking she was a severely but stylishly dressed woman with immaculately groomed hair and bright blue eyes. Born in 1894 she was the daughter of an Irish boot-and-shoe operative in Leeds. When twelve years old she became the 'mother' of her younger brothers and sisters after her mother died. When her father died four years later, she worked in the clothing trade to support the family. In 1915 at the age of twenty-one she was a full-time organiser and led a strike of 6,000 clothing workers at Hebden Bridge.

By the time she was twenty-six Miss Loughlin was made national organiser and witnessed the growth of her union to

102,000 in 1919 but saw it plunge to 45,000 in 1923. During the slump and Depression she reformed branch and shop committees, fought off the challenge of breakaways, coped with wage demands through Trade Board arbitration and called limited strikes in individual centres. She served on Royal Commissions and government committees dealing with such questions as holidays, equal pay, safety and unemployment insurance. Miss Loughlin later became General Secretary of the NUTGW and then the first woman President of the TUC and a Dame of the British Empire. Her life was a microcosm of women's trade unionism during the twenties and thirties.[38] The period examined of depression and revival was a prelude to another even greater war. Would its effects be any different?

F

7

World War II
and the Labour Government

THE period between 1940 and 1951 was marked by two
major events—World War II and the post-war Labour government. It also saw the number of women in trade unions exceed
the million mark for the first time since 1918, reaching 1,010,000
in 1939. By 1951 the figure would hit 1,790,000. A comparison
of the two World Wars and their immediate aftermaths reveals
contrasts that had an important impact on women's trade unionism: (1) During World War II the Minister of Labour was
regarded by the Labour Movement with trust while in World
War I the various Ministers of Munitions were regarded with
suspicion, (2) World War I witnessed industrial turmoil on the
home front while World War II after the German attack on the
USSR was characterised by a decrease in the number of workers
on strike and attempts to increase productivity, (3) after World
War I women were granted the vote but after World War II they
were not rewarded with equal pay, (4) after World War I the
numbers of women in trade unions decreased by forty per cent
within five years, while after World War II, following a slight
dip, they remained constant and the absence of a prolonged
post-war slump saw membership stabilised at over the million
mark, (5) after World War II the Labour part of the Coalition
came to power and was responsible for post-war reconstruction
whereas after World War I it was the Liberal-Conservative Coalition which made the decisions, (6) during World War II the
AEU allowed women to join its ranks in contrast to World War
I and (7) there was much more use and tighter control of
women's labour during World War II than during World War I.

Though this last generalisation was true, in September 1939
when war was declared, the government hoped to exercise less
government control of the economy than during World War I
in spite of the authority provided under the Emergency Powers

(Defence) Act of September 1939. After 1935, when rearmament started, the pool of unemployed skilled workers began to dry up and a shortage developed but most of the reserve supply of women were unskilled and in September 1939 the number of unemployed women increased by 175,000 and as late as April 1940 there were still a million men unemployed. In August 1939 in order to avoid problems in the assimilation of the new workers the AEU and Engineering Employers' Federation concluded a Relaxation of Customs Agreement (in World War I jargon, dilution), however it was not enforced by the Ministry of Labour which hoped that the Ministry of Supply would be responsible. General inertia prevailed during the so-called 'phony war' period until the Norwegian debacle caused the fall of the Chamberlain government. On 10 May 1940 Churchill became the new Prime Minister and appointed Ernest Bevin Minister of Labour and National Service. Bevin 'combined legislative audacity and administrative circumspection' to get things done. In May 1940 a joint Consultative Committee was created giving equal representation to the British Employers Confederation and TUC General Council to facilitate economic collaboration, recalling the days of the Mond-Turner talks.

During the first year of the war, before the German attack on the USSR, this unity was threatened by elements having roots on the Clyde in World War I. Trade Councils in Glasgow and Cardiff called an anti-war conference. Another conference at Birmingham on 7 April 1940 called for shop stewards to organise women being brought into industry to obtain equal pay for equal work.[1] The meeting led to the formation of the Engineering and Allied Shop Stewards Council which shortly after 22 June 1941, when Germany attacked the USSR, did an about-face to close ranks with employers and the TUC to form Joint Production Committees. Then *The New Propeller*, organ of the shop stewards, and Lord MacGowan of ICI, suddenly became sweethearts in an all-out effort to increase productivity. On 19 October 1941 a rally was held to increase productivity, sponsored by the Engineering and Allied Trades Shop Stewards' National Council. For the most part, aside from a strike by women aircraft engineers in the west of Scotland for equal pay against the wishes of the T&GWU, unity would prevail on the home front among women workers during World War II. The strike occurred at the new

Rolls-Royce factory at Hillington, Glasgow when the AEU took management before a court of inquiry which found that Rolls-Royce had evaded the 1940 agreement calling for the narrowing of wage differentials between female and male workers. A settlement reached in August 1943 was rejected by sixteen thousand men and women out of twenty thousand workers and a one-week strike ensued. A new agreement ended the dispute by setting wages on the basis of the machine worked rather than the sex of the operator.[2]

In spite of the fact that there was much more use and tighter control of women's labour during World War II than during World War I, Mary Agnes Hamilton felt that the status and conditions of women's labour were better than during World War I. One reason was that women's trade unions were more organised in 1939 than in 1914. Outside of the textiles unions in 1914 there were only 104,326 women trade unionists compared to 867,000 in 1939. The total number of women in trade unions climbed from 972,000 or 15.6 per cent in 1939 to 1,372,000 or 19.4 per cent in 1941, and in 1940 had reached 1,870,000.

In May 1940 the Emergency Powers (Defence) Act gave the government sweeping powers over persons and property. Under this Act, Defence Regulation 58A gave the Minister of Labour tremendous power for controlling labour. Miss Caroline Haslett was appointed Honorary Advisor to Bevin and a Woman Power Advisory Committee appointed to deal with the health and safety of women workers, the care of their children, feeding workers' families, shopping arrangements, lodging of women workers in remote industries, holidays, factory canteens, recreation and training of welfare and supervisory personnel.[3]

To ensure an adequate supply of labour to produce the complex machinery of modern warfare, the reserve supply of women's labour was tapped lightly at first and then plumbed to its very depths. On 19 April 1941 the Essential Work (Registration for Employment) Order No. 368 in effect mobilised all women, a more drastic action than any taken during World War I. No one could change jobs without the permission of the National Service Officer. It was the 'leaving certificate' all over again, but since it was administered by the National Service Officer rather than the employer as in World War I, it met with few objections. Until July 1941 it was applied only to women not already occupied in industry, but by summer 1941 there were few who were not affected. Women workers in retail distribution and woollen and worsted industries were released for more essential work. Early in 1942 the Employment of Women (Control of Engagement Order) stipulated that women between the ages of twenty and thirty years could obtain employment only through employment exchanges. In spring 1942 exemption from work was limited only to women looking after at least one other person. By October 1942 all women between the ages of eighteen and forty-five and a half were registered at employment exchanges and by 6 November 1943, to meet the demand for aircraft production, the registration of 'grandmothers', women up to fifty, produced another 20,000 workers. In addition the National Service (No. 2) Act of 1941 made all single women over twenty years old liable for military service. By autumn 1943 some forty-five per cent of all women were in the service or working.[4]

In another area of possible friction the Joint Consultative Committee in effect made strikes illegal when it provided that in disputes a National Arbitration Tribunal would make decisions which should be binding on both parties and in June 1940 an Order in Council 1305 was issued to prohibit strikes and lockouts. The year 1940 witnessed the fewest number of days lost to strikes since statistics were kept but the *number* of strikes rose throughout the war.[5]

The low number of strikes corresponded with the 'darkest hours' and munitions shortages in the period following Dunkirk but it was 'strikes as usual' as news from the front improved and 1944 set a record for the number of days lost by strikes, 3,700,000. The strikes were shorter and usually more isolated, affecting only one factory or one locality. Nine out of ten strikes in the engineering industries in 1943 and 1944 lasted for less than a week and were usually over piece rates.

	Number of Strikes
1940	922
1941	1,251
1942	1,303
1943	1,785
1944	2,194

As in World War I, women's trade unions used the occasion to try to obtain equal pay. Anne Loughlin (NUTGW), sounding much like Mary MacArthur, argued for the rate for the job on the ground that it was a protection for the wages of men called up.[6] Miss U. Hughes (Railway Clerks' Association) reminded the TUC that in her field men had refused to support the women's claim for equal pay during World War I and that as a result women's wages were lower and 11,000 men were displaced after the war. Men earned £260 a year alongside women getting £170.[7] Nevertheless, women in the bus and railway industry did fairly well, averaging four pounds a week at the end of the war.

Other unions faced similar problems connected with dilution. At the beginning of the war the T&GWU was forced to negotiate an increased rate for women engineering workers at Bristol and the NUGMW was confronted with a women engineers' strike at north-eastern war plants.[8] To avoid unrest the Extended Employment of Women Agreement was concluded in May 1940 between the NUGMW, T&GWU, AEU and the Engineering Employers Federation providing the 'rate for the job' for women doing men's work without extra help or supervision. The AEU signed even though it did not admit women. In December 1941 a national agreement was negotiated with the Engineering Employers Federation which provided for an increase of 9s. on all women's basic rates. Between October 1939 and August 1944 wages for women in the engineering industry (including bonus) rose from 32s. to 56s. a week. This represented an increase of from sixty-two per cent to seventy-four per cent of the wages paid male workers.

During the early part of the war the AEU was more interested in protecting the position of their male members than in the problems of women workers. A proposal to admit women in June 1940 was defeated by its National Committee by twenty-five to fourteen; however, two years later a postal ballot of 600,000 members saw a large majority favour admitting women who became eligible 1 January 1943.[9] Nevertheless in December 1942, when the Chairman of the National Conciliation Board awarded more money to women than men, it caused an outcry from the rank and file. To quiet their outrage, 'merit' increases were given them.[10] Finally in 1942–43 a Women's Section of the AEU was established and by 1944 added 139,000 women to its rolls.[11] Wal Hannington, the national organiser of the AEU admitted that it was the force of inexorable circumstances which compelled the AEU to give way. General unions were grabbing female members in engineering and the introduction of mass production techniques forced the skilled men to organise their semi-skilled brothers and sisters before they ousted them. To the credit of the AEU, all seven of its first delegation to the ACUCWW were women. It also held an Annual Women's Conference for its members and made them eligible to be elected to any position in the Union.

In other industries unions managed to telescope the training periods for women which meant that women reached their highest earnings more rapidly. In the quest for equal treatment the Engineering and Co-operative trade unions sought to have employers pay the difference in salaries between the military pay and civilian pay of women workers as was the case with male workers. In the transport industry women bus conductresses, as the result of a decision by the Industrial Court for Arbitration, established the principle that women doing men's work should get ninety per cent of men's rates for their first six months service and then a rate equal to men for a forty-hour week with everything in excess of that at men's overtime rates.[12]

Wage increases were necessary because of inflation. Between 1938 and 1946 the value of the pound sterling fell by forty-one per cent, while the women's basic rate between October 1939 and August 1944 increased by seventy-five per cent. In the cotton industry during October 1939 when the cost of living index stood at sixty-five points over the 1914 figure, the Northern Counties Textile Trades Federation negotiated a seventeen per cent increase effective as of 1 January 1940. On 16 January 1940 a sliding scale in wage movements tied to the cost of living was concluded and continued in effect until December 1946.[13] Generally speaking for all industries Bevin's call for wage restraints worked well and by spring 1944 wages had not increased more than eleven per cent above the cost of living.[14]

Although the numbers of trade unionists grew, organisers still encountered resistance from women who felt no obligation to join a union either because they were only working for the duration or because as munitions workers their wages were taken care of by the government. For every woman trade unionist in the engineering industry there were twelve women non-unionists.[15] In other industries what trade unions could not achieve by bargaining was accomplished by legislation. The Catering Wages Act (1943) brought about what Margaret Bondfield had attempted in 1931 by extending Trade Boards to the catering industry. This led the Shop Assistants Union to press for similar coverage. The result was a Wages Councils Act in 1945 converting Trade Boards into Wages Councils—statutory bodies consisting of three independent members and an equal number of representatives for employers and employees. It covered about 2,500,000 women or seventy-five per cent of the workers. The number of women covered by Wages Councils exceeded women trade union members by three-quarters of a million. But this raised the old complaint that the trade union movement was using its funds and energies to aid millions of non-members who would thus feel no great need to join a union. A case in point was the laundry industry where only 40,000 of the 190,000 workers were unionised.[16] Of the 40,000 organised, most had been recruited after guaranteed minimum wages in the industry were raised as part of an arrangement between Ernest Bevin and the laundry owners. This had been prompted by a shortage of workers which forced the owners to ask Bevin to apply an Essential Work Order to the industry, thus preventing workers from leaving the industry without permission.

Next to wages, hours were another concern for the TUC Women's Advisory Committee. While most of the labour movement favoured keeping the hours of women workers short, a deficit of munitions resulted in some working a sixty-five hour week. On the plus side the overtime wages resulted in some women workers earning £5 a week.[17] By summer 1941, after the ammunitions crisis eased a three-shift system was substituted with better travel facilities, canteens and hostels for women workers. The improvements in hours were not universal and Miss Hancock still complained about twelve-hour shifts.[18]

In order to allay anxieties over the effects of dilution a Restoration of Pre-War Practices Act was passed in 1942 providing that practices abandoned by unions would be restored if desired after the war. Included in it was a fair wages clause with punitive provisions for employers who failed to comply. Plans were also made for a more orderly demobilisation of women to avoid the

situation of the days following World War I. The TUC
advocated :

1. Women who volunteered for war service be given employment in the immediate post-war period.
2. A lump sum payment be made over a certain period to
women in industry during the war.
3. In the post-war period all women under fifteen shall remain
in school to prevent a flood of the labour market. It was
estimated that there would be three million more women than
men after the war and a total of about five million unmarried
women on the labour market.[19]

In 1944, with the war against Germany practically over, the
shock of the return to peace-time conditions was eased by a slow
winding down of the war effort rather than an abrupt halt as in
1918. As the ACUCWW looked to the post-war period at its
1944 meeting, Miss Dorothy Elliott (NUGMW), a member of
the WAC, noted that one in four women were unionised, making
1,219,543 women in the TUC, but urged each representative to
make sure that when women moved from one industry to another
after the war, they retained their cards. The Conference was
attended by ninety-four women and twenty-four men. Representation had been reapportioned in 1939 with unions of over
40,000 women allotted eight representatives, those with 30,000
women six representatives, 20,000 women four representatives
and 10,000 or less, two representatives. Mrs Wallace (Fire
Brigades Union) and Mrs Godfrey (Guild of Insurance Officials)
both called for the WAC to do something to increase the women's
representation of the TUC, where of 750 delegates only twenty
were women. In response both Miss Loughlin and Miss Hancock
warned that an attempt to seek greater parity at the TUC meeting might lead to an end of the Women's Conference, which
might in the long run be more disadvantageous. Miss Loughlin
felt that it was useful to have men attend the Women's Conference and hear what women had to say.[20] Within individual
unions greater women's representation was ensured by some
unions such as the Tobacco Workers who in 1942 passed a rule
requiring that of the two delegates sent to their Annual Delegate
Meeting one would have to be elected. The Tobacco Workers
during the war were a very innovative and active group especially

from 1943 to 1944 when they had to strike on a number of occasions in order to get Trade Union recognition. Especially notable was the sit-down strike at the Players cigarette factory in Nottingham.[21]

The general election held at the end of the war in 1945 saw the Labour Party triumph with 390 seats and win its first absolute majority. One of its first acts was the repeal of the Trade Disputes Act of 1927, and this resulted in the civil service unions rejoining the TUC (these included the Civil Service Clerical Association and Post Office Workers). World War II left the nation badly in debt (the interest alone ran to £73 million a year). The damage to housing came to £1,500 million and a large portion of the nation's industrial machinery and equipment was in need of replacement. Almost £900 million of depreciation had to be covered by new investment.[22]

In order to maintain a favourable balance of payments, exports had to be competitive in the new world economic markets. To assure this, the Minister of Labour continued to enforce Order 1305, making strikes illegal and forcing both parties in a dispute to abide by decisions of the National Arbitration Tribunal. Troops were used to break a strike of women laundry workers who were members of the Distributive and Allied Workers Union. The implementation of the Restoration of Pre-War Practices Act, 1942, was also postponed. A winter fuel crisis in 1947 and the abandonment of the convertibility of sterling were other events in the 'age of austerity'.

In February 1948, a *Statement on Personal Incomes, Costs and Prices* issued by Prime Minister Attlee called for a stabilisation of prices, profits and wages. The acceptance by the TUC of wage restraints during peacetime was facilitated by the euphoria surrounding the Labour government's nationalisation of industry, social reforms (i.e. the National Health Service and comprehensive National Insurance scheme) and the personal example and idealism of the Chancellor of the Exchequer, Sir Stafford Cripps. It is against this background that affairs on the women's trade union scene must be understood.

Between 1943, when the high point in women's employment was reached, and 1948, 1,250,000 women retired from industry. By the end of 1945, 98,501 women trade unionists left the rolls, with most of the losses occurring in the transport, engineering, distribution and agriculture unions. These were compensated for by increases in general and municipal, clothing, health services, textile, printing, tobacco and pottery unions. Thus in 1948 there were 683,000 more women in industry than before mid-1939 and approximately 750,000 more women in trade unions than in 1939. In 1948 growth continued to occur mostly among weavers, boot and shoe, distributive workers, civil service unions, actors, banks and clerical workers.[23]

If equal pay was the next step following women's suffrage in the progress of women's rights, women trade unionists planning for the post-war period had every right to expect equal pay would be their reward for service during World War II. They were soon to be disappointed, for while suffrage involved no financial sacrifice to the country, equal pay did. It was hoped that the government might take the lead and set an example but financial and 'paternalistic' considerations prevented this. The Education Act of 1944, passed by a majority of one, gave women teachers equal pay but both Churchill and the Chancellor of the Exchequer in the new Labour government postponed its implementation until the Royal Commission on Equal Pay, 1944–46, arrived at a conclusion about its effects. Its report, issued October 1946, recommended rejection of equal pay on the ground that employers would probably replace women with men and hire fewer women for new jobs. Anne Loughlin and two other women members of the Commission dissented, maintaining that women would hold their own. On the positive side, the Commission did recommend equal salaries for women in the 'common classes' of the civil service. In 1946 the 'marriage bar' upon women employed by the civil service was removed and they were admitted to the foreign service.

When it appeared that the recommendation for equal pay in the civil service was going to be ignored, two Equal Pay pressure groups were formed—the Equal Pay Campaign Committee composed solely of female white-collar workers and the Equal Pay Co-ordinating Committee composed of the mixed white-collar unions, the National Union of Teachers, the National Association of Local Government Officers and the Civil Service Clerical Association. Together in 1946 they mounted a campaign with petitions, public meetings and marches. Shortly after the Metropolitan Water Board initiated the practice of equal pay, further gains were halted by the wage freeze. Since the TUC General Council and the WAC generally followed the Labour government's lead, the raises necessary to bring women's wages to the level of men's were not implemented.[24] Thus a split occurred between some female trade unionists and the TUC establishment. In 1946 a deputation of women engineers who had demonstrated the day before at the offices of the National Arbitration Tribunal were refused admission to the ACUCWW because they were not members of delegations duly appointed by their organisations. Though pacified, they sent a resolution from a mass meeting outside to the platform urging the Conference to support their claim for the male rate to women engineers and expressed concern about falling production caused by thousands of women leaving the industry 'owing to the present iniquitous wages paid'.[25]

True enough, after World War II there was a labour shortage and women were asked by Charles Dukes, Chairman of the TUC, to remain in industry in an emergency not less burdensome than the war. The labour shortage complicated efforts to reduce hours from forty-eight to forty hours per week. Dame Anne Loughlin suggested the reductions be achieved in two stages; first to forty-four hours, then to forty.[26] Efforts to shorten shop hours ran into consumer protest from within the Women's Conference itself. Some working women who desired convenient shop hours such as Mrs M. H. Godfrey (Guild of Insurance Officials) suggested shops stay open fifty or sixty hours per week and adopt a shift system.[27] In 1947 the TUC Committee on the Forty-Hour Week supported use of a combination of voluntary and legislative methods to achieve its goal. In the area of individual negotiations unions were recommended to proceed in two stages with due regard to the separate characteristics of individual industries. In distributive trades the forty-hour week would have to be implemented in a form acceptable to both shop assistants and other sections of work people.[28]

In addition to shorter hours, four other major problem areas concerned women trade unionists after World War II : (1) organising domestic workers, (2) anomalies in the new National Insurance Act, (3) new methods in recruiting and (4) equal pay.

In 1946 Miss Dorothy Elliott assumed the job of running the Institute of Houseworkers set up by the Ministry of Labour and National Service to organise the domestic workers into a National Union of Domestic Workers. By 1950 it had trained 894 Associate Members holding the Institute's Diploma and established twelve Daily Houseworker Services in London and main provincial cities in which the Institute was the employer responsible for seeing the hours, pay, holiday and sick provisions were complied with.[29]

The ACUCWW also asked the TUC General Council to amend Section 58 of the National Insurance Bill. It provided that married women who worked and did not make forty-five contributions in one year forfeited all their accumulated rights whereas men could re-qualify after a period of only ten weeks.

Immediately following the war renewed attempts to improve recruiting through Local Women's Advisory or Organising Committees attached to Trade Councils were initiated. Eleven of these already existed at Ashford, Birmingham, Blackpool, Doncaster, Edmonton, Grantham, Manchester, Harrow, Leeds, London and Nottingham, but the Trades Councils had very little authority. Individual unions controlled their policies, they were badly attended and so were ineffective. The local Trades Councils did very little of significance, apart from passing resolutions and participating in May Day processions. Attempts to create Organising Committees to carry on local publicity among unorganised women workers were an uphill struggle and generally were unsuccessful even after valiant efforts. From 1945 to the sixties various Chief Women Officers made many tiring journeys across the country to dreary halls, where they tried to inspire small committees to attract new members.[30] The Blackpool Trades Council was an exception to this depressing assessment.

Besides recruiting, the major dilemma facing women trade unionists between 1946 and 1951 was the problem of how to continue the drive for equal pay in the face of the TUC policy of wage restraint. In 1946 before the real magnitude of the balance of payments problem became evident and the Royal Commission on Equal Pay made its report, women leaders such as Alice Horan (NUGMW) advocated the use of methods outside the constitution like those employed by the militant suffragettes.[31] Even in the middle of the 'age of austerity' a TUC statement indicating that equal pay could not be implemented in government departments, local government and teaching professions, because of its £24,000,000 cost was sharply criticised at the 1948 ACUCWW in the light of the fact that £78,000,000 had been returned by the government in tax reliefs for depreciation of machinery to industry, even though profits had increased by thirty-two per cent in 1948.[32] Miss A. Bone (Inland Revenue Staff Federation) called for an end to complacency and indifference, citing Ministry of Labour Gazette statistics showing that female wages during 1948 had deteriorated from being fifty-three per cent of male wages to forty-five per cent (wage increases awarded by negotiation on a percentage basis at this time only widened the gap since women's basic pay was less than that of male workers). She thought it was a disgrace that the Labour government should be the one to turn down equal pay after having made political capital out of it for so many years. The time was ripe during a manpower shortage to institute the principle—especially since in some instances in order to attract men to jobs where women were paid on piece rates it was suggested that the rate for the job should be increased.[33]

That the TUC policy line was maintained within the Women's Conference was due in no small measure to the powers of Miss Florence Hancock. For this reason September 1947 marked an important milestone for women trade unionists, for during that month by means of seniority and the rotation system used by the TUC Florence Hancock (1893–1974) became Chairman of the TUC General Council, the first woman to actually serve in that position—she had indeed come a long way. From the age of twelve Miss Hancock worked from seven in the morning to nine at night as a dishwasher in a café with a salary of 3s. a week and board. When fourteen she started work at 5s. 9d. a week at a Nestlé's milk factory in Chippenham until she reached 8s. 9d. at the age of twenty-one. Here she worked a fifty-five hour week. Following the death of both her parents she managed to keep herself, two brothers and a sister on these low wages.

Miss Hancock first became a trade unionist in 1913 in the Workers' Union. She was the only girl of twenty workers to attend an organising meeting of the union which saw two of its leaders fired but later reinstated. Within a fortnight a strike resulted over the issue of overtime pay during summer which was favourably resolved and also resulted in women receiving a minimum of 12s. a week pay. In 1917 Miss Hancock became

District Officer for Wiltshire which meant cycling hundreds of miles organising industrial and agricultural workers. She would always retain a pleasant west country burr in her voice.

After serving as District Officer in Gloucester and Bristol Miss Hancock became a member of the TUC General Council in 1935 and from 1942 to 1958 held the post of T&GWU National Women's Officer. She was reserved and considered by some a trifle aloof.

When the *Report of the Royal Commission on Equal Pay* was first made public in 1946 representatives of the AEU, USDAW, T&GWU and others at the ACUCWW Women's Conference were not only critical of Chancellor of the Exchequer Hugh Dalton and his plea that equal pay would be inflationary, but also criticised the new leaders of the trade union movement, who replaced those who had gone into government service, for failing to meet the needs of workers.[34] It was suggested that a deputation be sent to Mr Dalton to show him that the time for pious resolution was past and that action was demanded. Miss Hancock turned down the idea and instead advised placing their proposal before the TUC General Council. An attempt to change the Standing Orders of the Conference to make the Conference a policy-making rather than advisory body was rejected.[35] This decision doomed the ACUCWW to a position as an ineffectual sounding board for women's trade unionism. They were in effect isolated and outnumbered by male trade unionists. Women's leadership, the men's attitude, the state of the economy and government regulation all conspired to frustrate change.

It was Miss Hancock's difficult task at the ACUCWW in 1948 to urge the delegates to place national economic policy before the drive for equal pay. In 1948, 1949 and 1950 Miss Ethel Chipcase (Railway Clerk's Association) moved a compromise resolution supporting equal pay but not specifying a date for implementation. This was referred by the WAC to the Economic Committee of the TUC, which replied 'that a further approach to the government would be inappropriate at the present time'.[36] This brings us to an important point: much of the work done by the TUC was departmentalised and many issues affecting women which might have been handled by the Women's Advisory Committee were already within the province of the Economic Committee, Social Insurance Committee, the

Trade Boards Committee and the Education Committee. Also even while the TUC had passed a resolution in favour of equal pay very early in its existence, action to promote it rested with the affiliated unions who were more concerned to promote the interests of men.

In 1950 a proposal for the immediate introduction of equal pay by the National Union of Bank Employees was defeated, but the TUC General Council endorsed the principle of equal pay by a vote of 4,490,000 to 2,367,000. Nevertheless, once again equal pay for the 'common classes' of the public service was rejected by Hugh Gaitskell, Chancellor of the Exchequer.[37] The TUC represented its policy as one of increasing real wages rather than money wages. Later Miss Hancock praised the results achieved during the two years of TUC-supported wage restraint in increasing the productivity of industry, expanding export trade, closing the dollar gap, maintaining full employment and providing the means of meeting the still increasing costs of social services. Thus while a general scramble for wage advances on the principle of every union for itself had been avoided, some wage improvements had been made. By normal collective bargaining wages and salaries rose £670 million in 1948, £340 million in 1949 and £300 million in 1950, while productivity in 1950 was six and a half per cent higher than the previous year and nearly three times higher than predicted by the Economic Survey in 1949.[38]

The growth of white collar trade unionism after World War II could provide some awkward moments at the ACUCWW. In 1950 when some members urged the establishment of local liaison committees with the Labour Party to help with recruiting trade union members, Mrs I. Diffley (NUBE) took exception to stressing party politics at a trade union conference, explaining that the NUBE had no party affiliation and was not a worse member of the trade union movement because of it. Ethel Chipchase disagreed, feeling that since most unions were affiliated to the Labour Party there could be nothing wrong in even closer co-operation.[39]

Maintaining one's commitment to the Labour Party, TUC General Council and ACUCWW policy was often difficult for other members of the rank and file as well. An example was the occasion in 1949 when the militant Miss Horan expressed concern that many more men than women were entering the Factory Inspectorate due to the high standard set by the Civil Service Commission's examination—a standard beyond the normal working girl. Her complaint was answered both by its chairman Miss Hancock and by Mr A. Roberts (Amalgamated Association of Card, Blowing and Ring Operatives) who quickly challenged her logic. She was told that women had no right to demand both equality and preferential treatment and that the TUC had already secured the lowering of the educational standard and increased the age range but there were still forty-seven vacancies.[40]

Miss Hancock's career was a microcosm of the women's trade union movement during the period 1914–51. Beginning as a member of an out group, educated in the school of trade union politics during the 1920s and 1930s, she rose to prominence in the TUC establishment as a woman's leader in Ernest Bevin's powerful T&GWU. During the war she was Chairman of the WAC (1941 44) and again during 1948–52; for her many services she was showered with honours, an OBE in 1943, a CBE in 1946 and a DBE in 1951. She presided as chairman of the TUC General Council 1947–48 during a period when the Labour Party was in power. She even managed to help hold the reins on the equal pay movement in the interests of national recovery but at the expense of raising the status of the ACUCWW.

8

Equal Pay At Last
In A Stop-Go Economy

In 1970 the passage of the Equal Pay Act achieved one of the most important and long sought-after goals of women trade unionists. Its enactment took place not during the Age of Austerity, which had ended in the mid-fifties, but during a period of prosperity and low unemployment. However in the late fifties and sixties the British economy continued to be plagued by the problem of the international balance of payments. This resulted in a continuance of the managed economy instituted following World War II. Its chief characteristics were deflationary 'stop' policies aimed at halting inflation, or expansionist 'go' policies designed to stimulate production and maintain full employment. Despite monetary fluctuations, unemployment did remain remarkably low and the number of women trade unionists doubled—increasing from 1,322,000 to 2,613,139 between 1950 and 1974. The proportion of women in the TUC also soared from 15.4 to 26 per cent. By 1974 nearly

	1950	1970	Increase
Nat'l U. of Public Employees	40,000	173,000	133,000
Amal. U. of Engr. Workers	35,000	125,000	90,000
T&GWU	129,000	213,000	84,000
NUGMW	152,000	220,000	68,000
Civil & Public Services Ass.	73,000	117,000	44,000
Clerical & Admin. Workers U.	16,000	52,000	36,000
Electrical Electronic Tele-communication U.	5,000	41,000	36,000
Nat'l U. of Bank Employees	7,000	41,000	34,000
USDAW	136,000	158,000	22,000
U. of Post Office Workers	34,000	50,000	16,000[2]

a third of all women workers, compared to about half of all male workers, were in unions.[1] One of the major reasons for this phenomenal growth was the affiliation to the TUC of a number of white collar unions as can be seen from this list of the ten unions recording the largest increases in women's membership between 1950 and 1970.

One of the largest increases took place in 1969 when the total number of women trade unionists grew by 326,000 partly as the result of the affiliation of 212,000 members of the National Union of Teachers.

During this period two of the most influential women trade union leaders who aided in the growth of membership were Anne Godwin (1898–   ) and Margaret McKay (1911–   ). Appropriately Miss Godwin came from the rank of the white collar workers and started her career in the counting-house of a West End store at the age of sixteen earning 5s. for a six-day, forty-nine hour week, with tea and lunch provided. She later worked as a civilian clerk in the Army pay corps. At this time Miss Godwin requested a raise but was told by the officer that it was impossible unless she was in a union. She next worked as a stenographer in an engineering office and in 1920 joined the Association of Women Clerks and Secretaries. In 1924 Miss Godwin helped organise the extension of suffrage to women under thirty,[3] and in 1926 was one of the few women present at the TUC when it voted for the General Strike. In 1930 she joined the Clerical and Administrative Workers Union and later became General Secretary in 1941 of a union numbering 60,000 members. Though Miss Godwin gave vigorous support to its strike of the Automobile Association, she generally preferred arbitration to strikes.

Miss Godwin resembled a grey-haired headmistress; was well read and served on the Carr-Saunders Committee on Commercial Education. Miss Godwin's 'gentle-firmness' was instanced by her expulsion of the communist-dominated ETU from the TUC.[4] Her hobbies were collecting china and dancing and she was not intimidated by male members of the TUC. In September 1961 she became the third woman 'elected' Chairman of the TUC by means of the seniority rule.

One of the obstacles to trade union growth in the immediate post-war period among some white collar workers was the actions of Wages Councils, National Arbitration Tribunals and Industrial Courts upon whom workers relied for wage increases. These bodies also perpetuated the practice of unequal pay by awarding unequal wage increases to women. A way around this practice was the process of leap-frogging by which a Wages Council would set a wage minimum but a union would then secure a higher rate by collective bargaining. This wage rate then would be used to justify setting that level as the new Wages Council minimum and so forth. In order to practise leap-frogging a union had to win the right to collective bargaining. USDAW succeeded in obtaining collective bargaining for its members as the result of a fortnight's strike against George Masons, a subsidiary of International Tea in September 1951. The strike spread from South Wales to over 1,400 shops in London and Birmingham and established as a right that the existence of a statutory minimum did not preclude the right to collective bargaining. These efforts helped stimulate organisation. Later in 1961 and again beginning in South Wales USDAW succeeded in organising the F. W. Woolworth chain. Passage in 1963 of the Offices, Shops and Railway Premises Act which extended to shops and offices many of the regulations on heating, lavatories and lighting included in factories was another notable victory.[5]

While trade unionism expanded in the white collar sector of the economy another area ripe for trade union growth was the engineering industry. In 1951 out of a total of 22,250,000 workers in Britain, 7,250,000 were women and over 750,000 were in the engineering and associated industries.[6] That year the TUC launched a new effort to increase the number of women trade unionists. A special leaflet *Times Change* was circulated and a supplement to the TUC monthly journal *Labour* was initiated entitled *Notebook*. A one-week residential school for women at Ruskin College, Oxford was held for three years in succession and attended by 120 women.[7] In addition a series of TUC Women's Weekend Schools were held for rank and file members to teach them about trade union principles and methods of operation.

One of the leaders responsible for these and other innovative recruiting methods was Mrs Margaret McKay, a lively dark-eyed Irishwoman from Lancashire. During this period Mrs McKay produced *Women's Angle*, the AEU women's journal and also the women's pages of the shop assistants' magazine *New Dawn*. Her mother had been a weaver and her father a cotton spinner who died of tuberculosis at the age of twenty-nine. After starting work in a mill at the age of thirteen, she and her mother emigrated to the United States. This afforded her another standard of comparison but because of her mother's loneliness she returned to Lancashire, only to suffer from unemployment. In frustration she joined the Communist Party, visited Russia in 1927, 1928 and 1931, and studied at the Offices of the Red International of Labour Unions. In 1929 she was a leader of the Women's Hunger March to London. During the 1930s she broke with the Communist Party because of its ruthless methods and became an organiser of foreign workers for the T&GWU and later national organiser for the Civil Service Clerical Association.[8]

Mrs McKay became Chief Woman Officer of the TUC in 1950 and during her tenure helped stimulate union growth through the use of fashion shows, make-up lessons, outings for children, trade union schools and dances.[9] The National Union of Bank Employees also experienced similar success, interesting young women in trade unionism by hair style competitions, beauty and cooking demonstrations and above all rock 'n roll parties.[10] Mrs McKay's energetic organising efforts during this period were hampered by attempts by the TUC to subordinate the Women's Department to the Organisation Department where it would have become a small sub-section. The Organisation Department was run by Ray Boyfield, a university man, ambitious and an office empire builder. Mrs McKay waged an eleven-year cold war with Boyfield to maintain what little status the Women's Department was allowed. Her efforts were not aided by the fact that her brother had clashed with TUC Secretary George Woodcock while at Ruskin College. Mrs McKay and Woodcock had bitter quarrels over her efforts to secure trade union conditions and representation for members of the staff above typist level to whom up until then, union membership only had been permitted. At the time her annual salary was £1,150— less than any affiliated union paid their chief women officers. Woodcock and the General Council opposed her efforts to organise the staff and in 1962 she retired to work in public relations for Unilever.[11] She later served as a Labour MP for Clapham from 1964 to 1970 and was United Kingdom delegate to the United Nations Economic and Social Council's Commission on the status of women in 1965.[12]

Throughout the fifties and sixties the number of women trade unionists continued to increase and by 1974 they outnumbered men in eleven unions—six of these were predominantly white collar. These included:

	Women	Men	Total
Nat'l U. of Hosiery & Knitwear Workers	52,183	19,528	71,711
Nat'l U. of Tailor & Garment Workers	101,190	15,723	116,913
Ceramic & Allied Trade U.	20,436	18,229	38,665
USDAW	184,248	142,215	326,463
TobaccoWorkers U.	13,726	7,179	20,905
Nat'l U. of Public Employees	294,640	175,532	370,172
Conf. of Health Serv. Employees	80,722	40,428	121,150
Nat'l U. of Teachers	186,146	64,258	250,404
Civil & Public Serv. Ass.	147,549	68,153	215,702
Inland Revenue Staffs Fed.	30,309	22,776	53,085
Professional, Executive, Clerical & Computer Staffs Ass.	68,678	58,630	127,308[13]

The triumph of the Conservative Party in the 1951 election did not bring an end to the close co-operation between the TUC General Council and the government. Arthur Deakin, Secretary of the T&GWU, while not advocating a wages standstill, warned of the need to continue wage restraints,[14] and the General Council defeated efforts by left-wing unions to end wage restraints. However it rejected government attempts by Sir Godfrey Ince, Permanent Secretary of the Ministry of Labour, to initiate arbitration as a last resort in their negotiating procedure. As Dr Pelling observed, 'It was perhaps paradoxical, but it was inevitable, that the Conservative hopes of solving one of the most important economic problems with which they were faced should founder on the individualism of the trade union leaders'. Wage restraints did not last long and the mid-fifties saw an increase of disputes; many were unofficial or demarcation strikes. Chief among these were strikes involving the Hull dockers in August 1954, the

Merseyside in March 1955 when the T&GWU played an active part, another affecting the printing industry, the AEU and the Electrical Trades Union in 1955, and the Railwaymen and the Locomotive Engineers in the same year.[15]

As a result of these disputes the public reputation of unions went into decline. As early as 1953 the *Daily Worker* complained that the popular press was blaming trade unions for lower productivity and increasing the cost of living by demands for increased wages.[16] Women workers also took umbrage to what they considered unwarranted criticism from journalists and complained about the unfavourable image of women workers presented on BBC TV.[17] The late fifties was an age of self-criticism and satire epitomised by the popular programme 'The Rag Trade' whose shop steward heroine's motto 'Blow the whistle, and everybody out' was also taken to task for its portrayal of women trade unionists. They could hardly be faulted since oppressed segments of society intent on reform rarely enjoy a laugh at their own expense; although other women trade unionists were less thin skinned.[18]

The year 1955 marked a turning point in TUC leadership with the death of the influential, moderate Secretary of the T&GWU, Arthur Deakin. He was replaced by Frank Cousins, whose rhetoric at least was that of a left-wing militant. The late fifties were marked by the increasing influence of shop stewards and their committees especially among the motor, coal, docks, shipbuilding and engineering unions. The period also witnessed a struggle for power between left-wing and right-wing trade unionists within the TUC for control of the so called Big Six Unions (NUR, AEU, T&GWU, NUGMW, Mineworkers and USDAW). In the AEU the struggle was waged between the anti-communist William Carron and Hugh Scanlon a left-winger. Both supported women's equal pay claims but it is difficult to determine the proportion of women who favoured either leader or the attitude of women trade unionists towards communism.

The fifties witnessed continued contraction in the cotton industry, with unemployment reaching fifty per cent by 1952.[19] To permit greater use of the expensive machinery necessary to compete in international trade in 1955 a double day shift system was instituted and by May 1968 the industry resorted to treble and evening shifts. From 1952, when the number of members in the Amalgamation was 89,465, membership contracted to 55,647 in 1960 and 33,066 in 1968. The 1968 figure represented roughly one-third of the 92,540 workers in the industry. On the plus side average wages in the industry rose from 130s. per week in 1951 to 308s. per week in 1968.[20] Unfortunately much of the value of these wage increases was eaten up by inflation. In 1955 alone the cost of living increased by six per cent. The Conservative government's policy of reducing food subsidies and ending the granting of relief in direct taxation brought hardship to low income families.

Though the end of the Korean War in 1952–53 eased inflationary pressures a bit, trade unions opted to seek wage increases to make up for past restraint. Typically in 1953 the women in the engineering industry got a 6s. 5d. a week increase for a forty-hour week.[21] Though their increase did not equal that of male workers, they were thankful for it because for some it would reduce the necessity of weekend work. Soon, some women became aware that every round of wage increases set off another in prices, resulting in little gain in real wages. Increased costs for government services such as day nurseries were passed on to women workers and also had the effect of reducing net wage gains.[22] Overall from 1950 to 1961 personal income rose 106 per cent while retail prices went up fifty-four per cent.

Working mothers faced other problems. The emergence of juvenile delinquency as a social problem during the fifties somehow made them a target for blame from some moralists baffled by the phenomenon.[23] By 1960 there were close to four million married women working, a figure representing fifty-two per cent of all working women. The development of household appliances and processed foods made domestic work less taxing and the invention of the Pill enabled women to plan their careers with greater assurance. The figures for both single and married women workers also increased. For instance in the engineering industry over sixty-six per cent of the assemblers and press workers and stampers, forty-four per cent of the inspectors and testers and twenty-two per cent of the production process workers were women. Women comprised fifty-two per cent of clerical and administrative workers, stenographers, typists and office machine operators, while two-thirds of the workers in packing, bookbinding, pottery finishing, telephone services, laundries, catering services, office cleaning and lodging housekeeping were women.[24]

In 1959 the boom began to slow down and unemployment reached its highest point since World War II. A £455 million surplus in balance of payments dwindled to a deficit by 1960 causing the government to recommend a pay pause in 1961 implemented by the National Economic Development Council or Neddy. One outcome was the announcement in the summer of 1961 by Prime Minister Macmillan of Britain's application for membership in the Common Market or European Economic Community. Because of steps taken in 1961 by the Conservative government to restore the balance of payments, unemployment in 1962–63 climbed to 878,000. Deflationary policies always hurt women workers more than men because they were usually low on the seniority list. Out of frustration with government policies, Bessie Braddock, MP, and a member of the Liverpool Trades Council, led a march of women through the streets of London raising the cry of 'We Want Work'.[25] Women trade unionists even disputed official figures for unemployment during the boom period prior to 1959 because they did not include married women who had lost their jobs and had not registered at unemployment exchanges.[26]

In the midst of the pay pause of 1962 the AEU citing an increase in the cost of living called for a reduction in hours and an increase in pay for both men and women. To high-light their claims, a series of one-day strikes were staged in February and March of 1962. With the government's pay pause scheduled to come to an end in March 1962, Selwyn Lloyd, Chancellor of the Exchequer, decided to modify the policy to allow for a moderate and orderly advance which was interpreted as a two and one-half per cent increase.[27]

When women trade unionists were not fighting to keep up with the cost of living they sometimes fought among themselves. In 1961 there was a split between single and married women trade unionists over whether employers should make special arrangements to adjust the hours of married women to help them look after their families after school hours. Miss Nan Whitelaw (Post Office Union) objected that these 'privileges' would cause an extra burden on unmarried workers and make a mockery of the claim for equal pay. She made the point that single women also had responsibilities with relatives. The dispute was ended when Mrs S. Bird (National Union of Hosiery

Workers) reminded her sisters that 'we are busy fighting the men. Let us not show divisions among ourselves'.[28]

Nevertheless, women in fact had allies among men in the labour movement who sought to provide structural improvements in the TUC. In 1961 two male members of the LCC Staff Association audaciously proposed at a TUC meeting at Portsmouth to end the separate meetings of ACUCWW since it tended to produce only secondary emphasis upon the matters that emanated from it. Citing the example of the public service unions who had recently obtained equal pay for their women members they urged that equal pay could be achieved only by the full weight of the TUC. Their suggestion was not accepted. Miss Ellen McCullough of the TUC General Council defended the existence of the ACUCWW as an essential forum for discussing equal pay and improving trade union organisation among women.

Equal pay for public service employees became effective in 1961 but progress towards that end actually started with the temporary relaxation of controls in the early fifties. In 1952 the Labour-controlled London County Council introduced equal pay for its common classes. Their example was followed the next year by the other local governments represented on the National Industrial Council. In 1954 R. A. Butler, Chancellor of the Exchequer, after meeting with a deputation of the Equal Pay Campaign Committee, decided to begin its implementation in the civil service in 1955. To ease its effect on government finances, equal pay would be phased into effect over the next six years, however this applied only to England and Wales and did not include 'non-industrial' workers such as manual workers or telephone operators. Between September and June 1962 the latter group worked 'to rule' and finally were also included. Therefore the equal pay programme only applied to jobs undertaken by both men and women. Jobs performed exclusively by women (typists for example) were not included. The implementation of equal pay in government by the Conservatives mainly stemmed from pressure exerted by white collar unions, a 'middle-class' constituency whose votes the Tories traditionally courted.[29] For the remainder of the fifties and sixties neither political party, when in power, was able to further extend equal pay.

In April 1954 women engineers opened the door a crack to equal pay as the result of their claim to the Engineering and

Allied Employers Federation for a wage not less than the average male labourer's rate, which would be at least a step forward even if it was not equal pay.[30] The claim was made again in December of 1955. It was rejected. The Minister of Labour also refused to set up a Court of Inquiry but called upon the unions to negotiate the question with the Employers Federation.[31] Out of these discussions came the agreement of 19 December 1956 between the employers and the five unions covering women in the engineering industry modifying Clause 6 of the 1940 Extended Employment of Women Agreement.[32] The change reduced the waiting period for women able to work without additional supervision or assistance when they replaced a man from twenty-six to eight weeks before they received the men's rate for women doing men's work. The Agreement that became effective 27 May 1957 brought the average weekly rate for women to approximately 141s. a week for a 41.2 hour week and by 1959 the hourly rate for women engineers was 77.4 per cent that of males.[33]

Nevertheless, the average earnings of women in all industries between October 1959 and October 1961 decreased from fifty-two to fifty per cent of male workers, but since World War II some progress had been made.[34] A survey made by USDAW in 1960 listed twenty-one trades in which women and men were paid the rate for the job, while in ninety other trades women were paid seventy per cent or more; whereas in thirty-six of these in 1938 they were paid only fifty-six to sixty-five per cent.[35] By 1961 according to the National Women's Advisory Conference the climate for equal pay had worsened and employers opposition became hardened. Of forty-eight unions, containing seventy-seven per cent of those affiliated to the TUC who replied to a survey, nineteen said they got equal pay but half of these were civil service, while the remaining twenty-nine indicated they held out little hope of progress to equal pay.[36]

A major breakthrough took place in 1963 when the Confederation of Shipbuilding and Engineering Unions obtained a settlement giving women 1s. 6d. and men 1s. Another favourable sign was the agreement in the wholesale tailoring trade giving 1s. 6½d. in the pound to men and 2s. 3d. to women. Also as of March 1964 women received an increase in the boot and shoe industry of 7s. and men 5s. a week.[37]

Part of the reason for progress on the equal pay issue during the sixties came from the efforts of Mrs C. Marie Patterson (1935–   ) Woman Officer of the T&GWU. She had read classics at the University of London but decided against teaching and became a shorthand typist at the T&GWU in 1956. Her advancement was rapid and in March 1963 she was elected CWO of the T&GWU and in the same year became a member of the TUC General Council. Mrs Patterson was its only member with a university education. She was also able to mix her union work with married life as the wife of an insurance man.[38]

In 1974 she became President and Chairperson of the TUC and served on a host of other committees. At that time only one other woman was on the General Council and there was only one other woman officer out of 500 in the T&GWU. Though Mrs Patterson realised that women were often patronised with a type of tokenism she viewed it as her duty to use her post to further the cause of women's rights legislation. One of the major obstacles to be overcome was the problem of enabling more women to serve in executive positions in unions at the time of their life when most appointments were made; unfortunately a time when most women were least likely to be in the labour market. Thus it was particularly important to provide maternity benefits, nurseries and other facilities for working women who otherwise would be forced to the sidelines. Progress in this area was difficult because unions tended to consider fringe benefits as secondary to wage improvements.[39]

Another significant event during the sixties was the preparation in 1963 of an *Industrial Charter for Women* by the ACUCWW at the instigation of Mrs O. Smart, National Union of Tailor and Garment Workers. It was similar to a Charter adopted by the NUTGW[40] and called for : (1) equal pay based on the value of the job done and not on the sex of the worker, (2) opportunities for promotion for women, (3) apprenticeship schemes for girls in appropriate industries, (4) improved opportunities for training young women for skilled work, (5) re-training facilities for older women who return to industry, and (6) special care for the health and welfare of women workers.[41] The ACUCWW requested the next Labour government to implement the Charter within a specific period and ratify the ILO Convention 100. Nevertheless some delegates were impatient and vented their displeasure.

Mrs M. Veitch (NUGMW) called for something to be done to implement equal pay beyond endlessly passing resolutions. This practice, dating back to 1888, was obviously futile. Mrs E. M. Austin (LCCSA) urged increased militancy by forming a special committee on equal pay and opportunity, the use of newspaper publicity, marches and a rally in Trafalgar Square, and by picketing outside firms when negotiations for equal pay were taking place. Others urged that equal pay was but half the question and that equal promotion and training were just as important.[42]

Progress was made the following year in part of the engineering industry during negotiations between the Confederation of Shipbuilding and Engineering Union and Engineering Employers Confederation. Mrs Patterson succeeded in inserting into the National Agreement a provision that the minimum adult rate should apply to adult women. It recognised three distinct classes of women's labour—unskilled, semi-skilled and skilled—and that women doing skilled work would be paid the male rate. The Agreement was to be instituted over a three years period, but in 1968 a dispute between the Confederation of Shipbuilding and Engineering Union and the Engineers and Allied Employers Federation was settled by an agreement giving women a smaller settlement than men. Mrs Veitch, Chief Woman Officer of the NUGMW accused the Confederation of selling the women down the river. Her views had a marked influence on Barbara Castle, Secretary of State for Employment and Productivity and were important in generating the momentum leading to the passage of the Equal Pay Act in 1970.[43]

Help from the Labour government to implement the Woman's Charter was not immediately forthcoming for after its victory at the polls in 1964 it faced the same economic problems as its predecessor. In December the government's newly instituted National Board for Prices and Incomes decided to limit the norm for wage increases to three and a half per cent with the exception of increases in productivity in areas where workers had been exceptionally ill-paid or where there was a national need to stimulate recruitment. In spite of the loop-holes this afforded, Ray Gunter, Minister of Labour, chose not to institute equal pay and instead appointed an inter-department committee to consider its effects. Its findings were kept secret. Once again the TUC General Council had to place a higher priority on support for the Labour government than on demands for equal pay. By 1965 it had dropped support for the ILO Convention 100, calling instead for equal pay on piece work through negotiations at the local level.[44] In spite of this the TUC Women's Advisory Conference continued its efforts to have it implemented and a number of resolutions were moved to oppose the Labour government's wage freeze. Mrs Christine Page (USDAW) called for a mass deputation in the spirit of the suffragettes and it was only with difficulty that Miss W. Baddeley (AEU), Chairman of the National Women's Advisory Council, was able to contain these efforts by reminding the militants that only the TUC could authorise such a move.[45]

In the meantime a Royal Commission was set up in 1965 under the chairmanship of Lord Donovan to try to deal with the problem of industrial relations and particularly unofficial strikes called by shop stewards. Before it could present its findings a strike by the National Union of Seamen in May-July 1966 coupled with a sterling crisis in July 1966 resulted in the enactment in August of a Prices and Incomes Act freezing both prices and incomes. As a result Frank Cousins resigned from the Cabinet in opposition to compulsory government regulation to return to his old position as Secretary of the T&GWU. In 1968 a New Act imposed a ceiling of three and a half per cent on wage increases and empowered the Prices and Incomes Board to postpone increases for twelve months. This increased alienation between the Labour government and the TUC. In April 1968 Ray Gunter was replaced at the Ministry of Labour by Mrs Barbara Castle, a past advocate of equal pay, and a new Department of Employment and Productivity was established. In June the Donovan Commission Report was published and at about the same time a strike took place at the Ford Motor Company (Dagenham) which was a microcosm of many of the symptoms of industrial unrest which the Donovan Commission investigated—the role of shop stewards, demarcation disputes, sanctions, plus the problem of equal pay. The Donovan Report side-stepped most of these issues and assumed a laissez-faire position that there was little the state could do except advise disputants through a Commission for Industrial Relations. It viewed unofficial strikes as symptoms of a failure to devise institutions in keeping with changing needs.[46] It was an open invitation to continued industrial unrest.

The Dagenham strike began 6 June 1968 when some 187 women sewing machinists, led by their shop steward Mrs Rose Boland, struck for a 5d. an hour raise and for upgrading from semi-skilled B to skilled C ratings. At the Ford Halewood plant in Liverpool 200 other machinists called a sympathy strike. They received the official backing of the Amalgamated Union of Engineering and Foundry Workers Executive on 11 June. A recommendation was made by the Ford National Joint Committee (on which all unions with workers at Ford were represented : the leading union was T&GWU with forty-three per cent of the workers, followed by the AEF with the second largest percentage) to set up a five-man fact-finding committee under an independent chairman. It was rejected by the women and later also by the shop stewards of the Dagenham Body Plant. The women also received financial support from the Annual Conference of the National Union of Vehicle Builders to which most of the women machinists belonged. Ford Motor officials claimed that the NUVB had ignored their collective agreement with the company during the dispute to which William Kirkup (AEF) responded that equal pay was a fundamental principle, regardless of the sanctity of an agreement.

The dispute threw 5,000 workers out of work. It would have cost Ford £125,000 a year to implement the workers' demands or ten per cent of the cost of the strike to the company each day. On 1 July the strike was called off, after the majority of the trade union members of the National Joint Negotiating Committee, representing a minority of the workers, accepted a rise of 7d. an hour giving them ninety-two per cent of the male rate compared with the former eighty-five per cent and a phased agreement for equal pay for all women workers.[47] A Court of Enquiry headed by Sir Jack Scamp was appointed by Barbara Castle, Minister of the Department of Productivity, to investigate the dispute. Although the AEF claimed that the controversy revolved around equal pay for women, the Court concluded that it was about the grading of women. It viewed the action by the AEF as a serious breach of their obligations in declaring their official support for a strike which at that stage had not been presented or tabled by the National Joint Negotiating Committee. Ford's judgment was censured in negotiating, concurrently

with a return to work, an important change in the wage structure which had been decided on nine months earlier on the
basis that it should, save for exceptional circumstances, stand
for two years. The Court rejected complaints by the machinists
that their job profile (characteristics on which a job is evaluated)
was singled out for discriminatory treatment. Blame was laid for
the dispute at the door of a joint committee earlier recommending higher profile markings on five elements of the job, but it had
not been informed that their views were not accepted by another
joint committee which considered all of the completed profiles.
The Court recommended that a committee of management-
union representatives look into the matter of the five points under
dispute in the job profile.[48] The women deemed the Scamp
Report a waste of time and placed a ban on all overtime until
the issue was resolved.[49] It was not until 1974 that twelve out
of the 300 women were classed as skilled workers. In retrospect
the Dagenham strike epitomised the type of unofficial strike
which the Donovan Report viewed as caused by the failure to
keep pace with changing needs. For women the strike proved the
spark for greater pressure for equal pay.

A four weeks strike caused by a demarcation dispute in the
Girling brake factory rendered several auto companies idle later
in the year and in desperation in January 1969 Mrs Castle,
attempting to cope with the continued industrial unrest, published a White Paper, *In Place of Strife*, calling for a twenty-eight
days conciliation pause to delay walkouts, imposed settlements
in jurisdictional disputes that union leaders were unable to settle,
fines for unionists who defied a government order; and ordering
unions to hold a secret ballot whenever a major strike was
threatened. However, labour contracts were not to be made
legally binding and the attempt to implement these proposals in
an Industrial Relations Bill was unsuccessful, with Mrs Castle
backing down in the face of TUC opposition.[50]

The Dagenham strike occurred shortly after the British
Women's Liberation Movement was born in late 1967. The Movement was inspired by the outburst of American radical politics
in the 1960s; women's rights groups like Mothers in Action and
the Open Door International and the labour movement. The
Women's Liberation Movement received considerable publicity
from books like *The Female Eunuch* by Germaine Greer and

other elements of the media. At the 1969 TUC Conference the
T&GWU threw its weight firmly behind equal pay when it
used one of the two resolutions to which it was entitled to put
that issue before Congress.[51] In the same year the Trade Union
and Labour National Joint Action Committee for Equal
Women's Rights was established to campaign for equal pay
outside of the TUC and in May 1969 a march of over 1,000
women demanded that Parliament enact an equal pay bill which
received the support of Lady Summerskill.[52] It superseded the
Equal Pay Campaign Committee formerly led by Mrs Joyce
Butler, MP. It was in 1969 that the Institute of Personnel Management produced a comprehensive policy for the consideration
of the Department of Employment and Productivity.

Britain's possible entry into the Common Market was an
external stimulus for equal pay throughout the sixties. Article
119 of the Treaty of Rome required member nations to implement equal pay by 3 December 1964; however, by 1969 although
the six nations had made progress they still had a long way to
go. These nations were still ahead of Britain, where pay for
women compared with men was 59.5 per cent against the figure
for Germany at 69.3 per cent, Belgium 67 per cent, Italy 73.7
per cent and France 75.4 per cent.[53] In 1962 the British figure
had been 50 per cent, Germany 64 per cent, Belgium 57 per cent
and France 85 per cent. Clearly while equal pay legislation was
helpful it was no panacea. Among two million British women
in the manufacturing industry the 1969 average gross weekly
pay was £11 14s. 8d. while for men it was £23 18s. 5d.

The climate of opinion was indeed propitious for passage
of an Equal Pay Bill and in 1970 Mrs Castle managed to pilot
it through parliament. The Bill received royal assent in the last
hours of the Labour government; it gave women the right to
receive the same pay as men if their jobs were the same or
similar, or if their job was rated as equivalent in value. If the
employer refused, the employee had recourse to an industrial
tribunal. Pensions, retirement age and any special treatment
accorded to women in connection with birth were excluded.[54]

It was predicted by officials of the Department of Employment and Productivity that the direct cost to industry would be
between three and five per cent by 1975. While admitting that
it was morally right some employers vigorously opposed the Bill,

G

disagreeing with these figures, claiming that increases would reach thirty to forty-five per cent. Obviously the costs varied from industry to industry and in some probably would reach thirty-two per cent. The CBI claimed the difference between men's and women's wages was twenty per cent and that the increase in the annual wage bill would be over £1,000 million and that the direct cost would be six per cent.[55] Nevertheless the CBI also supported the Bill objecting only to the timing of its implementation.

A number of other results were forecast when the law went into effect: (1) That firms using cheap labour would be forced to automate to survive, (2) that male workers would receive proportionally smaller increments in their wages than the women working on the same job, (3) that there would be a large rise in union membership and thereby an increase in their bank balances and their power and (4) that some women might be dismissed because of their unwillingness to accept shift work.[56] The first and the last of these points had the greatest impact on women.

The issue of night work was one already under consideration by the Women's Advisory Committee, in 1965, in order to ready itself for the possible demand that the logic of equal pay carried with it the abandoning of women's protected status. The prohibition against night work for women dated from 1850 with its most recent amendment in the Factories Act (1961). It prohibited women from working more than eleven hours a day or finishing work later than 8 p.m. with the exception of women who cleaned factories. The fact that the Act applied only to women working in factories and not to non-manual labour such as nursing, air services, telephonists, etc., made it difficult to defend. In Sweden when the law providing for equal pay went into force the law prohibiting women from working at night was repealed; but later legislation was introduced under which neither men nor women could work at night except on certain essential work.[57] In 1974 only 31,000 women in Britain were exempted by orders allowing night work.[58] The CBI and senior women's rights groups favoured repeal of anti-night work legislation using productivity and anti-paternalism as their arguments while the TUC and Socialist women's liberation groups supported them in the name of health and safety.

On the possible loss of jobs due to automation, if the effect

of equal pay in public services was any example the number of
women workers would increase rather than decline. With a full
employment economy and women more willing to work because
of smaller families, labour-saving devices at home and the desire
for higher living standards, the number of women employed
promised to increase as had been shown by a London School of
Economics survey in 1962.[59]

Although Mrs Patterson led efforts to pass equal pay legislation she never was deluded into thinking it was a cure-all. The
EEC experience convinced her that the battle would be won
on the floor of the factory and office through trade union
strength and improved organisation among women.[60] She
realised that as many as two-thirds of women workers were
unlikely to benefit from the Act. This was true because an overt
discriminatory basic rate could be avoided by the more subtle
tactics of job evaluation (which often gave higher points to such
aspects as muscular strength and less points to female job
characteristics such as dexterity and detailed work), segregation
on sex lines in jobs, use of merit increases, long service increments and overtime bonuses to increase men's earnings.[61] A
more obnoxious method involved scaling down men's rates to
those of women and calling that equal pay.[62] To prevent this,
anti-discrimination legislation was needed to widen training and
job opportunities so that women could escape from low status,
low paid jobs and raise their average earnings closer to the male
rate. Even so women could never equal men's total wages as
long as restrictions on night work and overtime remained. Both
the Tory Government's Green Paper, *Equal Opportunities for
Men and Women*, and the Labour Party's White Paper, *Equality
for Women*, aimed at remedying this defect, even though the
Sex Disqualification (Removal) Act of 1919 already covered some
of the same ground. Because of the large expense in litigation
(£2,000 to £3,000), the law was little used. The Labour Party's
proposal also lumped the Race Relations Board and Equal
Opportunities Commission together in a Human Rights Commission.[63] These proposals were also supported by the CBI.

In 1972 the TUC decided to support unions taking industrial
action to achieve equal pay. Between 1972 and the date of the
implementation of the Equal Pay Act at the beginning of 1976,
a number of strikes of this nature took place. Typical was that

by the Society of Graphical and Allied Trades against the British Printing Industries Federation in September 1973. It obtained wages in some grades reaching within 97½ per cent of the male rate by March 1975. On some occasions women's strikes for equal bonuses, like the one at the Salford Electrical Instruments, Heywood in Lancashire by the AUEW, did not receive the whole-hearted support of men from their own union and even failed to persuade 800 women workers at another Salford plant to come out in their support. Everyone except the AUEW convener crossed the picket line and the women AUEW members soon assailed the men as 'Male Chauvinist Pigs'. [64] The sex war was far from over.

With the equal rights problem on its way to solution, another perennial problem area seemed ready for resolution—the organisation of domestic workers. After organising efforts during the fifties had yielded scant results, changes in the structure of the cleaning industry by the early seventies led to the first strike among the women cleaning workers who had previously proved so difficult to organise. The cause of the strike was the dismissal of two shop stewards attempting to organise women for the T&GWU. Undoubtedly the leader of the cleaners was a thirty-three years old colourful, coarse-tongued communist, May Hobbs, who had been blacklisted for eight years by the cleaning employers. A member of T&GWU since 1962, she accused the male-dominated union of indifference regarding women cleaners at the Workers Control Conference in Birmingham in October 1970. The women involved worked a forty-hour week from 10 p.m. to 6 a.m. for £13. They received no sick pay, and holidays and holiday pay were virtually non-existent.[65] The cleaning companies, Pritchards, Strand, Industrial Contract Cleaners and Initial Services, earned a profit after tax of £2,797,100 in 1969.[66]

The strike took place from the 3rd to the 10th of November and received support from the London Socialist Woman Group and Women's Liberation Workshop. The strike was settled when the two stewards were reinstated. The Union aimed to achieve the following demands : £16 minimum wage, full sick pay, union recognition, one day holiday for every month worked and adequate staffing on all buildings.[67] After some later success in organising women in government buildings and achieving better pay and conditions, May Hobbs's Cleaners' Action Group failed to raise enough money to expand and later a jurisdictional dispute between the NUGMW and T&GWU led to a bitter defeat of cleaning women at the University of Durham. Cleaning women were still difficult to organise but in this wave of organisation it seemed the union's bureaucracy was responsible for its failure.[68]

The passage of the Equal Pay Act had other consequences; some felt that the TUC Women's Conference had outlived its usefulness. In 1972 it discussed whether it should abolish itself but decided a separate Women's Conference was important, especially to assure implementation of the Equal Pay Act. During the debate the main objections to the separate Conference were: (1) While the Conference continued, no progress would be made towards increasing the number of women delegates at the annual Congress, (2) a separate Conference perpetuated the theory that women were second-class trade unionists and that there were women's problems which did not concern workers generally, and (3) the Women's Conference was advisory and because it could not make policy it had the effect of side-tracking women trade unionists.

Those who wished to continue the Conference but who looked forward to the time when it could be abolished made the following points: (1) there was no guarantee that abolishing the Conference would lead to an increase in the number of women delegates to the Annual Congress, (2) other minority groups (e.g. youth) were calling for separate conferences, (3) there were many women's problems which might not find a place on the Congress agenda and on which women did not necessarily want a solution imposed on them by men, (4) if the Conference was dissolved some feared the WAC might also be abolished, (5) the Conference served as an educative body, and (6) the Conference was essential to see that women had equal employment opportunities, to implement equal pay and to deal with problems stemming from entry into the Common Market.[69] While the Conference was not dissolved from the arguments presented, it was clear that women still differed amongst themselves as to the strategy they should adopt and position they should assume in order to attain their rightful place both in industry and in the labour movement.

Conclusion

IN the hundred years after 1874, the women's trade union movement made great strides. From its beginnings as mixed unions in the textile industry and later as small women's unions in the sweated trades it expanded gradually as more women entered an increasing variety of industries for the first time. During the nineteenth century the personality and ideology of its leaders were important factors in shaping its structure and policies—from the individualism of Emma Paterson to the government interventionist attitudes of Lady Dilke. In order to be successful when the economic climate and changes presented opportunities, both the leaders and those of the future had to accommodate their tactics and ideology in ways which would advance the interests of their members without unduly alarming either employers or male trade unionists. Miss MacArthur managed this role very well. A turning point occurred after the end of World War I due to the recession, the amalgamation of the separate women's unions with mixed unions, and the death of Miss MacArthur which deprived the movement of a leader of great genius. The inter-war period saw women trade unionists struggle to establish their identity within both mixed unions and the TUC. Even though the TUC male establishment paid lip service to the aspirations of women trade unionists, most of the male-dominated individual trade unions failed to give equal pay a high priority. After World War II, though the Labour Party favoured its implementation, economic considerations forced enactment of equal pay legislation to be postponed. It took the combined talents of Mrs Castle, from her position within the cabinet, and Mrs Patterson, as T&GWU leader, sparked by the example of the Common Market, the Women's Liberation Movement and what began as an 'unofficial' strike among the Dagenham sewing machinists, to achieve this goal.

In fairness to the other principal leaders during the period from the twenties to the sixties—Miss Bondfield, Miss Varley, Miss Adam, Miss Hancock, Mrs McKay and Miss Godwin— their failure to achieve this one major goal does not reflect upon their talent or dedication to the cause. It is merely another example in history where reputations are made and progress occurs as a result of action by those able to capitalise on the proper combination of circumstances. The other leaders did their best to build on the accomplishments of their predecessors to enable later leaders to deal from strength. The year 1969 was clearly propitious for an idea whose time had come.

It is significant that equal pay was achieved by legislative enactment, for reform legislation had been an important method used by women trade unionists to achieve their goals, ever since the days of Lady Dilke. Progress by negotiations was difficult to attain by women whose position in the labour market was always near the bottom. Protective legislation with regards to shift work or night work is still necessary because of their unique role in the home as cook and baby minder. As the state alleviated social evils among various interest groups in British society by assorted legislative enactments throughout the nineteenth and twentieth centuries, women too were beneficiaries. It was only a matter of time and circumstance before equal pay would be granted by one of the parties seeking power or attempting to stay in power. The morality and logic of their claim and the size of their voting block were too large to ignore indefinitely. Another sign of women's dependence upon legislation was their attitude toward Wages Councils. The USDAW and the NUTGW were reconciled to the role of the Wages Councils even though it seemed like an admission of weakness and reliance upon the state. On the other hand, the T&GWU and the NUGMW who were strong enough to bargain on behalf of most of their members, while acknowledging the importance of the Wages Councils dis-liked them because it was felt they produced a feeling of inferi-ority among members.

Two other factors having an effect on women's trade unionism were technological change and the state of the economy. As work became lighter, the number of women in the engineering industry increased and as the services sector of the economy grew the number of women in the economy increased accordingly. As wages in the blue-collar and blue-blouse industries rose in the period following World War II, due to prosperity and union efforts, increasing numbers of white-collar or black-coated workers dropped their attitudes of disdain towards trade unions and helped increase the strength of what was now no longer a shadow army as in the days of Miss MacArthur.

The economic climate affected both the growth of women's trade unionism and its legislative efforts. As the textile industry contracted so did the number of women in trade unions, but the expansion of the engineering industry made possible the replacement of these losses with new members in the general unions and after 1943 in the AEU. The recession following World War I, the depression, balance of payments crises and various pay pauses also all affected recruitment and the attainment of legislative objectives, such as equal pay, nursery care and pension reform. Some had both positive and negative effects. For example, the balance of payments crises eventually forced Britain into the Common Market and so contributed to the achievement of equal pay, which was required by those seeking membership.

The attitudes of male trade unionists, their leaders and of women themselves also affected the growth of women's trade unionism. After World War II as the result of full employment, men slowly began to regard women as equals and partners rather than as subjects for domination and rivals. Nevertheless, within unions women were usually either discriminated against or they deferred to men as far as leadership positions were concerned. Possessing only token representation on the TUC General Council, and with the WAC relegated to the status of an advisory body, women were still effectively under male control. The same was true in individual trade unions. The T&GWU, in 1968, had 200,000 women members out of 1,460,000 but no members on the Executive Committee. Even though over half of the members of the USDAW were female, of 120 officials it had only two full-time female officials.

Another factor affecting women's trade unionism was the attitude of women themselves that work was only temporary, an interlude and not a career. As a result, women were relegated to low-paid, unskilled, dead-end jobs. It was a circle similar to that described by Miss MacArthur: women were low paid because they were unorganised and unorganised because they were low paid. In this case, women were employed in low-skilled, low-paid work which led to high turn-over and in turn to indifference to trade union organisation. As more women began to look at their jobs as long-term pursuits, aided by day nurseries, their attitude towards union membership changed.

Although activist women trade unionists during the sixties were few in number, more seemed willing to become leaders. Husbands became more tolerant of wives playing a role in union activities. Still rank and file attendance by women at branch meetings remained low, except during crises, even where there was a high percentage of membership, but generally the younger generation seemed more militant than married women and those of the older generation. Whether larger numbers of women will end their deference to males as leaders in mixed unions as the result of a change in female or male attitudes, or by some mandatory quota system, is a question only the future can answer. Separate segregated women's branches are really an admission of inferiority and impotence. In the future, as in the past, any progress made will probably come as was the case with Equal Pay—when women leaders and an aroused rank and file co-operate.

Bibliography

MANUSCRIPT COLLECTIONS

MSS. Papers of Sir Charles W. Dilke, British Museum.
MSS. Lady Dilke's Trade Union Notebook : TUC Library.
MSS. Dr Marion Phillips, Labour Party Archives.
MSS. Standing Joint Committee of Industrial Women's Organ-
isation Minutes Feb. 1916, Sept. 1917. Labour Party Archives.
MSS. 'Gertrude Tuckwell and her *Reminiscences*', Unpublished
work at TUC Library.
MSS. Ellen Wilkinson, Labour Party Archives.
MSS. Beatrice Webb, British Library of Political and Economic
Science.

GOVERNMENT PUBLICATIONS

Katherine Graves Busbey, *The Women's Trade Union Movement in
Great Britain*, Bulletin of the Bureau of Labour, No. 83, Washing-
ton, July 1909.
*Reports on the Employment of Women by the Assistant Lady Com-
missioners, H.C., 1893–94*, XXXVII.
*Women in Industry, Report of War Cabinet Committee on Women
in Industry 1919* (Cmd. 135).
Ministry of Labour Gazette; Employment and Productivity Gazette.
*Report of a Court of Enquiry under Sir Jack Scamp into a
Dispute Concerning Sewing Machinists Employed by the Ford
Motor Company* (Cmd. 349), 1968.

ANNUAL REPORTS, YEARBOOKS AND
BIOGRAPHICAL DICTIONARIES

Bellamy, Joyce M. and John Saville (eds.) *Dictionary of Labour
Biography*, 3 vols., London 1970–76.
Dictionary of National Biography.
Labour Annual.
Open Door Council Annual Reports.
*TUC Report of the Annual Conference of Unions Catering for
Women Workers.*

TUC Conference on Equal Pay, 1973.
TUC Annual Reports of the Trade Union Congress.
TUC Report of Women's Trade Union Conference, 1925–7.
Woman's Rights, Employment in Engineering, 12 Jan. 1973, AEU.
Women's Year Book, 1924.
Women's Protective and Provident League (later *Women's Trade Union League) Annual Reports.*
Women's Trade Union League, Committee Minutes.

BOOKS
Alford, B.W.E., *Depression and Recovery? British Economic Growth, 1918–1939,* London 1972.
Anderson, Michael, *Family Structure in Nineteenth Century Lancashire,* Cambridge 1971.
Askwith, Lord, *Industrial Problems and Disputes,* London 1920.
Askwith, Betty, *Lady Dilke: A Biography,* London 1969.
Baernreither, J.M., *English Association of Working Men,* London 1889.
Bagwell, Philip S., *The Railwaymen: The History of the National Union of Railwaymen,* London 1963.
Banks, Olive and J.A., *Feminism and Family Planning in Victorian Britain,* Liverpool 1964.
Baylis, F.J., *British Wages Councils,* Oxford 1962.
Besant, Annie, *An Autobiography,* London 1895.
Best, Geoffrey, *Mid-Victorian Britain 1851–75,* London 1971.
Beauchamp, Joan, *Women at Work,* London 1937.
Bondfield, Margaret, *Unemployment,* New York 1930.
Bondfield, Margaret, *A Life's Work,* London 1949.
Boucherett, Jesse, 'Provision for Superfluous Women,' *Women's Works and Women's Culture,* ed. by Josephine Butler, London 1869.
Boucherett, Jesse and Blackburn, Helen, *The Condition of Working Women and the Factory Acts,* London 1896.
Branson, Noreen and Heineman, Margot, *Britain in the Nineteen Thirties,* St Albans 1973.
Brockway, A.F., *Bermondsey Story, the Life of Alfred Salter,* London 1949.
Brown, Phelps, *Growth of British Industrial Relations. A Study from the Standpoint of 1906–14,* London 1965.
Bryhner, Samson, *An Account of the Labour and Socialist Movement in Bristol,* Bristol 1931.
Bundock, C.J., *The National Union of Printing, Bookbinding and Paperworkers,* Oxford 1959.

Calder, Angus, *The People's War: Britain, 1939–45*, London 1969.

Checkland, S.G., *The Rise of Industrial Society in England, 1815–1885*, London 1964.

Clarke, A.F., *Lancashire and the New Liberalism*, Cambridge 1971.

Clegg, H.A., *General Union: A Study of the National Union of General and Municipal Workers*, London 1954.

Clegg, H.A., Fox, Alan and Thompson, A.F., *A History of British Trade Unions Since 1889*, Oxford 1964.

Coates, Ken and Topham, Anthony, *Industrial Democracy in Great Britain*, London 1968.

Cole, G.D.H., *Trade Unionism and Munitions*, Oxford 1923.

Cole, Margaret, *Women of Today*, London 1938.

Collier, Frances, *The Family Economy of the Working Class in the Cotton Industry 1784–1833*, Manchester 1964.

Corbett, J., *History of the Birmingham Trades Council, 1866–1966*, London 1966.

Davis, W.J., *British Trade Union Congress*, London 1910.

Dilke, Lady, *The Book of the Spiritual Life*, London 1905.

Drake, Barbara, *Women in Trade Unions*, London 1921.

Drake, Barbara, *Women in Engineering*, London 1918.

Fox, Alan, *National Union of Boot and Shoe Operatives, 1847–1957*, London 1947.

Goldman, Harold, *Emma Paterson*, London 1974.

Gore-Booth, Eva, 'The Movement Among Trade Unionists', *The Case for Women's Suffrage*, ed. *Brougham Villers*, London 1907.

Gwynn, Stephen and Tuckwell, Gertrude, *Life of Sir Charles W. Dilke*, Vol. II, New York 1917.

Hall, B.T., *Our Fifty Years, The Story of the Working Men's Club and Institute Union*, London 1912.

Halsey, A.H., *Trends in British Society since 1900*, London 1972.

Hamilton, Mary Agnes, *Margaret Bondfield*, London 1924.

Hamilton, Mary Agnes, *Women at Work*, London 1941.

Hamilton, Mary Agnes, *Mary MacArthur: A Biographical Sketch*, London 1925.

Hamling, W., *A Short History of the Liverpool Trades' Council, 1848–1948*, Liverpool 1948.

Hammond, B. and J.L., *The Town Labourer*, London 1917.

Hannington, W., *Industrial History in War-Time*, London 1940.

Harrison, Royden, *Before the Socialists: Studies in Labour and Politics, 1861–1881*, London 1965.

Hewitt, Margaret, *Wives and Mothers in Victorian Industry*, London 1958.

Higenbottam, S., *The Woodworkers, 1860–1960*, Manchester 1960.

Hinton, James, 'The Clyde Workers Committee and the Dilution Struggle', *Essays in Labour History, 1886–1932,* London 1971.

Holcombe, Lee, *Victorian Ladies at Work: Middle-Class Working Women in England and Wales, 1850–1914,* London 1874.

Hoffman, P.C., *They Also Serve,* London 1949.

Humphries, Betty V., *Clerical Unions in the Civil Service,* Oxford 1958.

Hutchins, B.L., *Women in Modern Industry,* London 1915.

Hutchins, B.L., and Harrison, A., *A History of Factory Legislation,* London 1926.

Hutchinson, H.G., *Life of Sir John Lubbock, Lord Avebury,* London 1914.

Hutt, Allan, *British Trade Unionism: A Short History,* London 1975.

Hyman, Richard, *The Workers' Union,* Oxford 1971.

Industrial Remuneration Conference: Report of the Proceedings and Papers, London 1885.

Inman, P., *Labour in the Munitions Industry,* London 1957.

Jacoby, Robin M., 'Feminism and Class Consciousness in the British and American W.T.U.L.', *Liberating Women's History: Theoretical and Critical Essays,* ed. Bernice A. Carroll, Urbana 1976.

Jenkins, Roy, *Dilke: A Victorian Tragedy,* London 1958.

Jephcott, Pearl; Seear, Nancy; and Smith, John H., *Married Women Working,* London 1968.

Jones, Peter D'A., *The Christian Socialist Revival 1877–1914, Religion, Class and Social Conscience in Late Victorian England,* Princeton 1968.

Kenny, Annie, *Memories of a Militant,* London 1924.

Knowles, G.C.K., *Strikes,* London 1952.

Lerner, Shirley W., *Breakaway Unions and the Small Trade Union,* London 1961.

Lloyd, T.O., *Empire to Welfare State: English History 1906–1967,* Oxford 1970.

Mallon, J.J., 'Women in Congress', *Sixty Years of Trade Unionism 1868–1928,* London 1928.

Markham, Violet, *Friendship's Harvest,* London 1956.

Markham, Violet, *May Tennant,* London 1949.

McCarthy, Margaret (pseudonym for Margaret McKay), *Generation in Revolt,* London 1953.

MacDonald, J. Ramsay, *Women in the Printing Trade,* London 1904.

McKenzie, K.A., *Edith Simcox and George Eliot,* Oxford 1953.

Mitchell, David, *Women on the Warpath: The Story of the Women of the First World War*, London 1966.

Musson, A.E., *British Trade Unions 1800–1875*, London 1972.

Neale, R.S., *Class and Ideology in the Nineteenth Century*, London 1972.

Neff, Wanda, *Victorian Working Women*, New York 1929.

Nethercot, Arthur H., *The First Five Lives of Annie Besant*, London 1961.

Pankhurst, Sylvia, *The Home Front*, London 1932.

Pearce, Cyril, *The Manningham Mills Strike*, Bradford, University of Hull 1975.

Pelling, Henry, *A History of British Trade Unionism*, 2nd ed. London 1971.

Phillips, G.A., *The General Strike*, London 1976.

Phillips, Marion, *Women and the Miner's Lock-Out*, London 1927.

Pollard, Sidney, *The Development of the British Economy, 1914–1961*, 2nd ed., London 1969.

Postan, M.M., *British War Production*, London 1952.

Ramelson, Marian, *The Petticoat Rebellion*, London 1967.

Roberts, B.C., *Trade Union Government and Administration in Great Britain*, London 1956.

Robson, Robert, *The Cotton Industry of Britain*, London 1957.

Rogers, Frederick, *Labour, Life and Literature: Some Memories of Sixty Years*, London 1913.

Rosen, Andrew, *Rise Up Women: The Militant Campaign of the Women's Social and Political Union, 1903–1974*.

Rover, Constance, *Women's Suffrage and Party Politics in Britain 1866–1914*, London 1967.

Rowbotham, Sheila, *Hidden from History*, London 1973.

Sandberg, Lars, *Lancashire in Decline*, Columbus 1974.

Saul S.B., *The Myth of the Great Depression, 1873–1896*, London 1969.

Seventy Years of Trade Unions, London 1938.

Sharp, I.G., *Industrial Conciliation and Arbitration in Great Britain*, London 1950.

Skidelsky, Robert, *Politicians and the Slump: The Labour Government of 1929–1931*, London 1967.

Soldon, Norbert C., 'Laissez Faire as Dogma : The Liberty and Property Defence League, 1882–1914' *Essays in Anti-Labour History*, ed. K.D. Brown, London 1974.

Stafford, Ann, *A Match to Fire the Thames*, London 1961.

Stewart, Margaret and Hunter, Leslie, *The Needle is Threaded*, London 1964.

Tate, G.K., *History of the London Trades Council, 1860–1950*, London 1950.

Thompson, L., *The Enthusiasts: A Biography of John and Katherine Bruce Glasier*, London 1971.

TUC History of Women's Trade Unionism, London 1955.

Turner, Benjamin, *A Short History of the General Union of Textile Workers*, Leeds 1917.

Turner, Benjamin, *A Short History of the Cotton Unions*, Heckmondwike 1920.

Turner, H.A., *Trade Union Growth, Structure and Policy; A Comparative Study of the Cotton Unions*, London 1962.

Webb, Sidney and Beatrice, *History of Trade Unionism*, London 1921.

Williams-Ellis, Annabel, *Women in War Factories*, London 1943.

Wolfe, Willard, *From Radicalism to Socialism: Men and Ideas in the Formation of Fabian Socialist Doctrines, 1881–1889*, New Haven 1975.

Wrigley, C.J., *David Lloyd George and the British Labour Movement*, London 1976.

Wynn, Niel, 'Working-Class Unrest Prior to World War I', *Popular Politics, 1870–1950*, London 1974

PERIODICALS AND JOURNALS

Abrams, P., 'The Failure of Social Reform, 1918–1920', *Past and Present*, 24 Nov. 1963.

Anderson, William C., 'Facts for Textile Workers', *Woman Worker*, 17 July 1908.

Bealey, F., 'The Northern Weavers Independent Labour Representation and Clitheroe, 1902', *Manchester School*, 25, 1957.

Bingham, Stella, 'Women in Trade Unions', *Nova*, Aug. 1971.

Black, Clementina, 'The Chocolate Makers Strike', *Fortnightly Review*, Aug. 1890.

Black, Clementina, 'The Organization of Working Women', *Fortnightly Review*, Nov. 1889.

Dilke, Lady, 'Trade Unions for Women', *North American Review*, Aug. 1891.

Dilke, Lady, 'Benefit Societies and Trade Unions for Women', *Fortnightly Review*, June 1889.

Dilke, Lady, 'The Industrial Position of Women', *Fortnightly Review*, Vol. 60, Oct. 1893.

Dilke, Lady, 'Trade Unionism Among Women', *Fortnightly Review*, Vol. 55, May 1891.

Dilke, Lady, 'Trade Unionism For Women', *New Review*, 2, Jan. 1890.

Dilke, Lady, 'The Seamy Side of Trade Unionism for Women', *New Review*, 2, May 1890.

Duffy, A.E.P., 'New Unionism in Britain, 1889–1890: A Reappraisal', *Economic History Review*, 2nd Series, Vol. XIV, Dec. 1961.

Firth, J.B., 'Weavers of Bradford, Their Work and Wages', *Economic Journal*, Vol. 2, 1892.

Fredeman, William E., 'Emily Faithfull and the Victorian Press: An Experiment in Sociological Bibliography', *The Library*, Fifth Series, Vol. XXIX, No. 2, June 1974.

Goldman, Harold, *Health Services Journal*, Vol. 22, No. 6, June 1969.

Harries, Edgar P., 'Organisation of Women in Industry', *Labour Magazine*, Apr. 1932.

Heather-Bigg, Ada, 'Women in the Nail and Chain Trade: a Victorian Viewpoint', *Blackcountryman*, 5, Summer 1972.

Hubback, F.W., 'Women's Wages', *The New Statesman Special Supplement on Women in Industry*, Vol. 2, 21 Feb. 1914.

Lewenhak, Sheila, 'Women in the Leadership of the Scottish Trades Union Congress 1897–1970', *Journal of Scottish Labour History*, Vol. 7, July 1973.

McAlmann, J., 'The Impact of the First World War on Female Employment in England', *Labour History*, 21, (1971).

O'Brien, J., *Women's Liberation in Labour History: A Case Study from Nottingham* (Spokesman pamphlet no. 24), Nottingham 1972.

Price, Richard N., 'The Working Men's Club Movement and Victorian Social Reform Ideology', *Victorian Studies*, Vol. XV, No. 2, Dec. 1971.

Richards, Eric, 'Women in British Economy Since 1700', *Historical Journal*, 59, Oct. 1974.

Simcox, Edith, 'Eight Years of Co-operative Shirtmaking', *The Nineteenth Century*, June 1884.

Tuckwell, Gertrude, *Labour Woman IX*, Feb. 1921.

Webb, Beatrice, *Labour Woman IX*, Feb. 1921.

Ph.D. DISSERTATIONS AND PAPERS

Bather, Leslie, 'A History of the Manchester and Salford Trades Council', Manchester Ph.D. 1956.

Bristow, Edward, 'The Defence of Liberty and Property in Britain, 1880–1914', Yale Ph.D. dissertation 1970.

Devine, Francis, 'Women in the Irish Trade Unions: A Note', a paper delivered to ICTU's Women's Advisory Committee, 4 May 1975.

Lewenhak, Sheila, 'Trade Union Membership Among Women and Girls in the U.K., 1920–1965, London Ph.D. 1971.

Mappen, Ellen F., 'Women's Work: Women's Industrial Life in London, 1890–1914', Rutgers Ph.D. dissertation 1977.

White, Joseph, 'The Lancashire Cotton Textile Workers During Labour Unrest of 1910–1914', University of California, Berkeley Ph.D. dissertation 1975.

NEWSPAPERS

Birmingham Gazette and Express; The Christian Commonwealth; The Communist; Daily Chronicle; Daily News; CBI Members Bulletin; Daily Express; Daily Herald; Daily Mirror; Daily Telegraph; Labour News; Englishwomen's Review; Financial Times; Individualist; Industrial Newsletter for Women; Industrial Review; Labour; Labour Weekly; Lincolnshire Echo; Manchester Dispatch; Manchester Guardian; Morning Star; N.U.G.W. Journal; New Dawn; New York Sun; Red Mole; Reynolds Newspaper; Shrew; Socialist Worker; Sun; Standard; The Times; TUC Times; The Way; Western Daily Press; Woman Worker; Woman's Angle; Woman's Dreadnought; Women Folk; Women's Trade Union Review; Women's Union Journal; Workmen's Times.

Notes

INTRODUCTION
(pp. 1–10)

1. H. A. Clegg, Alan Fox and A. F. Thompson, *A History of British Trade Unions Since 1889*, Oxford 1964, 44–6.
2. Frances Collier, *The Family Economy of the Working Class in the Cotton Industry 1784–1833*, Manchester 1964.
3. Geoffrey Best, *Mid-Victorian Britain 1851–75*, London 1971, 126.
4. Margaret Hewitt, *Wives and Mothers in Victorian Industry*, London 1958, 10–11.
5. *Women in the Trade Union Movement*, London 1955, 34.
6. *Industrial Newsletter for Women*, May 1952, 6.
7. B. L. Hutchins, *Women in Modern Industry*, London 1915, 92.
8. J. L. and B. Hammond, *The Town Labourer*, London 1917, 262.
9. Barbara Drake, *Women in Trade Unions*, London 1921, 4.
10. Wanda Neff, *Victorian Working Women*, New York 1929, 30–1.
11. Drake, *Women in Trade Unions*, 9.
12. *Ibid.*, 5.
13. *Women's Union Journal*, Aug. 1877.
14. J. Ramsay MacDonald, *Women in the Printing Trade*, London 1904, 33–7.
15. Drake, *Women in Trade Unions*, 8.
16. *Industrial Newsletter for Women*, May 1952.
17. J. M. Baernreither, *British Associations of Working Men*, London 1889, 225–7.
18. Benjamin Turner, *A Short History of the Cotton Unions*, Heckmondwike 1920.
19. J. A. and Olive Banks, *Feminism and Family Planning in Victorian Britain*, Liverpool 1964, 31–41; and Lee Holcombe, *Victorian Ladies at Work: Middle-Class Working Women in England and Wales, 1850–1914*, London 1974, 5–6.
20. S. G. Checkland, *The Rise of Industrial Society in England, 1815–1885*, London 1964, 216.
21. Eric Richards, 'Women in British Economy Since 1700', *History*, 59, October 1974, 337–57.
22. William E. Fredeman, 'Emily Faithfull and the Victorian Press: An Experiment in Sociological Bibliography', *The Library*, Fifth Series, XXIX 2, June 1974, 139–64.
23. Holcombe, *Victorian Ladies*, 18.

24. *Englishwomen's Review*, 15 April 1903.
25. Hutchins, *Women in Modern Industry*, 121.
26. Holcombe, *Victorian Ladies*, 16.
27. Richards, 'Women in the British Economy Since 1700', 345–51.
28. Jesse Boucherett, 'Provision for Superfluous Women', *Women's Works and Women's Culture*, ed. by Josephine Butler, London 1869, 33–49.
29. Holcombe, *Victorian Ladies*, 18–19.
30. Henry Pelling, *A History of British Trade Unionism*, 2nd ed. London 1971, 81–2.
31. H. A. Turner, *Trade Union Growth Structure and Policy*, Toronto 1962, 138.

CHAPTER ONE
(pp. 11–26)

1. Sidney and Beatrice Webb, *History of Trade Unionism*, London 1921, 336–7.
2. B. T. Hall, *Our Fifty Years, The Story of the Working Men's Club and Institute Union*, London 1912, 29–56, 275–81.
3. Frederick Rogers, *Labour, Life and Literature: Some Memories of Sixty Years*, London 1913, 93.
4. Harold Goldman, *Health Services Journal*, Vol. 22, No. 6, June 1969.
5. Fredeman, 'Emily Faithfull', 139–64.
6. MacDonald, *Women in the Printing Trade*, 27–31.
7. *Women's Protective and Provident League, First Annual Report*, 9 July 1875.
8. *WUJ*, Dec. 1886, 114.
9. *WPPL, 5th Annual Report*, 1879.
10. *WUJ*, 31 Jan. 1877.
11. *Ibid.*, Sept. 1886.
12. *Ibid.*, July 1878.
13. *WPPL, 2nd Annual Report*, 1876.
14. *WUJ*, May 1879.
15. Rogers, *Labour, Life and Literature*, 95.
16. *WPPL, 5th Annual Report*, 1879.
17. *WUJ*, July 1880, Jan. 1881 and Feb. 1881; and Harold Goldman, *Emma Paterson*, London 1974, 57.
18. *WUJ*, July 1886.
19. *Ibid.*, Aug. 1879.
20. *Ibid.*, Apr. 1879; and Edith Simcox, 'Eight Years of Co-operative Shirtmaking', *The Nineteenth Century*, June 1884.
21. *WUJ*, Dec. 1878.

22. *Englishwoman's Review*, 15 March 1876, 133.
23. K. A. McKenzie, *Edith Simcox and George Eliot*, Oxford 1961, 39–42.
24. Drake, *Women in Trade Unions*, 11; and Goldman, *Emma Paterson*, 70.
25. *WUJ*, Oct. 1877.
26. *10th Annual Trade Union Congress*, Manchester 1877, 12–19; and Drake, *Women in Trade Unions*, 15–20.
27. *WUJ*, Nov. 1878.
28. *Ibid.*, Aug. 1878.
29. *Ibid.*, Nov. 1878; and *Western Daily Press*, 13 Sept. 1878.
30. *Englishwoman's Review*, 15 Oct. 1883, 440–2.
31. W. J. Davis, *British Trade Union Congress*, London 1910, 128.
32. *WUJ*, Dec. 1886.
33. *Ibid.*, Dec. 1886.
34. *Ibid.*, Sept. 1878.
35. *Industrial Remuneration Conference: Report of the Proceedings and Papers*, London 1885, 200.
36. *Ibid.*, 199–221.
37. *Ibid.*, 204.
38. *Ibid.*, 85–95.
39. *Ibid.*, 208; and *WUJ*, March 1885.
40. *Englishwoman's Review*, Apr. 1886, 27 May 1887; and *WUJ*, Apr. and May 1886.
41. *WUJ*, July 1886 and *WPPL, 11th Annual Report*, 1885. The Unions were the Aberdeen Workwomen's Protective and Benefit Society, the Leeds Tailoresses' Society and the Glasgow Operative Tailoresses' Society.
42. A. E. P. Duffy, 'New Unionism in Britain, 1889–1890: A Reappraisal', *Economic History Review*, 2nd Series, XIV (Dec. 1961), 306–19; and Willard Wolfe, *From Radicalism to Socialism: Men and Ideas in the Formation of Fabian Socialist Doctrines, 1881–1889*, New Haven 1975, 93–109, 254–60.
43. *WUJ*, Oct. 1886.
44. *Ibid.*, Apr. 1886.
45. See S. B. Saul, *The Myth of the Great Depression, 1873–1896*, London 1969; and Peter d'A. Jones, *The Christian Socialist Revival 1877–1914, Religion, Class and Social Conscience in Late Victorian England*, Princeton 1968, 31–5.
46. Pelling, *A History of British Trade Unions*, 84–6.
47. *WUJ*, Dec. 1880.
48. *Ibid.*, July 1886.
49. Richard N. Price, 'The Working Men's Club Movement and

Victorian Social Reform Ideology', *Victorian Studies*, Dec. 1971, XV/2, 130–6.
50. *WUJ*, July 1886.
51. Norbert C. Soldon, 'Laissez-Faire as Dogma : The Liberty and Property Defence League, 1882–1914', *Essays in Anti-Labour History*, ed. by K. D. Brown, London 1974, 208–34.
52. *WPPL, 8th Annual Report*, July 1882.
53. *WUJ*, Oct. 1886.

CHAPTER TWO
(pp. 27–50)
1. Lady Dilke, *The Book of the Spiritual Life*, London 1905, 17. Sir Charles Dilke denies that Lady Dilke resembles Dorothea Brook in George Eliot's *Middlemarch*, except for her religious views; Roy Jenkins, *Dilke: A Victorian Tragedy*, London 1958.
2. 'The Art Work of Lady Dilke', *Quarterly Review*, Oct. 1906.
3. Stephen Gwynn and Gertrude Tuckwell, *Life of Sir Charles W. Dilke*, II, New York 1917, 229.
4. Ben Turner, *About Myself*, London 1930, 317; and Dilke, *Book of the Spiritual Life*, 112.
5. Lady Dilke, 'The Industrial Position of Women', *Fortnightly Review*, 60, Oct. 1893, 499–508.
6. Lady Dilke, 'Trade Unionism Among Women', *Fortnightly Review*, 55, May 1891, 741–50.
7. *Labour Annual 1896*, 231.
8. Gwynn and Tuckwell, *Life of Charles Dilke*, II, 228.
9. *WUJ*, July 1877.
10. *The Times*, 20 Dec. 1922.
11. *WUJ*, Nov. 1887.
12. Jones, *The Christian Social Union*, 184.
13. *WPPL, 12th Annual Report*, 1886.
14. Annie Besant, *An Autobiography*, London 1895, 334–6.
15. Ann Stafford, *A Match to Fire the Thames*, London 1961, 63–7.
16. *WUJ*, 16 July 1888.
17. G. K. Tate, *History of the London Trades Council, 1860–1950*, London 1950, 68.
18. Arthur H. Nethercot, *The First Five Lives of Annie Besant*, London 1961, 269–75.
19. *WUJ*, 16 July 1888.
20. See the interesting account of the activities of Miriam Daniell, Enid Stacy and Helena Born, in Samson Bryhner, *An Account*

of the Labour and Socialist Movement in Bristol, Bristol 1931, Part II, 15–19.

21. W. Hamling, *A Short History of the Liverpool Trades' Council, 1848–1948*, 1948, 25.
22. *WUJ*, 15 June 1889.
23. *The Times*, 4 Oct. and 14 Oct. 1889; and Clementina Black, 'The Organisation of Working Women', *Fortnightly Review*, 52, Nov. 1889, 704.
24. *The Times*, 21 Nov. 1890; and *Workman's Times*, 10 Oct. 1890.
25. Clementina Black, 'Chocolate Makers Strike', *Fortnightly Review*, Aug. 1890, 305–14.
26. *Ibid.*, 29 Nov. 1892.
27. *Ibid.*, 8 Dec. 1893.
28. Ellen F. Mappen, '*Women's Work: Women's Industrial Life in London, 1890–1914*', Rutgers Ph.D. Dissertation, 1977.
29. *WTUR*, May 1894.
30. *Ibid.*, Oct. 1902.
31. *WTUPL, 15th Annual Report*, 1889.
32. *WTUL, 18th Annual Report*, 1892.
33. *WUJ*, Jan. 1888, 15 Jan. 1889.
34. *Ibid.*, Oct. 1888; and *Woman Worker*, 7 Aug. 1908.
35. Ben Turner, *A Short History of the General Union of Textile Workers*, 80–4; and *WUJ*, Sept. 1889.
36. *TUC Annual Report*, 1888, 43.
37. *Ibid.*, Oct. 1889.
38. *Manchester Guardian*, 5 Sept. 1889, as quoted in McKenzie, *Edith Simcox*, 56.
39. *WUJ*, Jan. 1890.
40. Lady Dilke, 'Trade Unions for Women', *North American Review*, 1892, 4.
41. *WTUR*, July 1893.
42. Violet Markham, *Friendship's Harvest*, London 1956, 84–5; *idem*, and *May Tennant*, 12–35.
43. Jesse Boucherett and Helen Blackburn, *The Condition of Working Women and the Factory Acts*, London 1896, 1–39.
44. *WTUR*, July 1893.
45. Katherine Graves Busbey, *The Women's Trade Union Movement in Great Britain*, Bulletin of the Bureau of Labour, No. 83, Washington July 1909, 14, 32–3.
46. Dilke, 'Trade Unionism Among Women', 744–7.
47. Michael Anderson, *Family Structure in Nineteenth Century Lancashire*, Cambridge 1971, 70–6.
48. *WTUR*, Jan. 1895, Oct. 1896.

49. *Ibid.*, May 1894.
50. Dilke, 'Trade Unions for Women'.
51. *WTUL, 19th Annual Report*, 1893.
52. Lars Sandberg, *Lancashire in Decline*, Columbus 1974, 140.
53. Robert Robson, *The Cotton Industry of Britain*, London 1957, 2.
54. *WTUR*, Apr. 1893.
55. Lord Askwith, *Industrial Problems and Disputes*, London 1920, 187–193.
56. *WTUR*, Jan. 1902.
57. Busbey, *Women's Trade Union Movement*, 5–7.
58. *Ibid.*, 36.
59. Dilke, 'Trade Unions for Women', 8.
60. *Ibid.*, 17.
61. Turner, *Trade Union Growth*, 138, 218–23, 255; and Clegg et al. *History of British Trade Unions since 1889*, 183–5.
62. J. B. Firth, 'Weavers of Bradford, Their Work and Wages', *Economic Journal*, 2, 1892, 546–7.
63. Clegg, et al, *A History of British Trade Unions since 1889*, 183–5.
64. Cyril Pearce, *The Manningham Mills Strike, Bradford*, University of Hull 1975.
65. *WTUR*, Jan. 1901, July 1901.
66. Francis Devine, 'Women in the Irish Trade Unions : A Note', a paper delivered to ICTU's Women's Advisory Committee 4 May 1975, 1, quoting James Connolly, *The Re-Conquest of Ireland.*
67. *WTUR*, Oct. 1898.
68. *WTUL, 19th Annual Report*, 1893.
69. *Ibid.*, *22nd Annual Report*, 1895–6, May 1897.
70. *WTUR*, Jan. 1900.
71. Sheila Lewenhak, 'Women in the Leadership of the Scottish Trades Union Congress 1897–1970', *Journal of Scottish Labour History*, Vol. 7, July 1973, 4.
72. *WTUL, 19th Annual Report*, 1893.
73. *WTUR*, Oct. 1891.
74. *WUJ*, Sept. 1889.
75. *WTUR*, Oct. 1895.
76. *Ibid.*, Oct. 1896.
77. *Ibid.*, 1902.
78. *Ibid.*, Oct. 1891.
79. *Ibid.*, Jan. 1900.
80. *WTUL, 22nd Annual Report*, 1895–6, May 1897.
81. MacDonald, *Women in the Printing Trade*, 8.

82. Drake, *Women in Trade Unions*, 37.
83. *WTUL, 19th Annual Report*, 1893.
84. *WTUL, 20th Annual Report*, 1894, presented 6 Feb. 1895.
85. *WTUR*, Apr. 1895. One of the early WPPL members, Miss Mears, died 28 Feb. 1895 at age 54. She was a friend of Miss Addis. Both Miss Mears and her mother were working upholsteresses. One of her last acts was to expose a candidate for the LCC as a 'sweater'.
86. *WTUL, 22nd Annual Report*, 1895–6, May 1897; and *WTUL, 23rd Annual Report*, 1897.
87. Pelling, *History of British Trade Unionism*, 108.
88. *WTUR*, Oct. 1895.
89. *Ibid.*, Oct. 1897.
90. *Ibid.*, Oct. 1896.
91. *Ibid.*, Oct. 1899.
92. Lewenhak, 'Women in Leadership of Scottish TUC', 3–11.
93. *Reports on the Employment of Women by the Assistant Lady Commissioners, HC*, 1893–4, XXXVII.
94. *Dods Parliamentary Companion*, 1909, 359. F. W. Verney was born 1846, son of Rt Hon. Sir Harry Verney, Bart. MP, educated Harrow and Christ Church, Oxford, married 1870 Maude Sarah, daughter of Sir John Hay Williams, Barrister Bucks County Council since 1889, LCC 1898–1907. Unsuccessful candidate Liberal S.W. Kent, 1885, Norwich 1895, Liverpool 1900, elected N. Bucks 1906.
95. *WTUR*, Apr. 1893.
96. Markham, *May Tennant*, 32.
97. B. L. Hutchins and A. Harrison, *A History of Factory Legislation*, London 1926, 238–41.
98. *WTUL, 24th Annual Report*, 1898.
99. *Ibid.*, *18th Annual Report*, 1892.
100. Drake, *Women in Trade Unions*, 37.
101. Busbey, *Women's Trade Union Movement*, 59–65; and Drake, *Women in Trade Unions*, Appendix.
102. *WTUR*, Jan. 1900.
103. Drake, *Women in Trade Unions*, 43.
104. Betty Askwith, *Lady Dilke: A Biography*, London 1969, 190–6.

CHAPTER THREE
(pp. 51–77)

1. Mary Agnes Hamilton, *Margaret Bondfield*, London 1924, 23.
2. *Ibid.*, 40.
3. Margaret Bondfield, *A Life's Work*, London 1948, 28–36.

4. Marion Miliband, 'Margaret Bondfield', *Dictionary of Labour Biography*, Vol. 2, 39–45; *Woman Worker*, 12 June 1908. Mrs MacDonald was a founder of the Women's Labour League and a member of the Committee of NFWW and Women's Co-operative Guild.
5. Bondfield, *A Life's Work*, 32.
6. *WTUL, Annual Report*, 1900.
7. H. G. Hutchinson, *Life of Sir John Lubbock, Lord Avebury*, London 1914, 217.
8. Holcombe, *Victorian Ladies at Work*, 120–40.
9. Edward Bristow, 'The Defence of Liberty and Property in Britain, 1880–1914', Yale Ph.D. Dissertation 1970, 96.
10. B. V. Humphreys, *Clerical Unions in the Civil Service*, Oxford 1958, 55, 135, 235.
11. *Shop Assistant*, 22 Jan. 1921.
12. Margaret Cole, *Women of Today*, London 1938, 92–7.
13. Mary Agnes Hamilton, *Mary MacArthur: A Biographical Sketch*, London 1925, 1–5; and David Martin, 'William C. Anderson', *Dictionary of Labour Biography*, Vol. 2, 11–15.
14. L. Thompson, *The Enthusiasts: A Biography of John and Katherine Bruce Glasier*, London 1971, 164–5.
15. Hamilton, *Mary MacArthur*, 29, 60.
16. Gertrude Tuckwell, 'Reminiscences', unpublished work at TUC Library, 188–95.
17. Gertrude Tuckwell, *Labour Woman IX*, Feb. 1921, 22.
18. Beatrice Webb, *Labour Woman IX*, Feb. 1921, 22.
19. Hamilton, *Mary MacArthur*, 29–30.
20. *Ibid.*, 38.
21. Tuckwell, *Reminiscences*, 207.
22. David Mitchell, *Women on the Warpath: The Story of the Women of the First World War*, London 1966, 253.
23. *WTUR*, 12 Feb. 1914.
24. Hamilton, *Mary MacArthur*, 40–254.
25. *WTUR*, Apr. 1905.
26. Joseph L. White, 'The Lancashire Cotton Weavers during the Labour Unrest of 1910–1914', University of California, Berkeley Ph.D. dissertation, 1975, 79–83.
27. *Woman Worker*, 28 Aug. 1908.
28. Hamilton, *Mary MacArthur*, 39–40.
29. *WTUL, Committee Meeting*, Nov. 1908.
30. *Woman Worker*, 28 Aug. 1908.
31. Hamilton, *Mary MacArthur*, 66.
32. *WTUL, Annual Report*, March 1907.

33. *WTUL, Committee Meeting*, 23 June 1909, 8 July 1909.
34. *Lincolnshire Echo*, 11 Nov. 1910.
35. *Daily Telegraph*, 10 Nov. 1910.
36. *WTUL, Committee Meeting*, 16 June 1904.
37. *Labour Year Book*, 1916, 357.
38. Hamilton, *Mary MacArthur*, 57.
39. *Woman Worker*, 6 Jan. 1909.
40. *Ibid.*, 31 July 1908 and 15 Dec. 1909. Some light may be shed on his mysterious disappearance by his despondent article on death.
41. *Ibid.*, 28 Aug. 1908.
42. Hamilton, *Mary MacArthur*, 74.
43. *WTUL, Committee Meeting*, 9 July 1908.
44. Hamilton, *Mary MacArthur*, 39.
45. *WTUL, Committee Meeting*, 9 July 1905.
46. Alan Fox, *National Union of Boot and Shoe Operatives, 1847–1957*, London 1947, 312.
47. Drake, *Women in Trade Unions*, 66.
48. *Woman Worker*, 10 Feb. 1909.
49. Clegg, et al, *History of British Trade Unions since 1889*, 457, quoting *Cotton Factory Times*, 27 Dec. 1907.
50. Hopwood, *History of Lancashire Weavers*, 78.
51. William C. Anderson, 'Facts for Textile Workers', *Woman Worker*, 17 July 1908.
52. F. W. Hubback, 'Women's Wages', *The New Statesman Special Supplement on Women in Industry*, Vol. 2, 21 Feb. 1914, ii-iv.
53. *Woman Worker*, 5 May 1909.
54. *Ibid.*, 4 Sept. 1908, quoting *Manchester Guardian*, n.d.
55. *WTUR*, Jan. 1913.
56. Gertrude Tuckwell, *Constance Smith, A Memoir*, London, 1931, 19–28.
57. Tuckwell, *Reminiscences*, 204.
58. Margaret Stewart and Leslie Hunter, *The Needle is Threaded*, London 1964, 137.
59. Testimony of Miss Mary MacArthur in *Report from Select Committee on Home Work*, 18 July 1907, 134.
60. Drake, *Women in Trade Unions*, 44.
61. Amber Blanco White, 'Trade Boards', *Labour Year Book*, 1924, 338.
62. Hamilton, *Mary MacArthur*, 68.
63. *Ibid.*, 137–43.
64. J. J. Mallon, 'Women in Congress', *Sixty Years of Trade*

Unionism 1868–1928, London 1928, 58–62.
65. *Manchester Dispatch*, 16 March 1910; *Birmingham Gazette and Express*, 10 Jan. 1910.
66. Mary MacArthur, 'Slaves of the Forge : The Women of Cradley Heath', *The Christian Commonwealth*, 7 Sept. 1910, 81–90 and Hamilton, *Mary MacArthur*, 79–88.
67. *WTUL, Committee Meeting*, 8 Dec. 1910.
68. *Ibid.*, 11 May 1911 and 10 Oct. 1912.
69. J. Corbett, *History of the Birmingham Trades Council, 1866–1966*, 10 letters, 1966, 95.
70. *WTUL, Committee Meeting*, 9 Dec. 1909.
71. Mallon, 'Women in Congress', 61.
72. Hamilton, *Mary MacArthur*, 110–11, 113.
73. Mitchell, *Women on the Warpath*, 255.
74. Hamilton, *Mary MacArthur*, 117–25.
75. *WTUL, Committee Meeting*, 11 May 1911.
76. *Ibid.*, 14 March 1912.
77. *WTUR*, July 1912.
78. Phelps Brown, *Growth of British Industrial Relations, A Study from the Standpoint of 1906 14*, London 1965, 320–2.
79. A. F. Brockway, *Bermondsey Story, the Life of Alfred Salter*, London 1949, 12, 46–7.
80. *WTUL, Committee Meeting*, 14 July 1910; and Niel Wynn, 'Working-Class Unrest Prior to World War I', *Popular Politics, 1870–1950*, London 1974, 9–12.
81. *Daily Chronicle*, 11 Aug. 1911.
82. *Ibid.*, 15 Aug. 1911; and *Daily News*, 14 Aug. 1911.
83. Hamilton, *Mary MacArthur*, 105.
84. *Daily News*, 21 Aug. 1911.
85. *WTUL, Annual Report*, 1914.
86. Lewenhak, 'Women in Leadership of the Scottish Trades Union Congress 1897–1970', 12–13.
87. Devine, *Women in Irish Trade Unions*, 4–9.
88. *WTUR*, Apr. 1898; and P. F. Clarke, *Lancashire and the New Liberalism*, Cambridge 1971, 239–40.
89. Eva Gore-Booth, 'The Movement Among Trade Unionists', *The Case for Women's Suffrage*, ed. by Brougham Villers, London 1907, 50–67; and F. Bealey, 'The Northern Weavers' Independent Labour Representation and Clitheroe, 1902', *Manchester School*, 25 (1957); 26–60.
90. Marian Ramelson, *The Petticoat Rebellion*, London 1967, 131.
91. Leslie Bather, 'A History of the Manchester and Salford Trades Council', Manchester Ph.D. 1956.

92. *Woman Worker*, Sept. 1908, 13 Jan. 1909, 20 Jan. 1909.
93. Annie Kenney, *Memories of a Militant*, London 1924, 57; *Woman Worker*, 13 Jan. 1909; Andrew Rosen, *Rise Up Women: The Militant Campaign of the Women's Social and Political Union, 1903–1914*, London 1974, 47–57.
94. *Woman Worker*, 20 Jan. 1909 and *Women Folk*, 2 Feb. 1910.
95. Constance Rover, *Women's Suffrage and Party Politics in Britain 1866–1914*, London 1967, 150, 163.
96. WTUL, *Committee Meeting*, 16 June 1904, Nov. 1908, 13 Nov. 1913.
97. *Ibid.*, 13 May 1909.
98. Robin M. Jacoby, 'Feminism and Class Consciousness in the British and American WTUL', *Liberating Women's History: Theoretical and Critical Essays*, ed. by Bernice A. Carroll, Urbana 1976, 137–61; and Ramelson, *Petticoat Rebellion*, 158–9.
99. R. S. Neale, *Class and Ideology in the Nineteenth Century*, London 1972, 152–61.
100. *Ibid.*, 166–8.
101. White, *Lancashire Cotton Workers*, 83–4.

CHAPTER FOUR
(pp. 78–102)

1. *Women in Industry, Report of War Cabinet Committee on Women in Industry 1919* (cmd. 135), 79.
2. *Woman Worker*, Feb. 1916.
3. Hamilton, *Remembering my Good Friends*, 66–7.
4. *Labour Year Book*, 1916, 80–1.
5. Sylvia Pankhurst, *The Home Front*, London, 1932, 53–63.
6. *Contemporary Review*, Feb. 1921.
7. Drake, *Women in Trade Unions*, Table I.
8. Mitchell, *Women on the Warpath*, 249.
9. *Woman Worker*, July 1916.
10. Mitchell, *Women on the Warpath*, 261.
11. Richard Hyman, *The Workers' Union*, Oxford 1971, 84.
12. Mitchell, *Women on the Warpath*, 248.
13. H. J. Fyrth and H. Collins, *Foundry Workers*, London 1959, 145.
14. Drake, *Women in Trade Unions*, 70.
15. *Labour Year Book, 1916*, 50–3 and James Hinton, 'The Clyde Workers' Committee and the Dilution Struggle', *Essays in Labour History, 1886–1932*, 2, ed. by Asa Briggs and John Saville, London, 1971, 152–85.

16. C. J. Wrigley, *David Lloyd George and the British Labour Movement*, London 1976, 95.
17. Pankhurst, *The Home Front*, 346–50; and *Women in Industry* (cmd. 135), 200–7.
18. *Women in Industry* (cmd. 135), 83.
19. Drake, *Women in Trade Unions*, quoting from *Engineer*, Oct. 1915.
20. *Labour Year Book, 1916*, 85–6.
21. *Woman Workers*, Jan. 1916.
22. Hyman, *The Workers' Union*, 117–19.
23. Hamilton, *Margaret Bondfield*, 111.
24. *Engineering*, Mar. 1953.
25. *WTUL, Annual Report*, Sept. 1917.
26. *Ibid.*, 1916.
27. *WTUR*, 14 June 1917.
28. *Woman Worker*, July 1916.
29. *WTUL, Annual Report*, 1916.
30. Hyman, *The Workers' Union*, 87.
31. G. D. H. Cole, *Trade Unionism and Munitions*, Oxford 1923, 204.
32. Drake, *Women in Trade Unions*, 98.
33. Hamilton, *Margaret Bondfield*, 111–12 and *Labour Year Book, 1919*, 97.
34. *Women in Industry* (cmd. 135), 110–21.
35. *Labour Year Book, 1916*, 116.
36. *Woman Worker*, Jan. 1916.
37. Cole, *Trade Unionism and Munitions*, 113–14.
38. *Woman Worker*, Oct. 1916 and Dec. 1916.
39. *WTUR*, 14 June 1917.
40. *Woman Worker*, Sept. 1918.
41. *Ibid.*, Sept. 1916.
42. Hamilton, *Mary MacArthur*, 158–9.
43. *Women in Industry* (cmd. 135), 114–18.
44. *WTUR*, Jan. 1918; and Cole, *Trade Unionism and Munitions*, 152.
45. *Ibid.*, 93.
46. *Woman Worker*, Sept. 1918.
47. *Women in Industry* (cmd. 135), 114.
48. *WTUR*, Apr. 1917.
49. S. Higenbottam, *The Woodworkers, 1860–1960*, Manchester 1960, 46–7; Mendelshon and Pollard, *Sheffield Trades and Labour Council*, 74.
50. *Woman Worker*, Aug. 1918.

51. Mitchell, *Women on the Warpath*, 258; and *Woman Worker*, June 1916.
52. *Women in Industry* (cmd. 135), 220–53.
53. *Ibid.*, 107–8.
54. *Ibid.*, 239.
55. Drake, *Women in Trade Unions*, 84–5, quoting from *The Girl in Industry*.
56. *WTUR*, 11 Mar. 1915.
57. *Women in Industry* (cmd. 135), 88–90.
58. *Ibid.*, 98.
59. *Woman Worker*, Oct. 1918.
60. *WTUL, Committee Meeting*, 11 July 1918.
61. *WTUL, Annual Report*, 1918.
62. Drake, *Women in Trade Unions*, 90.
63. *Daily News*, 10 Aug. 1916.
64. Hinton, 'Clyde Workers' Committee', 165.
65. *Woman Worker*, June 1916.
66. *WTUL, Annual Report*, Sept. 1916.
67. Mendelshon and Pollard, *Sheffield Trades and Labour Council*, 74.
68. Hinton, *The First Shop Stewards' Movement*, 251.
69. Sheila Rowbotham, *Hidden from History*, 173, quoting J. T. Murphy, *The Workers' Committee, An Outline of Its Principles and Structure*, 1917, reprinted.
70. *Ibid.*
71. I. G. Sharp, *Industrial Conciliation and Arbitration in Great Britain*, London 1950, chapter IV.
72. *WTUL, Committee Meeting*, 11 July 1918.
73. *New York Sun*, May 1919.
74. F. J. Baylis, *British Wages Councils*, Oxford 1962, 16–22.
75. Cole, *Trade Unionism and Munitions*, 137, 217.
76. *WTUR*, Apr. 1917.
77. Mitchell, *Women on the Warpath*, 252.
78. *Woman Worker*, Feb. 1917 and Oct. 1918.
79. Mitchell, *Women on the Warpath*, 267.
80. Drake, *Women in Trade Unions*, Table I.
81. *Woman Worker*, Dec. 1918.
82. *Ibid.*, Jan. 1919.
83. *Ibid.*, Oct. 1918.
84. Mitchell, *Women on the Warpath*, 266.
85. *Ibid.*, 268.
86. *Woman Worker*, July 1918.
87. Mitchell, *Women on the Warpath*, 266–7.

88. P. Abrams, 'The Failure of Social Reform 1918–1920', *Past and Present*, 24 Nov. 1963, 62.
89. *WTUL, Committee Meeting*, 9 May 1918.
90. *Ibid.*, 8 June 1916.
91. Hyman, *The Workers' Union*, 79–83, 121.

CHAPTER FIVE
(pp. 103–132)
1. Allen Hutt, *British Trade Unionism: A Short History*, London 1975, 82–86.
2. *Woman Worker*, Dec. 1919.
3. *Daily News*, 21 Nov. 1919; *Reynolds Newspaper*, 3 Mar. 1919.
4. *WTUL, Annual Report, 1920*.
5. Stewart and Hunter, *The Needle Is Threaded*, 180.
6. *Ministry of Labour Gazette; Employment and Productivity Gazette*, 395.
7. *Ibid.*, July 1956.
8. *WTUL, Annual Report, 1920, Woman Worker*, Sept. 1920.
9. Hyman, *The Workers' Union*, 123–7.
10. *Woman Worker*, Sept. 1920.
11. *Ibid.*, Apr. 1921.
12. *TUC Annual Report, 1922*, 217.
13. Stewart and Hunter, *The Needle Is Threaded*, 180.
14. Fox, *A History of NU of Boot and Shoe Operatives, 1874–1953*, 309, 370, 410–16, 524–5.
15. Sheila Lewenhak, 'Trade Union Membership Among Women and Girls in the UK 1920–1965', London, Ph.D. 1971, 274–81; Baylis, *British Wages Councils*, 23–9; P. C. Hoffman, *They Also Serve*, London 1949.
16. *Women's Year Book, 1924*, 344–8.
17. *The Times*, 1 July 1921, 14 July 1921.
18. *Ibid.*, 3 June 1922, 14 June 1922, 20 June 1922; *NUGW Journal*, Jan.-Feb. 1923.
19. Sandberg, *Lancashire in Decline*, 140.
20. *The Times*, 6 May 1921.
21. *WTUL Annual Report, 1921; The Times*, 13 Jan. 1921.
22. *The Times*, 3 June 1921.
23. *Woman's Year Book 1924*, 350–5.
24. *TUC Annual Report, 1922*, 217; see also *Woman's Year Book 1924*, 336.
25. *Ibid.*, 218–21.
26. *Ibid.*, 218.
27. *TUC Annual Report, 1923*, 167.

28. Lewenhak, *Trade Union Membership*, 221, quoting *NUGMW Journal*, June 1927; *TUC Annual Report*, 283-8.
29. *TUC Rep. Women Advisory Conf. Report 1928*, 147-8.
30. Lewenhak, *Trade Union Membership*, 286-96; *TUC Annual Report, 1923*, 175; *ACUCWW 1955*, 26.
31. Clegg, *General Union*, 82-6.
32. *NUGMW Journal*, Ag. 1928, 116.
33. Bondfield, *A Life's Work*, 251.
34. *TUC Annual Report, 1924*, 232.
35. *Industrial Newsletter for Women*, July 1956.
36. *Seventy Years of Trade Unions*, London 1938, 73-4.
37. *Report of Women's Trade Union Conference, 1925*.
38. Bondfield, *A Life's Work*, 43-4.
39. *History of Women's Trade Unionism*, 96.
40. *Report of Women's Trade Union Conference, 1925*, 4.
41. *Ibid.*, 7-11.
42. Lewenhak, *Women in Leadership of Scottish TUC*, 14.
43. *Ibid.*, 6-15.
44. C. J. Bundock, *The National Union of Printing and Bookbinding and Paper Workers*, Oxford 1959, 336.
45. See Pelling, *A History of British Trade Unionism*, 173-8.
46. Hyman, *The Worker's Union*, 135n, 154; Bondfield, *A Life's Work*, 263-9.
47. Hopwood, *The Lancashire Weaver's Story*, 91.
48. Rowbotham, *Hidden From History*, 131.
49. Stewart and Hunter, *The Needle Is Threaded*, 180-3.
50. *Report of Women's Trade Union Conference, 1926*, 1-15. The 1925, 1926 and 1931 Conferences were all called 'First'.
51. *Englishwoman's Review*, Jan. 1906.
52. *Industrial Review*, Mar. 1930.
53. *Open Door Council Eighth Annual Report*, 1934.
54. Rowbotham, *Hidden From History*, quoting from Beth Turner, *The Communist*, Nov. 1927, 223.
55. Pelling, *A History of Br. Trade Unionism*, 188-9; Hyman, *The Workers' Union*, 136.
56. A. H. Halsey, *Trends in British Society since 1900*, London, 1972, 127.
57. *Daily Herald*, 5 Oct. 1928.
58. *The Times*, 13 Feb. 1929.
59. *Worker*, 19 Oct. 1928.
60. *Ibid.*, 19 Oct. 1928, 14 Dec. 1928.
61. Shirley W. Lerner, *Breakaway Unions and the Small Trade Union*, London 1961, 106-17.

62. *Industrial Review,* Apr. 1929.
63. *Ibid.,* Apr. 1929.
64. Sidney Pollard, *The Development of the British Economy, 1914–1961,* 2nd ed., London 1969, 225.
65. B. W. E. Alford, *Depression and Recovery? British Economic Growth, 1918–1939,* London 1972, 75.
66. Robert Skidelsky, *Politicians and the Slump: The Labour Government of 1929–1931,* London 1967, 71–2.
67. Baylis, *British Wages Councils,* 25–9.
68. Noreen Branson and Margot Heineman, *Britain in the Nineteen Thirties,* St Albans 1973, 31–2.
69. Skidelsky, *Politicians and the Slump,* 122–8, 231, 282, 310–11, 318–20.

CHAPTER SIX
(pp. 133–147)

1. *Daily Herald,* 24 Aug. 1932.
2. Branson and Heineman, *Britain in the Nineteen Thirties,* 107–14.
3. Hopwood, *History of Lancashire Cotton Industry,* 95–113; and H. A. Turner, *Trade Union Growth, Structure and Policy: A Comparative Study of the Cotton Unions,* London 1962.
4. *TUC Notes for Speakers,* 1934, No. 2.
5. *Industrial Review,* Oct. 1930; and B. C. Roberts, *Trade Union Government and Administration in Great Britain,* London 1956, 451.
6. *Industrial Review,* Feb. 1931.
7. *Ibid.,* Sept. 1932.
8. *Daily Herald,* 7 Feb. 1932, 18 Oct. 1932; and *Report of ACUCWW,* 1951.
9. Edgar P. Harries, 'Organisation of Women in Industry', *Labour Magazine,* Apr. 1932, 544.
10. *Daily Herald,* 27 Jan. 1934.
11. *Manchester Guardian,* 5 Dec. 1932.
12. *Daily Herald,* 18 Oct. 1932.
13. *Industrial Review,* Feb. 1933.
14. *Daily Herald,* 27 Jan. 1934.
15. *Ibid.,* 27 Jan. 1934.
16. *Ibid.,* 28 Jan. 1935.
17. *Daily Worker,* 26 Jan. 1935.
18. *Industrial Newsletter for Women,* 16 Mar. 1937 and Joan Beauchamp, *Women at Work,* London 1937, 24–8.
19. *Daily Herald,* 11 Apr. 1935; *Report of ACUCWW,* 1937, 12.

H

20. *Ibid.*, 3 Feb. 1936.
21. *Ibid.*, 18 Oct. 1937.
22. *News Chronicle*, 25 Apr. 1938.
23. *Daily Herald*, 26 Apr. 1936.
24. *Report of ACUCWW*, 8 May 1937.
25. Clegg, *General Union*, 86.
26. Bowley, *Wages and Income in the United Kingdom since 1860.*
27. Mary Agnes Hamilton, *Women at Work*, London 1941, 186.
28. *Daily Herald*, 3 Feb. 1938.
29. *Ibid.*, 26 Apr. 1938.
30. *Report of ACUCWW*, 1937, 13.
31. *Ibid.*, 1937, 24.
32. *Daily Herald*, 24 Oct. 1938.
33. *Ibid.*, 27 Jan. 1934.
34. *Ibid.*, 29 June 1938.
35. *TUC Times, Special Women's Edition*, No. 2, 1939.
36. *Report of ACUCWW*, 1939, 14.
37. Bowley, *Wages and Income in the United Kingdom since 1860*, 186–8.
38. Hugh Chevins, 'Anne Loughlin', *National Union of Tailors and Garment Workers: An International Women's Year Tribute to an Outstanding Pioneer Woman Member and Leader*, 21 Mar. 1975.

CHAPTER SEVEN
(pp. 148–163)

1. W. Hannington, *Industrial History in War-time*, London 1940, 113–19.
2. P. Inman, *Labour in the Munitions Industry*, London 378; Ken Coates and Anthony Topham, *Industrial Democracy in Great Britain*, London 1968, 139–195; *Daily Express*, 5 Nov. 1943; Angus Calder, *The People's War, Britain, 1939–1945*, London 1969, 403.
3. TUC, *History of Women's Trade Unionism*, 83–4; G. Thomas, *Women at Work*, Wartime SS, June 1944; Annabel Williams-Ellis, *Women in War Factories*, London 1943.
4. M. M. Postan, *British War Production*, London 1952, 99–100, 147–148, 218, 224.
5. G. C. K. Knowles, *Strikes*, London 1952, 54–55; P. Inman, *Labour in the Munitions Industries*, 292–9.
6. TUC, *Annual Report, 1940*, 247–50.
7. *Report of ACUCWW*, 1941, 19; ILO, *War and Women's Em-*

ployment, 64–7; Zelma Katin, *Clippie*, Guildford, Surrey 1944, 117.

8. Lewenhak, *Trade Union Membership*, 308. quoting *NUGMW Journal*, 1943, 358.
9. TUC, *History of Women's Trade Unionism*, 84.
10. Lewenhak, *Trade Union Membership*, 296–304, quoting from *New Dawn*, 3 July 1943, 210–12.
11. *Woman's Rights, Employment in Engineering, 12 Jan. 1973; AEU*, 12 Jan. 1973, 5; Calder, *The People's War*, 403.
12. *Manchester Guardian*, 7 Oct. 1940.
13. Hopwood, *History of Lancashire Weavers*, 130–1.
14. Pelling, *History of British Trade Unionism*, 217.
15. *Daily Herald*, 25 June 1941.
16. Baylis, *Wages Councils*, 60; H. A. Clegg, *General Union in a Changing Society*, Oxford 1964, 159.
17. *Manchester Guardian*, 7 Oct. 1940 and *Report of ACUCWW*, 1941, 1.
18. *Daily Herald*, 27 Apr. 1942.
79. *Ibid.*, 25 Apr. 1942.
20. *Report of ACUCWW*, 1944, 34.
21. *Industrial Newsletter for Women*, Mar. 1958.
22. T. O. Lloyd, *Empire to Welfare State: English History 1906–1967*, Oxford 1970, 271.
23. *Report of ACUCWW*, 1945, 5; *ibid.*, 1948, 3; *Daily Herald*, 22 June 1948.
24. Lewenhak, *Trade Union Membership*, 309–14.
25. *Report of ACUCWW*, 1946, 37; *Manchester Guardian*, 22 June 1946.
26. *Report of ACUCWW*, 1946, 4.
27. *Manchester Guardian*, 22 June 1946.
28. *Report of ACUCWW*, 1947, 9–12.
29. *Ibid.*, 1950, 11.
30. *Ibid.*, 1946, 12. Further research on Trade Council recruiting efforts is necessary.
31. *Ibid.*, 43.
32. *Ibid.*, 1948, 27.
33. *Ibid.*, 1949, 28–32.
34. *The Times*, 16 Apr. 1974; *Reynolds News*, 2 Feb. 1958.
35. *Report of ACUCWW*, 1947, 7, 30–2.
36. *Daily Worker*, 12 May 1949 and *Report of ACUCWW*, 1950, 7.
37. *TUC Annual Report, 1950*, 454–8 and Lewenhak, *Trade Union Membership*, 314–17.
38. *Report of ACUCWW*, 1951, 20–1.

39. *Ibid.*, 1950, 24–5.
40. *Ibid.*, 1949, 36–7.

CHAPTER EIGHT
(pp. 164–183)
1. *1974 Statistical Statement, TUC, Annual Report,* 1974.
2. *Report of ACUCWW,* 1970, 3.
3. *Standard,* 3 Sept. 1962.
4. *Daily Herald,* 8 Sept. 1961.
5. *New Dawn,* 12 Oct. 1951.
6. *Woman's Angle,* Nov. 1952.
7. TUC, *History of Women's Trade Unionism,* 89.
8. *Daily Herald,* 26 September 1957 and Margaret McCarthy (pseudonym for Margaret McKay), *Generation in Revolt,* London 1953.
9. *Daily Mirror,* 11 June 1952.
10. *Manchester Guardian,* 26 Apr. 1958.
11. *Reynolds News,* 28 Jan. 1962.
12. *Manchester Guardian,* 11 Apr. 1965.
13. *1974 Statistical Statement, TUC, Annual Report,* 1974.
14. *Daily Herald,* 10 May 1952.
15. Pelling, *History of British Trade Unionism,* 236–43.
16. *Daily Worker,* 18 May 1953.
17. *News Chronicle,* 14 May 1955.
18. *Daily Herald,* 28 Apr. 1967.
19. *Ibid.*, 10 May 1952.
20. Hopwood, *History of Lancashire Cotton,* 150–70, 189–91.
21. *Woman's Angle,* Jan. 1953.
22. *Ibid.*, 10 May 1953.
23. *Ibid.*, Mar. 1955.
24. *Ibid.*, July 1961.
25. *Ibid.*, Dec. 1962.
26. *Manchester Guardian,* 25 Apr. 1959.
27. *Woman's Angle,* Mar. 1962.
28. *Daily Herald,* 29 Apr. 1961.
29. Lewenhak, *Trade Union Membership,* 320–2.
30. *Woman's Angle,* June 1954.
31. *Ibid.*, May 1956.
32. *Ibid.*, Mar. 1957.
33. *Ibid.*, June 1957.
34. *Daily Worker,* 4 May 1963.
35. Lewenhak, *Trade Union Membership,* 329.
36. *Report of ACUCWW,* 1962, 1–2.

37. *Ibid.*, 1964, 4.
38. *Daily Express*, 29 Apr. 1963.
39. *Manchester Guardian*, 24 Oct. 1974.
40. *Report of ACUCWW*, 1966, 7–8.
41. *Ibid.*, 1962, 18–19.
42. *Ibid.*, 1963, 21–4, 31–2; and *Daily Telegraph*, 16 Apr. 1963.
43. M. Espinasse, 'Marian Veitch', *D.L.B.* Vol. III, 193–5; *G.M.W. Journal*, Jan. 1971, Aug. and Sept. 1973.
44. *Sun*, 19 Apr. 1965 and Lewenhak, *Trade Union Membership*, 334.
45. Report of ACUCWW, 1967, 52–3.
46. *Labour*, July 1968.
47. *Financial Times*, 7 June 1968, 5 July 1968.
48. *Report of a Court of Enquiry under Sir Jack Scamp into a Dispute Concerning Sewing Machinists Employed by the Ford Motor Company* (cmd. 3749), 1968 and *The Times*, 22 Aug. 1968.
49. *Morning Star*, 28 Aug. 1968.
50. Pelling, *History of British Trade Unionism*, 266–71.
51. *The Way*, 2 Jan. 1970, Oct. 1974.
52. *The Times*, 17 May 1969.
53. *TUC Conference on Equal Pay*, 1973, 2–3.
54. *Daily Telegraph*, 2 Feb. 1970.
55. Claire Hollingworth, 'Equal Pay—and its Price', *Daily Telegraph*, 2 Feb. 1970.
56. *Report of ACUCWW*, 1966, 9–10.
57. Anna Coote, 'Night Gains', *Manchester Guardian*, 17 June 1974.
58. Pearl Jephcott, Nancy Seear, John H. Smith, *Married Women Working*, London 1962.
59. *Labour*, June 1967.
60. *Manchester Guardian*, 24 Nov. 1974.
61. *Socialist Worker*, 1 Sept. 1973.
62. *Labour Weekly*, 9 Aug. 1974 and *CBI Members Bulletin*, 15 Nov. 1974.
63. *Morning Star*, 11 Sept. 1974.
64. *Manchester Guardian*, 10 July 1974.
65. Mary Hobbs, *Born to Struggle*, London 1973.
66. *Shrew*, Dec. 1971.
67. *Red Mole*, 30 Nov. 1970.
68. *New Statesman*, 21 Mar. 1975.
69. *Report of ACUCWW*, 1972.

Index